Why Cryptocurrencies?

What they are, what they do and why they matter

by Jonas Hietala

The full text of this book is available online at:

whycryptocurrencies.com

This is a self-published book, and if you're curious about the creation process I wrote a few blog posts about it:

jonashietala.se/blog/tags/why_cryptocurrencies/

Cover art by Brad Lark:

blark@blark.com

ISBN: 978-91-986762-0-4

To Veronica, who lights my way in darkness.

Contents

Acknowledgements

As usual, there is a great woman behind every idiot.

John Lennon

Sometimes, I'm an idiot, but it's clear that I have a great woman in Veronica that supports me, and without her this book would've never seen the light of day.

A big thanks to Filip Strömbäck, who proof-read everything and provided me with tons of good feedback.

And thanks to all others who gave me supportive comments, feedback, pull requests and donations. I'm forever grateful.

About the book
A perspective beyond the hype

What value does cryptocurrency add? No one's been able to answer that question to me.

Steve Eisman

Whenever the topic of cryptocurrencies—where Bitcoin and Ethereum are the most known—come up in conversations they're almost always misunderstood or dismissed.

If you're a cryptocurrency skeptic I honestly can't blame you. The only times you ever hear about it on the news is how Bitcoin rallies[1] and how Cryptocurrencies are about to become worthless[2]. Maybe you'll see claims that cryptocurrencies will lead to an environmental disaster[3] or how they're only used for illegal purposes[4].

Curiously enough, the news doesn't explain what cryptocurrencies are or what they can be useful for. But it's to be expected as the news today focuses on dramatic stories; it's why unsettling events like murder gets a disproportional amount of focus.

Maybe this is why most people—even cryptocurrency fans—only see cryptocurrencies as a form of investment? After all, there are few things as exciting as the possibility of becoming rich very quickly.

It's interesting when the news handles something you have a good understanding of—they're often completely wrong. Makes you wonder, how wrong are they about things you're not familiar with?

What hope does average Joe have when even the famous security technologist Bruce Schneier concludes that:

> Honestly, cryptocurrencies are useless

Bruce Schneier, "Blockchain and Trust"[5]

Schneier brings an interesting perspective and he's right about one very important aspect: contrary to popular belief cryptocurrencies don't remove **all** trust.

To counter his point that "cryptocurrencies are useless" all you have to do is provide one counterexample where they're useful. This book is full of them.

It's almost a universal phenomena. I've heard these arguments from students, co-workers, friends, family and in highly technical online communities:

1   It's a scam.
2   It's just a speculative bubble and cryptocurrencies are really worthless.

Here many draw parallels to Beanie Babies or the Tulip mania. And to be fair, cryptocurrencies have displayed bubble behavior—several times.

Beanie Babies is a type of fluffy toy that people used to speculate with. It became a mania where people would sell—and buy—these toys at 10x, 100x, or even 1000x their original price. The mania managed to make the creator, Ty Warner, one of the richest men in the world before it crashed (he's still insanely rich though).[6]

If you're looking for the digital version of Beanie Babies then look no further than CryptoKitties, a blockchain game running on Ethereum. There, someone spent $114,000 on a virtual kitten.[7]

Tulip mania is one of the first recorded speculative bubbles, which occurred 1636–1637 in the Netherlands. There, people speculated on tulip bulbs, which reached spectacular prices before crashing down abruptly.[8]

3   They don't do anything better than other payment systems like PayPal or VISA.
4   There's no legal use case.
5   They don't do anything valuable.

It seems everyone has an opinion but few are capable of explaining what they are or what they do differently. Of course, most aren't dismissive but simply don't understand what it's all about. Many are curious and want to learn more.

With this book, I hope to show how cryptocurrencies can be useful, what use cases exist, and how they can help people. I'll briefly go over how they work in a more conceptual level and I might throw in some historical notes here and there. I'm not trying to make anyone a cryptocurrency fan; I just hope to bring some nuance and help answer some common questions.

I must admit I'm also being selfish—writing a book is on my bucket list.

What this book is

This book tries to describe what value cryptocurrencies have using several examples. In particular I'll argue that:

1   Cryptocurrencies aren't just scams.
2   It's more than just a speculative asset.
3   They do many things better than any alternative.
4   There are legal use cases.
5   They have valuable use cases.

Please take care and do your research, there are **many** scams out there.

Of course, everything new brings positive and negative aspects with it. It's up to you to decide where on the global spectrum of good and bad cryptocurrencies lie.

What this book isn't

This isn't a deep dive on a technical level, and we won't focus on a single implementation. Bitcoin is the first cryptocurrency, but there are hundreds more.

Although there are hundreds and perhaps thousands, most are just copies or outright scams.

There are many problems with cryptocurrencies as they exist today, for instance:

- Why aren't cryptocurrencies used more?
- Bitcoin uses a public ledger where all payments are visible—what about privacy?
- How can a cryptocurrency scale globally?
- What about Bitcoin's energy usage?

I don't dismiss these problems, and I discuss them in more detail in the chapter *Challenges for cryptocurrencies* (p.191), but the focus of this book isn't to explain them or to look at how we might address them.

A problem-centric view is great for an engineer or a problem solver, but it also limits foresight. For example, the computer had many problems and drawbacks when first introduced, but today we ridicule statements like these:

I think there's a world market for maybe five computers

Thomas Watson, president of IBM, 1943

There is no reason anyone would want a computer in their home

Ken Olsen, founder of Digital Equipment Corporation, 1977

Instead of putting on blinders and getting stuck at these problems—which I believe can be addressed—we'll focus on the potential cryptocurrencies have. Only with this vantage point can we see if the problems are worth working on, or if we instead should scrap the whole idea.

And of course, none of this is investment advice.

Well, the only advice I'll give is to understand what you're investing in, and my hope is that this book can help with that.

Part I

Why cryptocurrencies in five minutes

ELI5 - what is the inherent values of cryptocurrencies?

While cryptocurrencies are mostly seen as speculative assets or get rich quick schemes, they have valuable properties and valuable use cases. For example:

- **Excellent monetary properties**

  Cryptocurrencies have better monetary properties (p.41) than anything else in history. In contrast to the fiat money we use today, cryptocurrencies have a limited supply and compared to gold, cryptocurrencies are much more portable, are easier to divide into small parts, and cannot be counterfeit.

  At first glance, this may seem insignificant, but money affects everything and even small improvements can have a massive effect.

- **Cheaper payments**

  Merchants have to pay a 1-4% fee for every credit card transaction, while cryptocurrency transactions only come with a small fixed fee (p.50).

  If you've heard about the ridiculously high Bitcoin fees, then don't worry—it's the exception not the rule. Please read the chapter *Cheaper & faster* (p.49) for more info.

- **Irreversible digital transactions**

  You receive money in under an hour (p.52), and after that the money is yours. In contrast, it may take days to receive other digital payments that can also be reversed weeks or months later.

  Thus merchants don't have to worry about having a purchase reversed, which usually means they have to swallow the loss.

  This is known as *charge back fraud* or *friendly fraud* (p.52) and is a big problem for merchants.

- **For anyone and anything**

  Cryptocurrencies can be used by anyone. It's for businesses who cannot accept credit cards (p.55), for people without a bank account (p.73), and people in dysfunctional countries. You can use it for truly uncensorable donations (p.63), and you don't have to worry that your payment processor or bank will freeze your account (p.59).

  Nobody can prevent you from sending or receiving cryptocurrencies.

- **Financial privacy**

  Banks, credit card companies, and payment processors have all your financial transactions on record. Cryptocurrencies allow you to reclaim some of your privacy (p.109) as they work like a swiss bank account in your pocket (p.133).

- **An alternative financial system**

  The traditional financial system rewards behavior that caused the 2008 financial crisis (p.83) and relies on being able to predict the unpredictable (p.91). Cryptocurrencies represent an alternative without a central authority that can manipulate the money supply, and they can be used to truly separate money from state (p.151).

- **Extensions**

  You can build applications on top of cryptocurrencies, such as provably fair gambling (p.169) or a timestamping service based on mathematics instead of social proof (p.157).

Of course cryptocurrencies don't perfectly solve everything, and there are many difficulties—both technical and social—that need to be resolved. As with all new technology, they will be associated with positive and negative change.

If you want to learn more and see more examples, just continue reading. You can also jump to whatever chapter interests you—they're supposed to be self-contained.

Please note that Bitcoin (and most other cryptocurrencies) are only *pseudo-anonymous*. There are others—like Monero—that improve the situation. Please see *the privacy and fungibility challenge* (p.193) for more information.

Part II
What is a cryptocurrency?
Peer-to-peer electronic cash

Bitcoin is the beginning of something great: a currency without a government, something necessary and imperative.

Nassim Nicholas Taleb

If we're going to talk about cryptocurrencies we need to know what they are. Otherwise how can we tell what value—if any—they have? I think the best description of what a cryptocurrency is can be found in the title of the original white paper: *Bitcoin: A Peer-to-Peer Electronic Cash System* (p.189). It's like cash, but in digital form.

The white paper is a good read. I recommend you look it up. If you prefer an annotated version or a podcast, there are those as well. (p.189)

In this part, we'll begin by looking at the properties cryptocurrencies have, which lay the foundation for the use-cases described in the book. Then we'll take a closer look at how cryptocurrencies work. Technical understanding isn't required to see their usefulness, but it helps us navigate the cryptocurrency space and to see through misleading information.

I'll try to back up my claims that cryptocurrencies are like cash by discussing what money is, the properties of money and if it's fair to classify cryptocurrencies as money. Not only will I proclaim that cryptocurrencies are money, but that they're potentially the best money we've ever seen, although they're held back by volatility and low adoption.

Chapter 1
Properties of a cryptocurrency
Trustless and permissionless

What is needed is an electronic payment system based on cryptographic proof instead of trust, allowing any two willing parties to transact directly with each other without the need for a trusted third-party.

Satoshi Nakamoto, "Bitcoin: A Peer-to-Peer Electronic Cash System"

These are the most important properties of cryptocurrencies as I see it:

- No more third parties
- No counterfeiting
- Predetermined emission rate
- Irreversible transactions
- Private
- Large and small amounts behave the same
- Borderless

They highlight the difference between cryptocurrencies and other payment systems and are ultimately what makes cryptocurrencies useful.

No more third parties

The important difference between a cryptocurrency and the digital payments we have today is the removal of a third-party. Payments are *peer-to-peer* just as if you gave someone a dollar bill or a gold coin.

Sending money to people via your bank isn't peer-to-peer as you rely on your bank to send it for you. VISA, PayPal, Swish, Apple Pay, and other digital payments have the same problem, all except cryptocurrencies.

Technically, you don't interact with each other directly but with a distributed ledger. You trust the system as a whole, not one particular entity.

Cash is given directly from hand to hand.

Regular digital payments are sent through a bank or different payment processors.

Cryptocurrencies are sent directly from device to device.

Transfers are therefore *trustless* and *permissionless*.

Trustless means you don't have to rely on a third-party to make or confirm the transfer for you, and permissionless means you don't have to worry about your transactions being blocked. Nobody can freeze your account (p.59) or prevent you from opening one (p.55). Cryptocurrencies are *uncensorable*.

You also don't have to trust a third-party to hold your money like you do when you have money in a bank. What you really have is an IOU from the bank where they promise to give you your money when you ask for it. With cryptocurrencies you can write down the keys to your wallet and you, alone, have access to it.

Some will be quick to point out that transfers aren't trustless. You need to trust your wallet, the OS, the hardware, etc. That is true. The context here is not having to trust a third-party to handle transfers for you, not eliminating trust of all kinds—which is impossible.

You can let a third-party hold them if you want, and it's probably a good choice for many.

Please make sure to encrypt your *seed* (a human-readable representation of your keys) (p.208) otherwise a thief can easily steal your coins if he finds it.

No counterfeiting

Problems with counterfeit coins and bills go far back. From biting coins to test their hardness to today's advanced techniques, counterfeit prevention has always been an important feature for cash.

With cryptocurrencies, anyone can independently verify the integrity of the coins you send and receive. Details on how is in the next chapter but I assure you no biting is needed. You cannot counterfeit coins and you cannot send the same coin to multiple people *(double spend)*. This is what allows cryptocurrencies to operate without a trusted third-party.

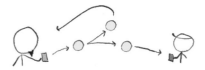

A double spending occurs when someone sends the same coin both to a merchant and back to himself.

Predetermined emission rate

As there's no trusted third-party, there's no single entity who controls the creation of new money and the inflation. Instead, new coins are minted following predetermined rules.

The new coins are rewards for miners who secure the network, but more on that in the next chapter.

Circulating supply

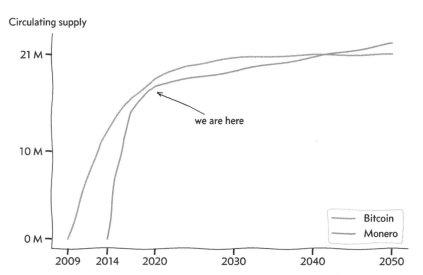

Bitcoin has a hard limit of 21 million bitcoins, while in Monero new coins will always be created.

The emission rate in Bitcoin approximates the rate gold is mined. In Monero, the tail emission is there to replace lost coins and to make sure rewards for miners don't run out.

If you're curious about Austrian Economics, which most cryptocurrencies follow, I can recommend the Bitcoin.com podcast with Jeffrey Tucker[11]. It's not something you hear about often, but it presents an interesting viewpoint and shouldn't be dismissed.

If inflation is good or bad depends on who you ask. Keynesian economists argue inflation is good[9] while the Austrian school argues inflation is bad[10].

I definitely don't know who is right. It's probably best to be skeptical of both camps—economics operate in an extremely complex and irregular environment. Economic theories are difficult, or impossible, to verify.

> acquisition of skills requires a regular environment, an adequate opportunity to practice, and rapid and unequivocal feedback about the correctness of thoughts and actions.

The book *Thinking, Fast and Slow* is fantastically thought provoking.

Daniel Kahneman, Thinking, Fast and Slow[Thi11]

Either way, it's not an argument against cryptocurrencies in general, as they can be made either inflationary or deflationary (although, all I know of becomes deflationary).

Irreversible transactions

Just like with cash, cryptocurrency transfers are irreversible. This means if you've sent someone coins, you can only get them back if they agree to give them back. It prevents *charge back fraud* (p.52) but it makes theft worse.

It's possible to reverse transfers... If everyone agrees. Ethereum famously altered their rules in the DAO hard fork. Many agreed but not everyone, so Ethereum split into two coins where Ethereum Classic kept the old rules.[12]

Private

Commonly used payment systems, like credit cards for example, asks you to give up your privacy as all payments are recorded. So they require you to tie your identity to them. But cryptocurrencies can be used privately— there's no need to disclose your identity or your transaction history—making them similar to cash in this respect.

Bitcoin, like most cryptocurrencies, do record all transactions in a public ledger. So, it's a little misleading to say that cryptocurrencies are inherently private, but some cryptocurrencies like Monero try to solve this problem (p.193).

Large and small amounts behave the same

In contrast to cash or gold where large amounts can be cumbersome to handle, there's no difference between large or small transfers in a cryptocurrency. Transaction costs are the same for small transfers as for large transfers. They are just as secure and wallets can store as much as you're comfortable with.

It's also easy to split coins into small parts. In fact, you don't have to think about dividing at all, you use a wallet just like a credit card—a transfer is always exact.

For example, one bitcoin can be divided into one hundred million parts—called satoshis (named after Bitcoin's inventor Satoshi Nakamoto). But there's no real technical limit, only a usability concern.

Borderless

Cryptocurrencies are inherently global. They're usable wherever you are as long as you have an internet connection. You can even send to wallets that are offline, but to retrieve them you need to access the internet. Technically, you could do transfers completely offline—on paper—but they would be unconfirmed and might not be valid when you do want to use them.

An offline wallet with no computer contact like a *paper wallet* is called *cold storage*. It's an excellent way to store large amounts you're not planning to use for some time.

Chapter 2
How do cryptocurrencies work?
Decentralized consensus

Price is the least interesting thing about bitcoin.

Roger Ver

This is my attempt to explain how a standard cryptocurrency like Bitcoin works. Other cryptocurrencies may diverge on various points, but the fundamentals are the same.

For example, Ethereum adds Turing complete smart contracts (p.155), and CryptoNote protocols like Monero hide transaction details (p.193).

As stated in the introduction the focus isn't on technical details, but it's a tight balance to make between keeping it simple and explaining how cryptocurrencies work. If this chapter is too technical, you can safely skip to the next chapter or just read the summary—it's not required knowledge.

Summary

The *blockchain* is a ledger that stores balances. The crucial problem is deciding between double spends (using a coin twice). Cryptocurrencies like Bitcoin use *proof-of-work* which makes miners expend energy and compete for rewards. This competition between miners is used to resolve double spends and to secure the chain, allowing the winner to extend the blockchain with new transactions that don't double spend.

What makes it all work is the incentives for the miners to work in the best interest of the network as it's the most profitable option. The security assumption is that most of the miners are honest and work for profit, otherwise the security model fails and transactions can be reversed.

The ledger

If you want to create a digital currency, you only really need to keep track of how many coins everyone have. For example, your bank might have entries in a ledger like this:

Person	Swedish krona
Sneaky Steve	7 000 SEK
Honest Harry	1 000 SEK

When Sneaky Steve wants to send 500 SEK to Honest Harry, the bank simply updates the ledger:

Person	Swedish krona
Sneaky Steve	6 500 SEK (-500 SEK)
Honest Harry	1 500 SEK (+500 SEK)

Cryptocurrencies work this way, as well. In fact, the ledger in a cryptocurrency, often referred to as the *blockchain*, contains the balance of all addresses.

It's a slight simplification to say the blockchain stores balances. It actually stores all transactions from which you can calculate all balances.

To lighten the load, you can run your software in a pruned mode which discards the transactions after validation and only keeps the balances.

Your keys, your coins

To be able to create a transaction, you need to have the *private keys* to the address you want to send from. Think of it as a secret password that unlocks your account. This prevents anyone else from stealing your coins, unless, of course, they steal your private key!

It uses *public-key cryptography* (p.204), which allows you to prove you control the private key without sharing the private key itself. Compare it to credit card numbers which act as both a private and public key. See *A hitchhiker's guide to cryptography* (p.201) for more details, but a low-level cryptographic understanding isn't required to understand how cryptocurrencies work.

Copying a coin & double spending

So far, cryptocurrencies don't do anything new. The hard problem is: how do you prevent someone from copying a coin, and sending the copies to two different receivers? Couldn't you just copy the hard drive to copy your coins?

For example, Sneaky Steve wants to buy a computer from Honest Harry and wants to pay with Bitcoin. The computer costs 1 BTC, and the Bitcoin ledger looks like this:

Address	Bitcoin
Sneaky Steve 1	1 BTC
Sneaky Steve 2	0 BTC
Honest Harry	0 BTC

What Sneaky Steve tries to do is send 1 BTC to the merchant, Honest Harry, and then send a copy of 1 BTC to his other address: Sneaky Steve 2. (It's possible to have as many addresses as you want—a consequence of the permissionless nature of Bitcoin.)

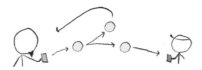

Sneaky Steve sends a digital coin both to Honest Harry and himself.

If we didn't prevent this, the ledger might look like this:

Address	Bitcoin	Diff
Sneaky Steve 1	-1 BTC	(-2 BTC)
Sneaky Steve 2	1 BTC	(+1 BTC)
Honest Harry	1 BTC	(+1 BTC)

We copied our coin and printed 1 BTC out of thin air, so now the ledger contains a negative balance. This is a form of *double spending*—spending the same coin twice.

This isn't really a problem with physical cash since you can't just copy gold coins or paper notes. It's not a problem for banks either since the bank can just deny one or both of the transactions. This is a hard problem for a digital currency that tries to remove the central authority, and this is why before Bitcoin no *decentralized* digital currency existed.

Decentralization is a common term used to refer to the lack of a trusted third-party. Instead, multiple unrelated entities come together and decide as a group.

There are different types of decentralization in a cryptocurrency to consider. For example:

1. Mining decentralization
2. Development decentralization
3. Node decentralization

The one we're interested in here is who decides which transactions to approve, which is the miners' job.

The Byzantine Generals Problem

To resolve double spending, it's enough to choose one of the double spending transactions. But how do you do that when there are many unrelated people—and some who want to cheat?

This is the same problem as the *Byzantine Generals Problem*[13]. Here's my description of a simple variation:

In the Eastern Roman Empire, also referred to as the Byzantine Empire, several generals surround an enemy city:

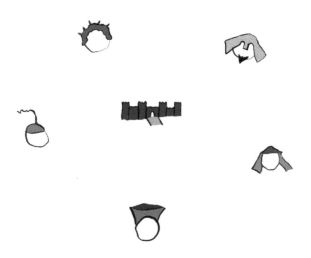

The five generals surround a well defended enemy city. They don't have direct contact and instead need to communicate by sending messengers.

The city is very well-defended and if they attack individually, they will be defeated. So, they will have to work together and coordinate to attack at the same time, or retreat as a unit. Doing nothing is not an option either as they have a limited food supply while the city is waiting for reinforcements.

If they try to act without a majority, they will surely face defeat—they must coordinate.

This would be very easy if they could trust each other. Unfortunately, they cannot trust the messages—either the messenger or the message itself could be replaced—and even some of the generals could be traitors.

One countermeasure to corrupt messengers is to *encrypt* messages (p.204). Unfortunately, it doesn't protect against a traitor who knows the code, like one of the generals. Also, in ancient times, encryption wasn't very advanced and could possibly be broken, see the *Caesar cipher*[23] as an example.

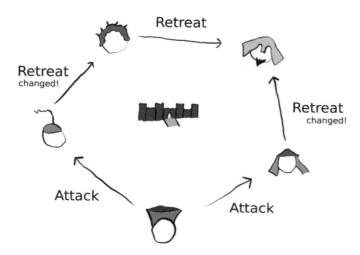

One general sends out messengers declaring his intent to attack to the generals next to him, who then sends messengers of their own, and so on, until all generals have received the message. However, two of the messengers are traitors and change the message from "attack" to "retreat".

In this simple example, three of the generals now believe that they will attack while two are preparing to retreat. In a more complex scenario, they might receive conflicting messages and notice something is amiss, but they don't know what's real and what's not and cannot decide what to do.

To relate it back to cryptocurrencies, the choice between "attack" and "retreat" is similar to choosing between two transactions in a double spend. You know there are bad actors, but who can you trust?

The resistance to this kind of problem is called *Byzantine fault tolerance (BFT)*. There's a big difference between systems with known actors and systems with unknown actors, like with cryptocurrencies, but they both fall under the BFT umbrella.

Sybil attack

You may think most users in the network are honest, so can't you just ask everyone?

Unfortunately, there's a serious problem here. As there's no barrier to participate in the network and no identity control, a single person can have multiple identities:

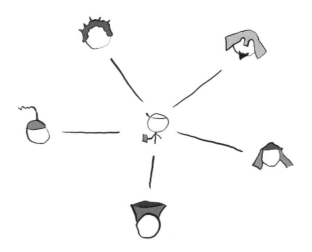

This is what Honest Harry sees; a diverse group of honest individuals.

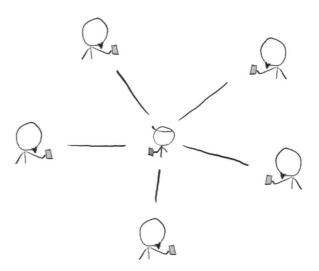

But in reality they're all controlled by Sneaky Steve.

This is called a *Sybil attack*. Think of how one person can use multiple online identities to troll or attack people online—it's hard to know who is real.

Proof-of-work

If you've heard about cryptocurrencies, then maybe you've also heard about *cryptocurrency miners* or *Bitcoin miners*. This is how Bitcoin provides sybil resistance and prevents double spends.

The core idea is: if you want to choose which transaction is valid you have to do work. The process is known as *proof-of-work*, shortened to POW.

The work is to find a solution to a computing problem. The problem itself is not that important, and it doesn't have any meaning outside of mining. There's some important properties it should have:

- **Hard enough**

  In Bitcoin, one solution is expected every 10 minutes. The difficulty is continuously adjusted to allow miners to join and leave.

  An example is playing a game of Yahtzee, where the goal is to cast dice and get them all to have the same number, and you change the number of dice in play.

- **Easy to verify**

  While a problem should be hard to solve, it must be very easy to verify. It should be easy to verify on mobile phones, for example.

  For instance while multiplying two prime numbers is easy, it can be very difficult to determine which two primes given only the product. This is used to make a type of *public-key cryptography* (p.204) safe.

- **Memoryless**

  Knowing earlier outcomes shouldn't give any advantage. Finding a solution should essentially be random.

  It's similar to how you're just as likely—or unlikely—to get a Royal Flush on your first hand as on your 1000th hand. Whatever you got the other 999 hands doesn't matter.

Cryptographic hash functions are excellent choices, Bitcoin uses SHA-256, for example. See *Hash functions* (p.202) for more details. For an in-depth explanation of Bitcoin's proof-of-work, I recommend Ken Shirriff's blog post *Mining Bitcoin with pencil and paper: 0.67 hashes per day*, which shows how to mine Bitcoin with pen and paper[14].

It's very common for cryptocurrency communities to be flooded by trolls pushing their own agenda.

Remember that to resolve double spending one transaction must be chosen, which one doesn't matter.

In Bitcoin, specialized hardware, called *ASICs*, are used which are many magnitudes faster than regular computers at solving POW problems.

They can only be used for a specific type of POW algorithm and cannot be used to mine any other cryptocurrency unless that currency also uses the same POW algorithm.

It's difficult to create a problem that satisfy the POW properties while having a useful side-effect. For example, *The Protein Folding Problem* is not easy to verify, and it's hard to adjust the problem difficulty.

Additionally, if there was a useful side-effect, it might alter the economic incentives of mining. If mining is purely done to secure a cryptocurrency, then the miners' investment rests on the success of the cryptocurrency while a secondary use for specialized mining hardware lessens the incentive to secure the chain.

A solution is proof that you've done the work—it's proof that you've expended energy. It's like a lottery and you can get lucky, but in the long run it balances out. Since you require a significant investment to find a block, this can be used as sybil resistance; you can't just create thousands of fake identities for free.

It's important to note that the system is permissionless so there's nobody to prevent you from becoming a miner, but you also don't have to be. The blockchain is open for anyone to read and validate, it's only writing that's exclusive to miners.

Updating the blockchain

When a miner finds a solution, she can update the ledger by adding a block to the blockchain. A block is basically a collection of transactions.

A blockchain is what it sounds like: a chain of blocks where a new block builds on previous blocks. When a miner searches for a solution, she must target a block on a specific height—the POW problem includes a reference to the previous block and it only fits at a specific position in the chain. When a new block is added, all miners need to work on a new problem targeting that block.

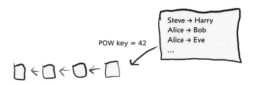

The blocks in the blockchain are linked with a key obtained by solving the POW problem.

The transactions must follow common rules, called consensus rules, otherwise other miners and users who use the blockchain will discard the block. For example, a transaction cannot send coins from an empty address or spend coins without having access to the private key of that address.

In return for adding the block, you get to collect the rewards. One for finding a block and you can collect transaction fees for the transactions you include in the block.

The blockchain is public and anyone can see all transactions. You can use a blockchain explorer, such as blockchair.com, to see for yourself; try for example to lookup this transaction that has one input and two outputs:[15]

```
0c4c723ea0b78722a79c3e34fb714b92e5aac355041f490cd56937c14458d44f
```

As I'm writing this in February 2021, the current *block reward* for Bitcoin is 6.25 BTC, or about $250,000. With one block expected every 10 min that's about $36,000,000 per day. Bitcoin mining is big business.

One output is usually a *change output* where you send change back to one of your own addresses.

Cryptocurrencies, like Monero, that hide transaction amounts and the source and destination of coins also have a public blockchain, see the `xmr-chain.net` blockchain explorer, for example[16]. While you cannot see what the transactions are doing, you can still verify that the transactions are valid and aren't sending coins from empty addresses. The math on how exactly that works is outside the scope of this book—I can't say I fully understand it either.

The blockchain is duplicated, stored, and maintained by many different people; you might think of it as similar to how torrents work. When you send and receive transactions, you're really interacting with the block-chain and not with each other directly.

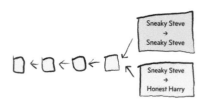

A payment is sent to the network and not directly to the receiver. The transaction then gets forwarded to miners who eventually add it to the blockchain. The receiver then confirms the payment in the blockchain, without trusting the payee.

Forks

What happens if two miners find a block at the same height? For example, one where Sneaky Steve sends money to Honest Harry and one where Sneaky Steve sends money to himself?

Two blocks at the same height with different transactions.

The chain will split, and there will be a *fork*. Each miner will independently choose which one they will build on and one will eventually become longer:

Here there are two chains after a fork, one of length two and one of length four.

There are several different ways to interact with the blockchain. For the end user there are three main ways, with different trade-offs:

1. Run a full node
2. Use an SPV wallet
3. Use a light wallet

A full node stores a complete copy of the blockchain on your computer and verifies all transactions. This is the most trustless way but also the most resource intensive.

An SPV wallet confirms that the proof-of-work is valid and that your transaction is inside the block, but it does not validate the transactions. This means it's trusting that the longest chain is always valid—a reasonable assumption—and is much less resource intensive.[24]

A light wallet interacts with a third-party node but does not validate anything itself. It's the least resource intensive but you also need to trust a third-party service.

Forking a cryptocurrency is different from forking the code, although both are common.

When a shorter chain gets abandoned, we say it gets *orphaned*. It's a natural consequence of the system but high orphan rates are problematic because they hurt smaller miners more than larger miners.

In the credit card world, this type of fraud is called *charge back fraud* or *friendly fraud* (p.52).

The longer chain is to be considered "the correct" chain and the shorter chain will be abandoned. Coming to consensus by following the longest chain is often referred to as *Nakamoto consensus*.

Because rewards on each chain can only be used on that particular chain, any rewards on the abandoned chain will be effectively worthless. Therefore, the miners are heavily incentivized to work on the longest chain and so the shorter chain will get abandoned quickly.

In the example, Honest Harry should wait until he knows which chain is longer and decide from there.

Reversing transactions

If Sneaky Steve can't trick Honest Harry by showing him a fake transaction, he can try to reverse his payment after receiving goods from Honest Harry.

It works like this:

1   Make a transaction to Honest Harry that's confirmed on the blockchain.

2   Create a longer hidden chain where Sneaky Steve keeps the money.

3   After receiving the goods, Sneaky Steve publishes the second chain.

    Because people automatically follow the longer chain this effectively reverses the transaction to Honest Harry and Sneaky Steve has successfully commited fraud.

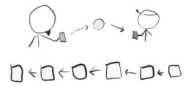

Sneaky Steve pays Honest Harry and they wait until the transaction has two confirmations.

Satisfied, Honest Harry gives Sneaky Steve a new pair of beautiful jeans.

Sneaky Steve walks away with his jeans, all while secretly working on his own chain.

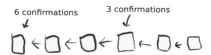

After Sneaky Steve has walked away he releases his hidden chain of length four, which **doesn't contain his payment to Honest Harry**. Since the new chain is longer, the old chain will get discarded and the payment to Honest Harry will also disappear. It will seem like the payment never happened.

This is a different type of double spend, and it's the primary attack vector the white paper (p.189) is concerned about. It's called a *51% attack*, for reasons we'll soon explain.

Transaction security

The deeper a transaction is in the blockchain—the more confirmations it has—the harder a transaction is to reverse.

6 confirmations   3 confirmations

Confirmations for different blocks.
Each block added to the blockchain makes every existing block—and transactions—more secure.

Bitcoin's security isn't absolute but probabilistic. One way to think about it is to find one block you need to get lucky. To find more blocks you need to get lucky several times, which you have to do if you want to reverse a transaction with more confirmations.

Bitcoin's white paper (p.189) goes into more details and recommends 6 confirmations—roughly one hour—to be sure you don't get defrauded. Today for most normal payments, a single confirmation is enough.

A crucial mistake people make is to think more miners, or more energy used, means more transactions can be handled. This is not true. Miners **only** care about securing the chain preventing transactions from being reversed.

In fact, we could spend 100x more energy on mining and process the same amount of transactions, or we could spend 1% of the energy and process more transactions. Transaction throughput is a separate problem.

You can even accept transactions without any confirmation, called *0-conf*. They are much less secure than a confirmed transaction, but since most miners respect the first-seen-rule it's fairly safe for small purchases.

There are investigations on how to make 0-conf more secure. One of the more interesting proposals is *0-conf forfeits* where you provide a larger sum as hostage and if you try to double spend, you lose them.[25]

There is some correlation here. Because each transaction contains a fee the miner can claim, more transactions means the reward is bigger which, in turn, supports more miners. But the reverse is not true, more energy does not mean higher transaction throughput.

The 50% security assumption

The whole system relies on a majority of miners being honest—it's the core security assumption behind proof-of-work.

Honest miners work for profit so they absolutely don't want to risk their blocks being rejected by the other miners and lose their reward. Therefore, the rational thing to do is to work on the longest chain.

This means for Sneaky Steve to successfully reverse a transaction he needs to control more than half of all mining power—otherwise his hidden chain can never become the longest. It's called a *51% attack* because you need to control at least 51% of all mining power to pull it off consistently.

This touches on the immutability of the blockchain. As long as more than 50% of miners don't want to change the chain, it will always be longest and correct. But if they do then they can reverse transactions.

Economics of a 51% attack

How secure is Bitcoin, really? What do we need to pull off a 51% attack?

Here's some quick napkin math to estimate the cost for 51% mining power:

Total Bitcoin hash rate[17]	152,810,000 TH/s
Antminer S9i hash rate[18]	14 TH/s (+-5%)
Antminer S9i cost[19]	$400
Number of S9i to cover the whole network	10,915,000
Total network miner cost	$4,366,000,000
Cost to reach 51%	> $2,183,000,000

So that's more than two billion for just the miners themselves (assuming you could purchase that many—a big task as all miners are sold out!). On top of that, we need power supply, cooling, storage, and maintenance for millions of miners. We're looking at a massive warehouse or several. Safe to say it's a very large investment, but maybe not impossibly large.

If we manage to get enough miners, it should allow us to double-spend and defraud exchanges and merchants. It almost sounds like we can get free money, but it's not that simple.

A 51% can be detected and there can be severe negative consequences:

- The Bitcoin price might crash.
- Exchanges might blacklist the stolen funds.
- The community might change POW and make all mining rigs worthless.
- It's hard to keep warehouses full of mining rigs of that scale a secret—there's a big risk to get caught.

Bitcoin Gold was successfully 51% attacked and exchanges were double spent. The attacker managed to reverse transactions 22 blocks deep.[26]

This is the danger for smaller cryptocurrencies that don't have much mining power securing the chain. 51% attacking Bitcoin would be **much** harder.

I made the estimation in January 2021, but the math changes quickly. I encourage you to make an estimate on your own, with more up-to-date numbers.

As an example, Monero has changed POW several times bricking existing ASICs. The expensive mining rigs used on Monero are now practically worthless.

Bitcoin miners are rewarded in bitcoin and they also can't be spent until after 100 blocks—roughly 16 hours. Executing a 51% attack that crashes the price would directly affect the rewards. If the community goes for the nuclear option and change POW, then the massive initial investment into mining equipment might be lost.

These risks needs to weighed against what profits a 51% attack could generate. Maybe exchanges could get defrauded for $100 million (roughly a 5% return on investment)? A 51% miner would make that back in about one week—risk-free.

The economic incentives are so strong that it might be rational even for a 51% for-profit miner to be honest. In fact Bitcoin has had pools with 51% before[20] without incidents.

The biggest security risk for Bitcoin might instead be state-level actors who wants to destroy it no matter the costs. For example if the United States would spend billions on a "War on Bitcoin".

The case is a little different for cryptocurrencies that share POW algorithm with others. The miners could attack the minority chain and jump back to the majority chain after executing the attack.

An economic innovation

While cryptocurrencies combine several different technologies in an interesting way, the real innovation is how they're secured by economic incentives; the most profitable way for miners is to follow the network rules.

As noted earlier, the current block reward for Bitcoin is 6.25 BTC, or around $250,000. Losing out on just one block reward is a big loss in the cutthroat mining business, so miners are heavily incentivized to always work on the longest chain.

For example, in a fork with two competing chains, the most profitable move is to jump to the longest chain as quickly as possible. This ensures that a double-spend gets resolved quickly.

It also doesn't make sense for a minority miner to try to double-spend, it will only cause them to lose money in the long run. Therefore, only a miner with 51% can compromise the network security, and even then it may even be more profitable to play by the rules.

Network upgrades and new cryptocurrencies

There's another situation where forks can arise: when consensus rules are changed. Here are some examples of consensus changes:

- Removing the 21 million supply cap in Bitcoin.
- Blacklisting or stealing coins from an address.
- Allowing a new transaction type.
- Tweaking the POW algorithm.
- Raising the 1 MB blocksize limit in Bitcoin.

Some cryptocurrencies, like Monero and Bitcoin Cash, have regular network upgrades where consensus rules are changed.

Because a network upgrade is a fork, there will be two chains (as long as someone mines them). Sometimes, the minority chain lives on as a new cryptocurrency; Ethereum Classic is the continuation of the old chain after an Ethereum fork[21].

Other times, the fork is initiated by people who want to create a new cryptocurrency from another one, but the mechanism is exactly the same. This means you can fork Bitcoin at any point if you want, the tricky part is getting other people to join you.

You may then wonder; what decides which is the correct chain? There's no clear answer and social consensus decides which of the chains is called "Original Coin" and which is called "New Coin". Social consensus may be very messy, and cryptocurrencies won't help us there.

Alternative consensus models

There are alternatives to proof-of-work but none have so far been proven to work well. The most popular is *proof-of-stake* where instead of miners expending energy, you have coin holders who vote.

One problem is the *nothing at stake problem* where a coin holder can vote on all forks while a proof-of-work miner can only vote on one of the forks[22]. It causes a situation where everyone is incentivized to vote on all forks, and an attacker can abuse it to reverse a transaction by only mining on their fork, which is initially a block behind, to overtake the main chain and reverse their transaction. This only requires a small percentage of total voting power in contrast to proof-of-work where you need 50%.

I've deliberately simplified my usage of fork terminology. On a technical level, it's useful to distinguish between two types of forks: *hard-forks* and *soft-forks*.

A hard-fork is a backwards incompatible change and all nodes must upgrade to avoid ending up on the old chain. Bitcoin Cash forked off from Bitcoin using a hard-fork for example.

Instead, a soft-fork instead doesn't break older node implementations. They will simply ignore the new soft-fork rules—they will not fully validate the chain anymore but they will follow it. The rules are instead enforced by the miners who must upgrade. For example, SegWit in Bitcoin was implemented using a soft-fork.

More details

In this chapter, I've focused on a high-level understanding and I've skipped out on details occasionally. If you want to go deeper I encourage you to do more research on your own.

Bitcoin's white paper (p.189) is always a good place to begin, and there are also many good resources online. I've tried to include key concepts which you can use as starting points in your search.

Chapter 3

Look out for snake oil
The space is new, hyped and full of misleading information

So I mean for today, you could have, some Bitcoin business have a tab, so you pay them and then you work your tab there and presumably you cash your tab out if you don't use it.

If you have repeat custom... or maybe the shops in the local area could make a shared tab or something in anticipation of... you know somebody in the local area ... technology expert could make a local Bitcoin tab that's interoperable between the shops and some sort of app to do it.

Adam Back, Baltic Honeybadger 2017 Bitcoin Conference[27]

A snake oil salesperson sells, or promotes, a valueless or fraudulent solution. The cryptocurrency space is full of such people and broken solutions.

Not really cryptocurrencies

There are many projects in the cryptocurrency space that, curiously enough, aren't actually cryptocurrencies. Some even go so far as to call them cryptocurrencies even though they don't fulfil the criteria. For example I don't consider these real cryptocurrencies:

- OneCoin and Bitconnect—they're simple pyramid schemes
- Ripple
- Stablecoins like Tether or JP Morgan's JPM coin
- "Second layer solutions" like the Lightning Network
- Smart tokens like the ERC20 tokens running on top of Ethereum
- Facebook's Diem (renamed from Libra due to bad publicity)

Some might be useful, but they don't have the same properties as cryptocurrencies like Bitcoin, and they don't work the same way.

For example, stablecoins depend on a third-party issuer and redeemer—the very thing cryptocurrencies are meant to remove. Second layer solutions have fundamentally different security trade-offs and they work differently; they're built on top of—but they are not—cryptocurrencies.

Be very skeptical of sites like `coinmarketcap.com` that says it lists the "Top 100 Cryptocurrencies by Market Capitalization" because most of the coins listed aren't real cryptocurrencies. Like how Tether is currently #3 on the list (2020-09-21), but that's meaningless since they can be printed out of thin air, significantly warping the market cap.

The blockchain hype

There's the phenomena where a technology gets hyped up and businesses all over rush to adopt it in any way they can, even if it's totally the wrong solution for their problems.

Removing the consensus mechanism from a cryptocurrency, so they can just use the blockchain, removes what makes cryptocurrencies useful. The blockchain data-structure by itself is neither new nor interesting, yet that's all people seem to focus on.

Be aware of "the blockchain" being used only as a buzzword.

Leaders of OneCoin got charged for operating it as a pyramid scheme[28] and I'll recommend BBC's podcast series *The Missing Cryptoqueen*[29] for a fascinating account of the scam. Meanwhile, the FBI is seeking victims who invested in Bitconnect[30].

In 2021 the SEC charged Ripple and two executives with conducting an unregistered securities offering.[32]

After years of suspicion Tether finally admitted it's only backed 74% by cash.[31]

Smart tokens are often used in *Initial Coin Offerings (ICOs)* where you invest in a project by sending them money and in return get these tokens. The hope is they become valuable or the project buys them back so you get returns on your investment.

Many ICOs have been declared illegal as they're classified as securities and many more are very scammy. Bitconnect is for example an ICO.

You could say the popular version control system git uses a blockchain, but it has nothing to do with cryptocurrencies.

Warning signs to look out for

When evaluating cryptocurrencies, here are some red flags to look out for:

- Heavily slanted initial coin supply

  Like only creating 21 million coins, but keeping 20 million for yourself.

- Central authorities

  A "centralized cryptocurrency" is an oxymoron because it's not trustless or permissionless and it doesn't prevent a single entity from manipulating the supply, the very things that define a cryptocurrency. A "private block-chain" has the same fatal flaws.

  If someone can freeze your coins, prevent them from being used in a particular country or generate them from thin air then it's not a crypto-currency.

- Bad consensus algorithms or centralized governance protocols

  If a cryptocurrency isn't working as I describe in *How do cryptocurrencies work?* (p.11), then chances are it's not actually decentralized and calling it a cryptocurrency might be a stretch.

- Promises that sound too good to be true

  For example promising instant transactions and infinite scalability, while compromising the decentralization and security of the network. *Proof-of-stake* coins are usually guilty of this.

- Propaganda

  Social media is chock-full of users who try to sell snake oil to you. Slander, lies and censorship is a daily occurrence.

- Large drawbacks

  Like having expensive and unreliable transactions or having to be online to receive payments.

- Problems are hand-waved away

  "We'll figure it out" or "It'll be ready in 18 months" (forever).

There are many traps to fall into in this space. I think the best antidote is to try and learn as much as possible, and never be afraid to question everything.

Slanting the coin supply comes in many variants. It's common to assign large parts of the initial supply to the creators or to mine the chain in secret before releasing it to the public.

A more sinister tactic is to introduce a bug in the code that allows miners to mine extremely fast—and only fix it after you've mined a big portion. This is what Dash did in a so-called *instamine*[33].

Imagine the irony of censorship being a problem in communities supporting censorship-free money. Unfortunately, examples of censorship on Reddit are plentiful.[34][35][36][37]

Chapter 4

What is money?

It's subjective

Money is gold, and nothing else.

J.P. Morgan, 1912

Money is something completely necessary in our society, and most people come in contact with money every day. We might use it to buy things, worry about our expenses, that we don't have enough, or even be glad for how much we have. But we seldom stop and think of what money really is.

Not just how the physical coins and pieces of paper are made, but why does money exist? What makes it valuable? Are there different kinds of money? And are some forms of money better than others?

Before getting interested in cryptocurrencies I too had never asked these questions and with this chapter, I hope to provide some insight into this admittedly complex topic.

The terms money and currency are often used interchangeably. Although I might be sloppy in my usage, there's a subtle difference. Money refers to an intangible concept—you cannot reach out and grab it. Currency instead refers to the physical coins themselves.

If that's the definition then maybe cryptocurrencies should instead be called crypto-money?

Even though we cannot reach out and grab them, the coins do exist. Similar to how digital pictures exist—they're not an abstract concept. Therefore I, as much as the community, will still call cryptocurrencies a type of currency.

Historical examples of money

First, let's look at some interesting historical examples of items that have been used as money. Some are quite fascinating.

Sea shells 1200 B.C.

Sea shells have been used as money for centuries and were commonly used in parts of Africa and Asia but also in other parts of the world[38]. In West Africa, they saw significant use until the 20th century[39].

Coins in ancient Greece 500 B.C.

The Greeks used coins made from precious metal like silver, bronze, and gold. They also stamped the coins with beautiful portraits for a truly modern look.[40]

Rai stones 1000 - 1400 A.D.

Rai stones is a form of stone money on the Yap Islands. They can be up to 4 m in diameter but most are much smaller, down to around 3.5 cm in diameter. Instead of moving the big ones, you simply tell people you've transferred them, like a social ledger.[41][42]

A 20kg copper coin 1644

Another example of—let's say interesting—form of money is the world's largest coin. It's a copper coin weighing 20kg, issued in Sweden.[43]

Since copper was worth much less than silver, very large coins had to be made to offset the difference. At that time, coins did contain raw materials according to their value, which isn't the case today.

A 100 billion mark note 1924

Bank notes—paper money—are easy to use but they do have problems of their own. Unless kept in check, by for example *the gold standard* (p.34), they can be mass produced to cause *hyperinflation* (p.122).

This is what happened in Germany after the first World War. They had massive debts after losing the war, so they tried to print enough money to pay off the debts.[44]

While the inflation was slow at first it quickly ramped up. It culminated in 1924 with a 100 billion mark note[45], while only four years earlier 100 mark notes were used.

There are many interesting stories[46]. For example, kids playing with stacks of money, how it was cheaper to use the notes themselves as wallpaper, or how kids created kites with the notes.

Cigarettes in prison 20th century

Like depicted in the movie Shawshank Redemption cigarettes are used in some prisons as a form of money[47]. Today, some prisons have started to ban smoking, so they instead use things like stamps or ramen[48][49].

Euro bank notes 21th century

There are many kinds of *fiat currencies*, for example the Euro. Modern coins aren't made of valuable metal and paper notes are used for large denominations.

There is a popular classification of money into different types. *Fiat money* is what we typically use today—government-issued money.

Commodity money refers to money which derives its value from the commodity it's made of. For example, coins made of gold. The fact that the value comes from the commodity itself is questionable, see the *subjective theory of value* (p.35).

Dogecoin 2013

Dogecoin is a cryptocurrency and while created as a "joke currency", it quickly gained popularity as a tipping tool online. You can still find merchants who accept it today for things like domain names, web hosting, VPNs, or games.

Marbles on the school yard 2017

Kids on the school-yard often come up with interesting forms of money. For example collectible card games or game components. Another example is marbles used in a Swedish game where you win your opponents marbles. (And those with many marbles had higher status in class.)

I'm not up to date with the games kids play these days. I still live with the memories of skipping class to play Pokémon. Good times.

The gold standard

There's an important historical point to make about fiat. First used 1821 in the United Kingdom, the *gold standard* made sure to back each currency unit with gold. So if you had 1,000 bank notes, you could exchange them for a specific weight in gold bullion. This was used in various ways up until 1971, when it was finally abandoned completely.

Like a lot of things we'll touch, whether the gold standard is preferable or not is hotly debated.[50]

Bartering, and why do we need money?

What would life look like if we didn't have money? We would have to turn to bartering—trading goods or services directly.

Bartering can happen on a small scale today. For example, in your social circle, you might trade favors instead of money.

In an economical collapse, like in the case of hyperinflation or a zombie invasion, bartering might make sense on a larger scale as well.

Imagine if you're a farmer and you have a bunch of pigs. To buy a new chair, you need to trade with the carpenter, and maybe you can buy the chair for a single pig.

But there are problems with this system:

1 What if the carpenter doesn't want your pig?

   You would have to trade with others and find something the seller would accept.

It can sometimes be very cumbersome to trade for something the carpenter wants—in this case a bottle of rum. Each step in the process needs a matching buyer and seller.

2 What if you want to buy a loaf of bread, worth much less than a single pig?

   You would have to kill a pig and offer parts to him. It's undesirable if the pig hasn't grown up yet and you'll get stuck with leftover parts.

In short, it's extremely inefficient.

This is why we as a society prefer to use money. Even if the thing we use as money itself is basically worthless—like pieces of paper—the function it serves is very valuable.

State theory of money

One common answer to the question "what gives money value?" is the *state theory of money*[52] (many refer to it unknowingly).

The basic thesis is that it's the state that gives value to money:

- Fiat currency is declared by the state to be *legal tender*.

  Which, among other things, means merchants have to accept it by law.

- The state is responsible to regulate inflation.

- Banks are insured by the state, increasing safety of the currency.

  During the gold standard the state ensured that fiat currencies were backed by gold.

In the US, it's actually the *Federal Reserve System*, a central bank, that controls printing of money. Most other countries use a similar system. In the EU, it's called the *European Central Bank*.

While this might on the surface explain why fiat currencies are valuable, it fails to explain why other forms of money become valuable.

Subjective theory of value

Instead, a better explanation is given by the *subjective theory of value*[53]. It describes how goods are valued, but it serves just as well to explain why money is valuable.

In short, it says that *value is subjective*.

It might sound too simplistic or like a tautology. But what it means is there's no global deciding function that gives value. Instead, each person independently assigns value.

For instance, medicine can be extremely valuable for those who need it, but could have little value to others. So if you have the medicine, but don't need it, you'll gladly sell. But someone who needs it would be reluctant to sell, unless it's for a very high price.

In the context of commodity money it means they can be more valuable than what they're made of. This can happen if their value as a medium of exchange is more than the value of the raw materials.

A related fact is that the material in US nickels can be worth more than the value of the nickel itself. (The melt value varies).[51]

What does it mean for money? That **the value of money is emergent from a group of individuals**. If, for example, everyone in your social group declare that tomorrow they'll use Pokémon trading cards as money, then the trading cards suddenly become very valuable to you. The more people that use a form of money, the better it works and the more value it will have.

States don't give money value, but they can contribute. For example, declaring fiat legal tender makes more people accept it, which in turn increases its value.

What functions does money serve?

If anything can be used as money, it makes more sense to look at how money is used. Knowledgeable people[54] seem to agree money has three major functions:

1   **Medium of exchange**

    It can be used to intermediate the exchange of goods and services.

    For example, the use of sea shells as money. The shells themselves aren't particularly useful, but their use as a medium of exchange is.

2   **Unit of account**

    A standard unit to measure the market value of goods and services.

    For instance, car prices in across Sweden can be compared in SEK.

3   **Store of value**

    It maintains its value over time.

    A piece of gold could, for example, buy clothes in both ancient Greece and today.

Medium of exchange is the most important defining property of money, the other properties follow.[55]

Note that these are functions of usage and adoption. For instance, if something has been a store of value for a period of time, it doesn't mean it will continue to be a good store of value in the future.

Now we may wonder, can anything be used as money? And are there "good" and "bad" forms of money?

As seen from historical examples, I think it's safe to conclude that yes, basically anything can be used as money. But if we want to compare how well different forms of money work, we need to look at other properties.

Some also use a fourth function: *standard of deferred payment*[56]. I chose to focus on the three functions; it seems to me it's the popular way.

Used cars are usually cheaper in the south of Sweden, for some reason unknown to me.

Gold is the classical example of a store of value. But it has also seen large up and down movements in valuation. This is the yearly closing price of gold[57]:

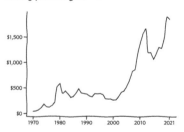

For example in 2010 it increased 27.74% and in 2013 it decreased 27.79%.

What properties does good money have?

To function as money, money should have these properties:

1 **Acceptable**

Everyone must be able to use the money for transactions.

If only the very rich can use it, then it's not good money.

2 **Divisible**

Can be divided into smaller units of value.

If it's difficult to subdivide, then it's hard to use in practice. It's why cash always come with coins and notes with different values.

3 **Durable**

An item must be able to withstand repeated use.

Food is not durable and makes for poor money.

4 **Fungible & Uniform**

Two items of the same type should always be considered equal.

All shares in a company should be worth the same, even if bought at different times and at different prices. All gold coins of the same denomination should contain the same amount of gold.

5 **Limited in supply**

There should be a limited and predictable amount of money.

A limited amount is needed for the money to hold its value.

6 **Portable**

It's easy to carry around money and to transfer it to others.

Money should be practical.

7 **Recognizable**

Money should be easy to identify and difficult to counterfeit.

You should be able to differentiate between different types of money, so you don't mistake Dollar notes for Euro or Monopoly notes, and you should be able to separate real from fake notes. This is sometimes referred to as *cognizable*.

We can summarize the properties as: money should be practical and efficient.

It makes sense as the point of money is to increase efficiency. If money isn't practical, it's not a good medium of exchange.

What properties money should have also differ. Some list *stability in value* as a property, but I chose to go with *limited in supply* as I wanted to focus on intrinsic properties that don't change with time. Other popular descriptions leave out *recognizable,* but I felt counterfeit-resistance is too important to leave out.[58]

The difference between *fungibility* and *uniformity* is confusing, so I'll bundle them together.

Fungibility refers to one unit being interchangeable with another while *uniformity* refers to two versions of the same denomination having the same purchasing power.

Perfect uniformity implies fungibility, but non-uniform goods can still be fungible. For example, barrels of oil aren't uniform—their quality differ. But oil can be classified into different qualities, where they are treated as the same. Thus oil of the same quality is fungible.

In the ideal situation money should function as a medium of exchange between goods and services, in a closed system. Therefore, it's important that money cannot be created out of thin air—the supply should be limited. The only way to earn money is to trade for it somehow.

Food or sand would be examples of really bad money. Food spoils quickly while sand exist in extreme quantities.

Both Rai stones and the Swedish copper coins have smaller versions as well, making them more practical.

Let's run a thought experiment: what if we wanted to use marbles as money on a global scale?

If we control the creation of a special kind of marble, we can make them durable and uniform. We can also add some sort of counterfeit protection—maybe embed holograms with cryptographic messages—to ensure a limited supply. Of course, it's easy to create different kinds of denominations.

Then, let's consider the shape—a sphere isn't very good. It might roll away and it's hard to carry in the wallet. So, why not make it a flat cylinder?

Now we've reinvented the coin. A coin is actually remarkably efficient!

How well do our historical examples work as money?

How do our historical examples of money hold up? They don't include examples of outright bad forms, but some are indeed better than others.

The large **Rai stones** and the **20kg copper coin** are great examples of money that isn't portable. Therefore, they don't work very well as money.

Cigarettes, marbles, stamps and other types of commodities are decent forms of money—on a small scale. They have some durability issues (wear and tear) and they're not perfectly uniform. But most importantly, they can be mass produced which prevents their use on a larger scale.

Sea shells work well as money—assuming they're not too plentiful. If used in a local market—for example on an island—there's always a risk of the market being overrun by shells from other islands, where they're more common. But they're durable, lightweight and easy to use, which are great properties for money to have.

Metal coins is a very good form of money, especially if made by scarce material. Gold is naturally very scarce, ensuring a limited supply, and coins are easy to use and very durable. This is the reason coins have been the dominating type of currency for over 2000 years.

How well cryptocurrencies work as money is a topic for the next chapter (p.41).

The problem with fiat currencies

The money we usually use today is a little different from coins made of precious materials. We use coins made with cheap metal or paper notes, and our money is often just stored digitally at a bank. After abandoning the gold standard, there's nothing physically backing up the value of money.

It's not a requirement that the money must be backed by something, or have intrinsic value like *commodity money*. The real problem is that the supply isn't limited. Banks inflate the supply using *fractional banking* (p.100) while central banks can print money, both physical and digital, without any limit.

The term *sound money* refers to money that isn't prone to sudden changes in long term purchasing power, and the value is determined by the free market. If the supply of money differs from the demand, which will happen with fiat due to the disconnect between banks and the market, then there might be sudden changes to the purchasing power.[59]

While fiat has many positive properties, after the move away from the gold standard, it's now considered unsound money.

Why do we need good money?

Outside of curiosity, why does it matter if there are better forms of money? If fiat is good enough, why bother?

I see two major reasons:

1   The point of money is to increase economic efficiency.

    Better forms of money are more efficient.

2   Money with poor properties can lead to large economic problems.

    For instance how the ability to print fiat money from thin air can lead to hyperinflation.

In our context, knowing what makes money perform well helps us reason about cryptocurrencies, and to see if they can live up to their namesake.

Some say cryptocurrencies can't be money because it lacks intrinsic value—like gold has. But fiat currencies don't have intrinsic value either. The only value comes from the function as money.

See Gary North's *The Fallacy of "Intrinsic Value"* from 1969.[60]

There are those who argue that Fractional Banking is a net positive for society.[61] And those who disagree.[62] Regardless, it's a negative with respect to the properties of money I've chosen.

Chapter 5

Are cryptocurrencies money?

How well do they work as money?

One man's trash is another man's treasure.

Proverb

As we saw in the previous chapter, practically anything can be used as money. Therefore, it's more useful to ask if cryptocurrencies have the properties of good money, and how well do they function as money today.

In this chapter we'll see that cryptocurrencies have excellent monetary properties, but their function as money is held back by volatility and adoption.

Evaluating the properties of money

To decide how well cryptocurrencies can function as money, we'll take a look at the properties good money should have and see how cryptocurrencies hold up. See the previous chapter for historical context and a discussion about the properties (p.31).

1 **Acceptable**

Nobody's excluded from using cryptocurrencies—they're open to everyone by design. The drawback is that you need a device with internet connection.

2 **Divisible**

A fairly small requirement given the stated purpose being *digital* cash, but it's undoubtedly a drawback.

There's no real technical limit to how much a cryptocurrency unit can be divided, and it's all automatic.

3 **Durable**

Coins can be used an infinite amount of times. The only drawback is keeping your private key secure, so you don't lose your coins.

4 **Fungible & Uniform**

Because phones can break or be stolen, you should write down your private key as backup. It's a good idea to secure it from fire, theft and simply losing it.

For most cryptocurrencies, fungibility is problematic. If all transaction history is public, like it is in Bitcoin, it could be used to blacklist certain addresses[63], and in the long run break fungibility if coins having touched a blacklisted address become less valuable.

Cryptocurrencies like Monero tries to solve this problem (p.193), so I'll say that cryptocurrencies are fungible.

5 **Limited in supply**

Cryptocurrencies follow predetermined emission rates, ensuring a limited supply.

6 **Portable**

You can carry any amount you want in your wallet. One billion worth of cryptocurrency is as easy to carry as one cent. There's no difference in transacting large amounts or small amounts.

7 **Recognizable**

Cryptocurrencies are impossible to counterfeit and if implemented correctly, they're easy to separate from each other.

While at a low level it may be difficult to tell which cryptocurrency a number belongs to, all necessary data is public so you can differentiate them. Wallet apps do this automatically, making them easy to identify.

Traditionally sound money refers to money backed by precious material. Cryptocurrencies are instead backed by cryptography, and in Bitcoin's case, the supply mimics the gold supply.

All in all cryptocurrencies fulfil the properties excellently.

Cryptocurrencies can also be considered to be *sound money*—the value is entirely market driven and there's no manipulation of the supply.

Comparing properties with other forms of money

This is a table of how I think cryptocurrencies compare to other forms of money. I differentiate between the two forms of fiat—digital and physical—because they have different properties. Gold can be either gold coins or gold bars—basically some suitable physical form of gold.

	Fiat (digital)	Fiat (physical)	Gold	Cryptocurrencies
1. Acceptable	Poor	Excellent	Excellent	Excellent
2. Divisible	Excellent	Good	Good	Excellent
3. Durable	Excellent	Good	Excellent	Good
4. Fungible & Uniform	Excellent	Excellent	Excellent	Excellent
5. Limited supply	Poor	Poor	Excellent	Excellent
6. Portable	Good	Good	Good	Excellent
7. Recognizable	Excellent	Good	Good	Excellent

I know this might be controversial, so let me motivate some of the entries:

1 Digital fiat gets a poor score on **acceptable** because it requires a bank account to use. This isn't something everyone can get (p.73) as banks are in the right to reject you if they want (p.55).

2 Digital money is inherently easier to **divide** than physical variants. You can always send an exact amount without having to mix and match change.

3 Paper notes can easily wear out or burn up. While cryptocurrencies cannot themselves burn up or deteriorate, the security backups and your phone can. Therefore they score lower than gold on **durability**, which is near indestructible.

4 I see no major problems with **fungibility** or **uniformity**.

5 Both digital and physical fiat gets a poor score on **limited supply**. Per the discussion in the previous chapter (p.39) fiat money is unsound.

6 Cryptocurrencies are simply much more **portable** than the other options. Carrying large amounts in cash or gold is cumbersome and digital fiat isn't easy to move across borders.

7 While it's possible to check for fake cash and gold coins, it requires expertise and certain tools. Therefore they get a lower **recognizable** score.

You could argue that because you need a device with internet access, cryptocurrencies should get a lower score on *acceptable*. But you could also argue that having to transact in person is another drawback, and to me they cancel out.

The definition of *durability* is only concerned with reuse, where cryptocurrencies score excellently. I wanted to include the storage drawback that didn't fit anywhere else.

I note again that there exists fungible cryptocurrencies (p.193).

Moving money across borders will be handled in the chapter *A global currency* (p.119). I'll just note that it's extremely difficult, or impossible, to send fiat digitally to countries like North Korea or Venezuela.

Even if you disagree about certain choices, it's hard to deny that cryptocurrencies come out of the comparison pretty well. Of course, this doesn't give the whole picture. There are other significant differences, for example:

- A big difference between cryptocurrencies and gold is that cryptocurrencies are digital. This isn't only positive—cryptocurrency implementations can have bugs that might have severe negative consequences.

- Digital fiat can get frozen any time by your bank (p.59), while physical payments and cryptocurrencies are uncensorable.

- Gold has stood the test of time. It's been used as money for thousands of years, while cryptocurrencies are just more than a decade old.

Do cryptocurrencies function as money?

We've looked at the properties—but how well do they function as money, today?

1 **Medium of exchange**

Cryptocurrencies work well as a medium of exchange, but they're not commonly used.

2 **Unit of account**

Most who use cryptocurrencies still convert the amounts to fiat.

3 **Store of value**

The valuation is highly speculation driven and has been notoriously volatile.

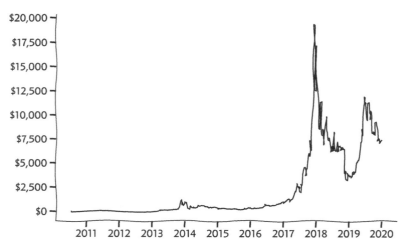

Bitcoin price per week up to the beginning of 2020.[64]

The price peaked in December 2017 to $19,870, and some exchanges had it even higher. A year later the price had dropped to $3,177, a drop of over 84%.

A bug is a programming fault in the software. As a developer, I can assure you that bugs will happen. The question is, how can you avoid the most severe ones, and what do you do when they appear?

Both Monero and Bitcoin has for example had major bugs that could have allowed an attacker to create coins for free. Neither were exploited... this time.[67][68]

I find it interesting that the average life expectancy for a fiat currency is 27 years.

There's a clique of Bitcoin supporters who claim the primary, and sometimes even the only, function of Bitcoin is as a store of value. Unfortunately it's based on wishful thinking (from a short-term investment view) and not reality.

While cryptocurrencies are used as money in certain communities and for certain goods, they're not in widespread use. They don't function very well as money globally, today.

There are mainly two things holding cryptocurrencies back today:

1 **Large volatility**

It's hard for merchants to accept cryptocurrencies if they might lose a large percent of this months profit due to market movements.

2 **The network effect**

Money is better the more people who accept it. Getting people to start accepting a new form of money is difficult—even if it's better than the alternatives.

Both of these are functions of how new cryptocurrencies are. When the market matures, the volatility will naturally decrease. Barring any large weaknesses the network effect will only grow larger as cryptocurrencies have a unique value proposition.

Perhaps it's to be expected that cryptocurrencies aren't global money yet—they're only a decade old after all.

How well do other forms of money function?

Again, let's try to compare cryptocurrencies with the other forms of money. This time I'll combine digital and physical fiat, since they function the same in practice.

	Fiat	Gold	Cryptocurrencies
1. Medium of exchange	Excellent	Good	Good
2. Unit of account	Excellent	Poor	Poor
3. Store of value	Poor	Excellent	Poor

With the motivations:

1 Both gold and cryptocurrencies can work well as a **medium of exchange**. But they're not commonly used as such, which lowers their score.

There's a feedback loop here: the more they're used the better they are, and the reverse holds true as well.

2 Nobody prices goods as "0.2 ounces of gold" or "0.13 BTC". Neither gold nor cryptocurrencies are currently used as a **unit of account**.

3 Fiat isn't a good **store of value**. If you store money in your bank account or beneath your mattress inflation will eat away the value. Cryptocurrencies, despite the historic increase in price, are far too volatile.

Cryptocurrencies are quite popular for privacy-concerned users. For example, most serious sellers of VPNs, domain names and VPS hosting accept payments via cryptocurrencies.

For a different perspective of how technology gets adopted, I recommend *The Shock of the Old* by David Edgerton. He argues that technology must be significantly better than the previous to see use, and even then the adoption is not as swift as one might think. [Old06]

Another perspective on network effects is given by Kevin Simler in his blog post "Going Critical". [69]

Marc Levinson writes in *The Box* that 20 years after the invention of the light bulb, arguably one of the most important inventions of all time, only 3% in the U.S. were using it. [Box16]

Cryptocurrencies are still in their infancy.

While cryptocurrencies match up poorly, there's no perfect alternative.

Note that unlike the fundamental properties that don't change that much, how well money functions change with time. For example a few hundred years ago gold coins would be used everywhere.

What do lawmakers say?

Several countries—like Sweden[65]—have ruled that Bitcoin isn't a currency. The reason is there's no responsible issuer and it's not *legal tender* in any country.

Cryptocurrencies just don't fit into existing rules of fiat currencies. This often happens with new innovations that break the mold—laws cannot keep up. For instance cryptocurrencies remove the third-party requirement, something previously thought impossible.

There are others who've ruled in favor of Bitcoin as a currency. For example the EU ruled that VAT is not applicable to the conversion between fiat currency and Bitcoin, however VAT still applies when used for goods and services.[66]

So, are cryptocurrencies money?

Cryptocurrencies fulfil the properties of money very well—in fact, they fulfil them better than any alternative in history. Unlike fiat they can also be considered sound money as the valuation is entirely market driven.

While they are used as money in certain communities, they do not function well as global money today. They're very volatile and adoption isn't there yet.

I personally think cryptocurrencies is the best form of money we've ever seen, but they haven't reached their potential yet.

Maybe a bad example as cryptocurrencies and modern fiat didn't exist so far back. But hopefully you get my point: gold was once an excellent medium of exchange and unit of account, but not anymore. It changes.

Legal tender declares that you have to accept it as money by law.

Another beautiful example of laws not keeping up with technology is patents. Software patents work horribly[70], yet software is continuously pushed into the existing framework that doesn't really fit.

One example is Amazon's one-click checkout patent.[71]

Part III

Better digital payments

Benefits over existing payment systems

When money is coming your way, you don't ask questions

Frank Underwood, "House of Cards"

In this part, we'll explore benefits cryptocurrencies have over other digital payment systems, such as VISA, Mastercard, PayPal or Apple Pay.

The big benefit is cryptocurrencies being *permissionless* (p.6): anyone can pay and anyone can accept them—for any business. Certain types of businesses, like pot stores or gambling sites, have problems accepting credit cards. Small businesses are also always at risk of having their accounts frozen without warning or recourse. Similarly, there are people who cannot get bank accounts—and are in effect frozen out of large parts of the society.

When I say small business, I do mean it. If PayPal freezes the account of a large or popular business, like freezing the account of Minecraft, the social backlash will make sure they're unblocked quickly. Small businesses— who can't gather outrage on social media— will simply be ignored. (p.61)

But there are other benefits as well. Cryptocurrencies have lower fees and by becoming irreversible very quickly they reduce and often eliminate the risk of charge back fraud, which is a big expense for merchants.

Chapter 6

Cheaper & faster
Avoids middleman fees and settles quickly

A penny saved is a penny earned.

Attributed to Benjamin Franklin

Cryptocurrencies provide two major advantages compared to other digital payments: they have lower fees and they settle faster, made possible by cutting out the middleman. But there's a trade-off—it shifts the risk management from the merchant to the customer. Merchants no longer have to worry about *charge back fraud*, but instead customers lose the ability to do charge backs.

Cryptocurrency fees

Fees in cryptocurrencies are relatively straightforward: each transaction has a fixed fee, independent of the transaction value. The one who sends the transaction pays the fee.

Bitcoin Cash	Monero	Dogecoin	Litecoin	Bitcoin
$0.0012	$0.0028	$0.003	$0.0162	$2.46

The median transaction fee for common cryptocurrencies 2019-05-25.[72][73]

Because cryptocurrencies are so volatile, the expected fee converted to fiat varies. The fees are also set by demand, but most cryptocurrencies have enough capacity to keep the fees very low.

There are cryptocurrencies boasting zero fees, but they use unproven consensus algorithms or centralized governance. That's why I only include coins using proof-of-work.

For the most part, cryptocurrencies have very low fees—enough to call them negligible. But there's an elephant in the room: Bitcoin has large and unpredictable fees.

In fact, Bitcoin fees of $2-3 is still low compared the fees during the bull run in December 2017, which reached an average of $50(!!) per transaction. This is because transaction throughput in Bitcoin is maxed out, and to get your transaction accepted you need to pay more than others.

You may think the fees are so high because Bitcoin is much more popular than other cryptocurrencies, but that's not the whole story. In fact, it would be easy to lower the fees—Bitcoin Cash can for example handle at least 20 times the transaction count of Bitcoin, while keeping the same low fees. See the discussion of the scalability challenge (p.195) for more details.

Bitcoin just doesn't work well as a currency with these high and unreliable fees, but it's not representative of cryptocurrencies in general.

Who pays the fees?

> Visa has been misusing its position and charging retailers excessive fees for a long time. They conceal from customers what Visa and its banks charge retailers to accept Visa credit cards.

Mike Schlotman, Kroger's executive vice president and CFO, Mars 2019[74]

Wait a minute, isn't paying with credit cards, debit cards, PayPal etc already free? I've never paid a fee except for a yearly fee for having a card. Many credit cards even give you a bonus for every purchase, so what's the deal?

That's because you as a customer don't see the high fees—but the merchant does. Fees of 1-4% per transaction can be very demanding, especially for low-margin businesses. To make up for the fees (and to compensate for charge back fraud) merchants instead raise their prices. So you as a customer actually pay for the fees, they're just indirect and hidden from view.

Fee comparisons

It's difficult to compare the fees of different digital payments in a complete and fair manner. This is my attempt, but please be aware it's a generalization.

There are different types of cards; debit and credit cards, and different providers like VISA, Mastercard or American Express. I'll treat them as one category for simplicity, even though they have slightly different fees. Wire transfer fees also vary a lot and international transfers outside of SEPA can be very expensive depending on your bank and country.

There are some Bitcoin developers who claim high fees are necessary for the survival of Bitcoin. Gregory Maxwell was famously "pulling out the champaign" when Bitcoin had $50 fees in 2017.[82] He thought it was a sign that the market supported the "fee market" idea (which is more a blockspace market).

The issue is that Bitcoin's block reward will eventually run out (after several decades), so who will pay the miners to secure the network? The "fee market" idea says that transactions must be very expensive for it to be worth it for miners to secure the chain.

There are other possible solutions:

1. Many cheap instead of few expensive transactions
2. Prevent the blocksize reward from going to zero

See John Blocke's "The fee market myth" for more info (it was written a year before the ridiculous $50 fees).[83]

Fees can differ depending on the amount of transactions, the transaction value, the type of your business, your country and your chosen fee model. Not to mention different providers have different fee structures.[84]

Mobile payments have become popular recently. As a representative, I'll choose Swish, which is used everywhere here in Sweden. It's connected to your bank and have free person-to-person transactions, but unsurprisingly there are fees for businesses.

	Transaction Fee
Wire Transfer[75]	$0–50
Cards[76]	1–4%
PayPal[77]	2.9–4.4% + $0.30
Swish[78]	$0.16–0.26
Bitcoin Cash	$0.0012

A summary of transaction fees of various payment systems.

I've also left out any monthly and yearly fee, common for regular payment systems. For example, merchants might rent credit card terminals and Swish—with comparatively low transaction fees—also has a $10–50 yearly fee (the fee varies depending on your bank).

As we can see, cryptocurrencies are decidedly cheaper than the other options. Even Swish, which is much cheaper than PayPal or cards, is 100 times more expensive than Bitcoin Cash. There are also no yearly fees of any kind just to receive payments in it (but there might be fees if you want to convert it to fiat).

As the purpose of money is to increase economic efficiency (p.31), a 1–4% tax on nearly all digital payments is really counter-productive. Therefore a move towards cheap payment solutions like Swish or cryptocurrencies would be beneficial economically.

Payment speed

Shifting focus a little, let's take a look at payment speed. We can identify different stages of a digital payment:

1   Notification

2   Settlement

3   Irreversible

You'll get a *notification* a few seconds after your payment. For a credit card this ensures the customer has a valid card and has entered the right PIN-code, but no money has been transferred yet. The money changes (virtual) hands during the *settlement*, which might be several days later. Finally, a transaction might still be reversed much later. When this is no longer possible, I call the transaction *irreversible*.

The popularity of mobile payments is easy to understand. They're convenient, cheap and fast. In fact they work exactly like cryptocurrency wallets do—just pay with a simple app on your phone.

A definite advantage over cryptocurrencies is mobile payments are directly linked to your existing bank account.

Bank accounts also come with a fee. For example, I pay a $30 yearly fee just to have my bank account, which includes a debit card and the ability to do banking online.

Yes, parts of the fees represents fraud protection. But that too comes with a cost, and if viewed from a global economic perspective it might even be detrimental.

Credit card payments are more complex. See the blog post *How Visa's Payment System Works* for an overview of VISA's payment system.[85]

Accepting a cryptocurrency transaction which haven't any confirmation yet, called *0-conf*, is often criticized in the cryptocurrency community. But it's really no different than accepting a credit card payment instantly—they're both uncertain.

Charge back fraud

For us customers, it's a feature that transactions can be reversed. If someone steals your credit card or a merchant is fraudulent, you can reverse the transactions by calling your issuer. But this can also be abused, which is called *charge back fraud* (or *friendly fraud*).

It goes something like this:

1　Place an order

2　Receive item

3　Claim your card was stolen

4　Get your money back

This can be a big problem for some merchants, especially those serving digital goods, who often have to swallow it as a loss.[79] To make matters worse merchants also have to pay non-negotiable and non-refundable charge back fees even when disputing.[80]

It's also common that banks are the ones who have to eat the cost of the fraud.

Speed comparisons

Credit card transactions can take days to settle, and they can be reversed several months after via charge backs.[81] Mobile payments—via Apple Pay and similar—are often tied to credit cards and share their properties while others—like Swish—instead connect to your bank account directly.

Inside the EU, SEPA has massively improved the state of wire transfers across borders. Transactions often go through the same day and they're cheaper than other types of wire transfers.

Wire transfers aren't usually used for payments, but it's still a useful comparison to make. They are typically much slower than other payment systems but they're generally harder to reverse as they don't offer the same charge back protection as credit cards do.

A unique property of cryptocurrencies is they become irreversible very quickly (p.21). In Bitcoin it usually takes 10–60 min.

	Notification	Settlement	Irreversible
Wire Transfer	days	days	days
Cards	seconds	days	months
Mobile payments	seconds	days	days–months
Cryptocurrencies	seconds	an hour	an hour

A summary of the speed of various payment systems.

There's a risk of having transactions reversed (double spend (p.13)) before they're confirmed. This can happen when delivering goods immediately after payment notification.

Because transaction security is probabilistic, there's always a risk of having a transaction reversed even for confirmed transactions, but in practice it's **very** low (p.21).

The speed that cryptocurrencies settle and become irreversible significantly reduces the risk of charge back fraud and eliminates it for most use-cases.

The risk management trade-off

It seems payment systems needs to choose between these two options:

1 Provide costumer protection but merchants might suffer from charge back fraud.

2 Protect merchants from charge back fraud but don't provide protection for customers.

Traditional payment systems have chosen to protect customers (or maybe that's the only option they can realistically choose—for social and technical reasons). Cryptocurrencies try to prevent transaction reversal and charge back fraud instead.

While it's of course bad to not have customer protection, there might be other solutions. For example, offering optional fraud insurance or offering *custodial wallets* with extra protection. (A custodial wallet is managed by a third-party, similar to a bank account.)

In addition, it might make risk management more practical. While it's basically impossible for merchants to audit all their customers, it's plausible for customers to check out a merchant. In fact, we do it all the time: "this website looks shady!" or "my friend uses them all the time". Merchants are known and have a reputation while customers are innumerable and anonymous.

I haven't seen any "fraud insurance" yet, but don't see a reason why it can't be created if there's a need for it. Especially when combined with a custodial wallet.

Conclusion

We've seen three large benefits to cryptocurrency payments:

+ Cheaper

+ Settles quickly

+ Reduces or removes the risk for charge back fraud

And one large drawback:

– No inherent fraud protection for customers

The drawback might be alleviated with optional systems in the future, giving us the best of both worlds.

Chapter 7

"Undesirable" businesses
The ones payment processors don't want to do business with

@DirectorJoshua something has to be done. #chase has fucked with people before with other issues. Should not get away with shit like this.

Dakota Skye, April 22, 2014[86]

If you want to accept digital payments today you need to partner with a payment processor, for example Stripe or PayPal. Usually, that's not a problem, but what if they say no?

This is the reality for certain businesses with high charge back rate (p.52) or that exists in a legal and moral gray area[87]. If you view it from the payment processor's point-of-view it might make sense—they're just minimizing their risk. But that's of little comfort to those being rejected.

Here are some examples of affected businesses:

- Adult entertainment (anything remotely related to porn)
- Auctions
- Cannabis
- Cryptocurrencies (how ironic)
- Gambling

For whatever reason, these businesses are deemed high risk and undesirable; despite them being legal, they might not be able to accept digital payments. This is something that cryptocurrencies solve.

While we'll focus on payment processors in this chapter, the problem is much bigger than that. Often banks don't want anything to do with the business either. Sometimes they even close personal accounts of business owners—because of the nature of the business.

For example, Chase closed hundreds of porn stars' accounts[94] and Wells Fargo closed the bank account of a supporter of medical marijuana[95].

There are many stories of banks closing down your account if they find out you've traded cryptocurrencies. Naturally without warning, explanation or recourse.[96][97]

Pot stores are cash-only

Pot stores in the United States are in a weird legal place. While they're legal—to various degrees[88]—in many states, they're illegal under federal law. Kind of like Schrödinger's cat: they're legal yet simultaneously illegal.

Because banks in the US are regulated both on a state and federal level, banks don't want anything to do with them. Payment processors take a similar stance, forcing the stores to be entirely cash-only.

Not having access to banks means they also have to store the cash themselves and have trouble getting loans.

We're talking large amounts of money here, for example two businesses in Denver generated $250,000 to $350,000 in monthly sales—all in cash[89]. This all needs to be counted, recounted, transported and stored. Large amounts of cash needs large amounts of secure storage, which means renting warehouses and hiring armored trucks and armored guards.

They are absolutely dependent on nearby ATMs, because the move towards cashless payments mean people don't usually carry that much cash. In fact many stores have an ATM inside the store itself, to sort-of allow people to pay with credit cards.

The ATMs are run by separate businesses and usually don't have any problems with banks.

Not having access to digital payments hurts, but there are workarounds. Cash does work in physical stores. There might also be (uncertain) ways to accept digital payments[90], a basic requirement for online stores.

Expensive and dubious workarounds

But some "undesirable" companies do accept credit cards. Does that mean the problem has been solved? Unfortunately, not really.

For example, porn is a business with very high rate of charge backs (p.52). Just think about it: what happens if your significant other would come across a charge to "XXX-Teens" or similar? Of course, you'd exclaim "my card must've been compromised!" and quickly call your bank to freeze your card and issue a charge back.

There was a popular blog post detailing the struggles for porn sites to accept digital payments.[98] The post itself has been deleted because of people accusing him of admitting to fraud[99] (the workarounds are of dubious legality). If you're savvy you might be able to find the original post on the Wayback machine.

Therefore, most payment processors explicitly forbid porn sites[91], making it very difficult to accept credit cards directly.

PornHub (according to Alexa one of the top 100 websites in the world) has been dropped by PayPal, MasterCard and VISA, and now only accept payments in cryptocurrencies.[100][101][102]

Payment processors usually don't want anything to do with porn sites.

Instead, they have a third-party request the payment on their behalf and do some shady stuff. They can for example claim the payment is for another type of business, which isn't banned by the payment processor.

Another party acting as an intermediary might get accepted by the payment processor, especially if they disguise themselves.

These things are in the gray area legal wise, so the companies that do this have high fees—VERY high fees. While regular payment processors may have ~3-4% fees, these intermediary fees can be as high as **30%**. That's ludicrously expensive for low margin businesses.

I don't know if this practice is legal or not; I just want to note they don't really have many options.

Why does it matter?

> First they came for the socialists, and I did not speak out—
>> because I was not a socialist.
>
> Then they came for the trade unionists, and I did not speak out—
>> because I was not a trade unionist.
>
> Then they came for the Jews, and I did not speak out—
>> because I was not a Jew.
>
> Then they came for me—
>> and there was no one left to speak for me.

Martin Niemöller, a poetic form of a post-war confession[92]

You might wonder what does it matter if these businesses disappear. Maybe you don't gamble, don't use cannabis and find porn deplorable—which is fine. But what about the thoughts of other people?

The cannabis business is experiencing explosive growth[93], hinting at how many people do care. Porn is another thing that is very popular—but very few would admit they watch it. I can see why some people object against them... but what's the problem with auctions? (Other than being an easy target for charge back fraud.)

Incidentally, it's also a powerful argument for privacy. Maybe you personally don't have anything to hide—but others do.

For example, a gay teenage boy who would get thrown out if his parents found out or even get killed if he lives in the wrong country. Doesn't he have the right to privacy?

The argument for privacy is examined in more detail in the chapter *Private money* (p.109).

Why should people running and using **legal** businesses be punished for arbitrary reasons? A society that punishes people for doing something legal seems insane to me. (Yes, legality is different from morality, a topic we'll revisit in the chapter about *Darknet markets* (p.127).)

Are cryptocurrencies the solution?

Cryptocurrencies give you permissionless digital payments; they solve the problem of accepting payments very well. But they're not a complete solution, at least today.

As we discussed in *Are cryptocurrencies money?* (p.41), they're very volatile and not widely accepted. Businesses still need to convert cryptocurrencies to fiat to be able to pay their bills and salaries, and the workers in turn need to pay their bills. To sell them for fiat, you still need to go through exchanges who—you guessed it—can refuse to do business with you.

It's not as big of a problem if an exchange blocks you compared to being able to accept money in the first place—it's easier to move to another exchange. There are also peer-to-peer variants where you can trade cryptocurrencies in person, bypassing the problem.

While cryptocurrencies improves the situation today, we would really need to bypass all third-parties for a great solution. This means you should be able to pay all expenses with cryptocurrencies so you can't get blocked by a third-party anywhere on the line.

But there are related problems cryptocurrencies can't solve. Banks serve a very important function: they lend businesses money, and there's no good solution if they say no. It can also be more secure to let banks store large sums of money than keeping it yourself.

Chapter 8
Freezing of merchant accounts
The account your business relies on can be frozen at any time

Considering that the project operates with minimum margins, just having most of its assets frozen for an unknown amount of time would be disastrous.

PayPal freezes Neo900 funds, Dec 2015[103]

This chapter continues on the same idea as the previous one, but we'll view the issue from another angle. Instead of focusing on getting permission to accept payments at all, we'll focus on the problem that accounts can be frozen at any time, for arbitrary reasons. This isn't a problem with crypto-currencies, as they cannot be frozen.

Freezing funds, not just payments

Imagine coming in to work one day and having this conversion with your boss:

- I'm sorry John, but we'll pay you in 6 months.

- What?

- Don't worry, you'll still get your full salary, but we'll pay it in 6 months.

- But why?

- You apparently didn't put one of the new coversheets on your TPS reports.

- TPS reports...??

Don't worry if you don't know what a TPS report is, the point is you got your salary **frozen for 6 months** for an **arbitrary** and **unknown** reason.

Now imagine the consequences.

Would you be able to pay your rent? Buy food for yourself and your kids? Repair your fridge if it breaks? Given that only 39% of Americans have enough savings to cover a $1,000 emergency[104] you should be glad if you can honestly answer yes to these questions. Many would panic if their salary was just a little bit late, let alone half a year.

Yet, this has played out again and again for businesses all over the world who have gotten their account frozen for an unknown amount of time for arbitrary or unknown reasons. Actually, let me take that back. What happens is actually much worse—businesses also get **funds** frozen. It's like if your employer would freeze your credit card, your savings account and hold off your salary.

Imagine what you would do now, without a salary and without your savings...

The TPS report is a reference to movie *Office Space (1999)*, a black comedy about working in an office. There a worker gets reprimanded for an extremely minor and unimportant issue.

You think 6 months is too long? PayPal freezes your account for 180 days by default. There are also several stories of PayPal **never** releasing the funds.

This is possible because PayPal isn't really a bank (in many countries) and can get away with more than regulated banks can.

Confiscating future payments

Just to be a little gratuitous and to drive home my point on how bad this can be—it doesn't end there. When PayPal freezes your account, they don't block incoming payments. People can continue paying for stuff, but you're not getting their money and yet you still have to give them the stuff they've paid for.

> There's over 600000 euro in there. Money I was planning on investing in the new company.
>
> [...]
>
> I withdraw everything from paypal every week. They limited my account just as sales started spiking, so this money has accumulated since they limited the account.
>
> Notch, creator of Minecraft, Sep 2010[105]

They didn't just freeze the account, they're making it worse by confiscating future payments as well!

Small businesses & projects may be ruined

If you run a very popular business like Minecraft, you'll probably get through without much issue. You're already making enough money to cover expenses and the attention in news and social media will make sure the issue gets resolved quickly.

But what happens if you run a small business? If your startup gets their account frozen, with no new money coming in? Obviously, you'll be in a world of hurt. Maybe you'll take a hit and survive but it could also kill your business.

What about the Neo900 project I quoted at the start of this chapter? They missed a bunch of supplier deadlines, and the project is still crawling along—but as a shell of what it once was. It was indeed a disaster.

It might be easy to deliver digital goods, but physical goods may be created on demand. In addition salaries, rent and other expenses needs to be paid. Cash flow is a very important issue for most companies.

And even if you get all your money back eventually, you still have to deal with ruined reputation, missed opportunities and customers suing you for delayed deliveries.

Creating an uproar on social media is still the best way to resolve issues with companies that have very poor customer service. For example if you have an issue with Google hopefully your post on Hacker News gathers enough attention to catch the eye of someone working there.

Other examples

If you search for it online, there are thousands of stories like these. Here's a few examples to get the curious started:

- PayPal Know Your Customer failure[106]
- We got banned from PayPal after 12 years of business[107]
- PayPal just froze over $70,000 in my account[108]
- PayPal destroyed my business of 8 years in a day[109]
- Why Should Startups Avoid Stripe?[110]
- Why Stripe is the worst choice for your new startup business[111]

Some of these had a happy ending but others did not.

Money under your mattress

With cryptocurrencies, you can accept digital payments that go directly into a wallet that you—and you alone—control. Then, it's impossible to get your cryptocurrency account frozen; it's really like storing them under your own (digital) mattress.

As always, there are trade-offs. Storing money at home drastically increases the risk of theft so keeping it at a trustworthy bank might be a wise choice.

With cryptocurrencies, a good compromise might be to receive payments to your own wallet and automatically transfer them to a more secure storage when the sum becomes too large.

This of course requires that you use a wallet that holds the coins itself, and not a custodial wallet—which a third-party manages for you. It's why so much emphasis is placed on controlling your own keys, otherwise you won't get all benefits.

I'm not advocating either way; just realize there are trade-offs with controlling your own keys or not. If you want the ease of use of a custodial wallet, then you'll sacrifice control of your account.

With cryptocurrencies, at least you have a choice and a possibility to avoid your account getting arbitrarily frozen.

Chapter 9
Uncensorable donations
Donations governments cannot stop

Open government is strongly correlated to quality of life. Open government is compelled to answer injustice rather than causing it. Plans by an open government which are corrupt, cause injustice or do not alleviate suffering are revealed and so opposed before implementation. If unjust plans cannot reach implementation then government will be a force for justice.

WikiLeaks[112]

In the last two chapters, we looked at the issues with digital payments, but when you think about donations you wouldn't assume they have the same problems as payments have. For example, when donating money to a charity, like Charity Water, they don't have to be worried about charge back fraud (p.52) because you're voluntarily giving them money. But the same problem with third-party censorship is relevant here as well.

Imagine a country doing something really horrible, like purging intellectuals and political opponents[113], that would put the government in a bad light. Journalists trying to report on this event may find it difficult or impossible to accept donations to continue their work. A payment processor (which is necessary for digital donations)—perhaps under pressure from the government—might block donations or break the journalist's anonymity, making donations to truth-seeking journalists very difficult or outright dangerous.

Donations are an excellent use case for cryptocurrencies, as they cannot be censored even by the most powerful nations in the world. And as I'll argue in this chapter, this is a real concern.

Most payment processors have lower fees for charities, but they're still more expensive than the low cryptocurrency fees (p.49).

However even charities can be prosecuted for not fulfilling their promises, an experience the founder of Charity Water writes in his book *Thirst*[Wat18]. So charge back fraud isn't a completely irrelevant worry.

Some cryptocurrencies also give better privacy than other digital payment systems (p.193).

Censorship is real

A powerful example of censorship is the Tiananmen Square Massacre in China in 1989. It was a student-led protest which was forcefully suppressed by hundreds of thousands military troops, killing large numbers of demonstrators and bystanders.

> "This gun-happy soldier, he's firing indiscriminately into the crowd and three young girl students knelt down in front of him and begged him to stop firing," she says quietly, gesturing with her hands in a praying motion.
>
> "And he killed them."
>
> Margaret Holt, BBC: Tiananmen 30 years on - China's great act of 'forgettance'[114]

Some have drawn parallels between the recent protests in Hong Kong and Tiananmen, but with smartphones everywhere it would be close to impossible to cover up a similar massacre.

The Hong Kong Free Press, an independent news source in China, accepts Bitcoin donations.[146]

China has gone to great lengths to cover up these events. Twitter is censored by default in China and anyone caught tweeting about Tiananmen might get arrested. On the anniversary they have police escorts for the victim's families who want to visit the graves—to keep them away from journalists.[115]

Censorship is a global problem and is a big problem in for example Eritrea, North Korea, Saudi Arabia and Ethiopia.[116] A more modern problem is manipulation on social media, with the goal to control public opinion. One way is to use trolls (fake user accounts) and another is to censor opinions[117] that don't fit your narrative.

The censorship in China is absolutely massive. They try to scan and filter all internet traffic in China, often called "The Great Firewall of China", and they're doing a pretty good job. For example they completely ban Facebook, Twitter, Snapchat, Google, Youtube, Wikipedia, WikiLeaks, Netflix and **many** others. It might be possible to work around the restrictions using a VPN, but many don't work in China either.[147]

If caught, you'll probably be placed in a "re-education camp", which are quite similar to camps in Stalin's Soviet or Hitler's Germany.[148]

A short history of WikiLeaks

WikiLeaks is a relevant example for illustrating the importance of uncensorable payments as it shows the influence powerful actors have over payment processors and, in turn, the funding for WikiLeaks. We will focus on the Chelsea Manning leaks and the aftermath, where WikiLeaks got their donation channels shut down for exposing government atrocities.

I'll bring up the events surrounding Julian Assange[118], because they give context and might be relevant to the story of government abuse, but it's not about him or any other person in particular. Even if Julian Assange is guilty of rape, it does not change the importance of the leaks or WikiLeaks as a concept, which goes above individuals.

Trying to discredit WikiLeaks by discrediting Assange is *guilt by association*—a logical fallacy.

If we think that good deeds can only be done by perfectly good people then it follows that only Superman can do good. But in reality people are flawed like Iron Man, who is narcissistic and alcoholic, but also a hero.

This is **not** a glorification of WikiLeaks—they have endangered individuals[119] via their leaks. Instead I hope to show that uncensorable donations are important, because exposing government atrocities can lead to your donations being blocked (and government atrocities should be exposed).

Beginning Oct 4, 2006

WikiLeaks was launched as a news site for collaborative editing, similar to how Wikipedia is edited by volunteers. Despite their similar names the sites aren't related. In 2010 WikiLeaks stopped being a wiki, but the name remained the same.

Today many equate WikiLeaks with Julian Assange, but he's only one of many people involved. Sometimes he's described as the founder, editor-in-chief, or director.

The Chelsea Manning leaks July 5, 2010

First I must caution you: it's very easy to become numb when you read about these leaks. The sheer amount of horror is enough to over-whelm you and might cause your brain to suppress your emotions, maybe out of self-defense. But try to remember that this happened to real people—it's not just a mass of text and numbers. Please don't relegate this as just another forgettable statistic.

Chelsea Manning (formerly Bradley Manning) is a former soldier of the United States who provided WikiLeaks with nearly 750,000 military and diplomatic documents. They were released in batches and spread out over a period of time. Some of the content was absolutely shocking and caused global outrage, I've tried to pick out some notable leaks:

- **Collateral murder**[120]

    WikiLeaks uploaded a video of a Baghdad helicopter attack in July 12, 2007 with the title "Collateral murder". It's a video of how an attack hel-icopter killed a dozen innocent people, including two Reuters news staff.

    Here are some transcripts[121] of the full video[122] with my comments on the events:

    | 02:34 | He's got an RPG [Rocket Propelled Grenade]? |
    | 02:35 | All right, we got a guy with an RPG. |

    Except now we know it's not an RPG but a camera held by a Reuters jour-nalist.

    | 03:45 | All right, hahaha, I hit [shot] 'em... |
    | ... | |
    | 04:55 | Oh, yeah, look at those dead bastards. |
    | 05:00 | Nice |
    | .... | |
    | 06:57 | Come on, buddy. |
    | 07:01 | All you gotta do is pick up a weapon. |

It's hard to do justice as there are **many** more leaks, I find it overwhelming. See for example:

1. Torture and abuse in the Guantánamo naval base.[149]
2. How the U.S. avoided the U.K. cluster bomb ban.[150]
3. The Abu Omar abduction.[151]
4. Political corruption in Tunisia.[152]
5. Saudi urged U.S. to attack Iran.[153]

At 2019-08-28 the transcript timestamps are slightly off compared to the full video, I've tried to match them up better.

After killing a bunch of people, they're looking at an injured person crawling on the ground wanting him to pick up a weapon—so they're allowed to kill him.

07:59	Picking up the wounded?
08:01	Yeah, we're trying to get permission to engage.
08:04	Come on, let us shoot!

Then, a van enters the scene and they're rushing in to help the wounded. But now the rules aren't that important anymore—they want to shoot!

10:35	Oh yeah, look at that. Right through the windshield!
10:37	Ha ha!
10:39	All right. There were uh approximately four to five individuals in that truck, so I'm counting about twelve to fifteen.

There were two children behind that windshield who got seriously injured. Their father was killed for trying to help the wounded on the street.

When Reuters tried to get answers for how their reporters died, the U.S. military claimed they didn't know how they got killed, and that all dead were insurgents. They also didn't know how the children got injured, despite having the video footage.

Afterwards, the military investigated the issue and concluded that the actions of the soldiers where in accordance with the law of armed conflict and its own "Rules of Engagement".

- **Execution of children**[123]

In 2006, a group of U.S. soldiers entered a house in Iraq where they executed at least 10 people (9 civilians), including an infant and four other children—all five years or younger—and elderly women. They called in an airstrike to cover up the evidence, but postmortems showed they had been handcuffed and shot in the head.

Even the infant was shot in the head. A photographer captured pictures of the bodies.[154]

We're quick to call them terrorists, but viewed from another angle the U.S. soldiers are the terrorists. Just imagine foreign soldiers entering your neighbour's house and executing everyone there, including the children...

The soldiers were cleared of any wrongdoing by the U.S. military, after the military initially denied that the events happened at all.

One man's terrorist is another man's freedom fighter

Unknown

- **Civilian deaths in Iraq[124]**

  While U.S. officials had previously said no logs existed of civilian deaths in Iraq, leaked cables told another story. 66,081 civilian deaths had been logged out of a total of 109,000 deaths between 2004 and 2009. That's 60.6% of all dead being innocent people—a horrifyingly bad ratio.

  Leaked cables also indicated that U.S. authorities had failed to investigate hundreds of reports of torture, rape, abuse and murder by Iraqi security officials.

66 thousand innocent people dead in six years. That's like 22 World Trade center attacks (where 2,977 people died)—more than three a year. Or 31 innocent people dead every day during the six years.

Countless numbers of civilians killed—while soldiers are laughing—and systematic cover-ups to hide it all.

To me, Chelsea Manning is a hero for bringing this to light. Yet how was she thanked? Like all whistleblowers, she was made an example of; she was court-martialed and sentenced to 35 years in prison.

You just can't help but wonder—for what purpose? Imaginary nuclear weapons, bringing "democracy and peace" to Iraq, securing oil supply, helping U.S. allies or simply needing a purpose for their massive war machine?

The value of non-American lives in this war is ridiculously low.

Sexual assault allegations against Julian Assange Aug 2010

Shortly after the massive leaks, Julian Assange was accused of sexual assault in Sweden.[125] The timing might be a coincidence; or if you're a conspiracy theorist you might say they're manufactured by the U.S. government, in a way to reach Julian Assange.

In November, when Assange had already traveled to London (the charges were dropped to be picked up again after he left Sweden), an international arrest warrant was issued by the Swedish police via Interpol.[126]

Like the saying goes: "truth is stranger than fiction".

PayPal freezes WikiLeaks donations Dec 4, 2010

Later, PayPal freezes WikiLeaks donations[127] with the reason:

> Our payment service cannot be used for any activities that encourage, promote, facilitate or instruct others to engage in illegal activity.

As far as reasons for shutting down services, PayPal doesn't have a good record (p.59). This excuse is at least believable on the surface.

Even if you don't like conspiracy theories, it's not a stretch to say the U.S. government put pressure on PayPal in their effort to shut down WikiLeaks.

Banking blockade Dec 7, 2010

This further developed into a Banking Blockade that the Bank of America, VISA, MasterCard and Western Union also joined.[128] WikiLeaks claim this destroyed 95% of their revenue, and they had to resort to cash reserves.

The blockade was later found to be illegal[129] and today WikiLeaks again accept donations via PayPal and credit cards, but they suffered large damage at the crucial time when the world was in uproar over the leaks.

WikiLeaks accepts Bitcoin Jun 14, 2011

After being shunned by banks and payment processors, WikiLeaks turned to Bitcoin, because nobody—not even the U.S. government—can block Bitcoin transactions.

Why did it take almost a year before WikiLeaks started accepting Bitcoin? Satoshi made this appeal in the de-facto discussion forum at the time:

> Basically, bring it on. Let's encourage Wikileaks to use Bitcoins and I'm willing to face any risk or fallout from that act.

> No, don't "bring it on".

> The project needs to grow gradually so the software can be strengthened along the way.

> I make this appeal to WikiLeaks not to try to use Bitcoin. Bitcoin is a small beta community in its infancy. You would not stand to get more than pocket change, and the heat you would bring would likely destroy us at this stage.

Satoshi, Dec 5, 2010[130]

Which Assange cites as the reason they held off introducing Bitcoin donations.[131]

Assange applies for political asylum from Ecuador June, 2012

A couple of weeks after the Supreme Court's final ruling in U.K. that Assange should be extradited to Sweden, he walked into the Ecuadorean embassy in London and applied for political asylum. The stated reason was fears that Sweden would send him to the U.S. where he would risk the death penalty under espionage charges.[132]

Assange was granted asylum on August 16th [133] and his stay at the embassy would be longer than anyone would have thought.

If the goal was to divert attention and to put breaks on WikiLeaks until the whole thing blew over, you might say it was a success.

For instance today, in 2021, the torture and abuse still continues in Guantánamo, despite ex-president Barack Obama's promise to close it[155].

The fears of Sweden extraditing Assange to the U.S. might not be unfounded. In 2001 the Swedish police watched CIA forcefully detain two Egyptian refugees on Swedish soil, who later faced torture in Eqyptian prisons.[156]

Chelsea Manning's sentence is commuted Jan 17, 2017

President Barack Obama commutes Chelsea Manning's prison sentence.[134] Important to note it only reduced her sentence, it doesn't change the fact that she was convicted. She spent almost 7 years of her original 35 year sentence in prison.

In contrast, a *pardon* would completely absolve her of any wrongdoing.

Chelsea Manning is jailed again Mar, 2019

Chelsea Manning is jailed again for her refusal to testify against Julian Assange. She objected to the secrecy of the grand jury process and says she has already revealed everything she knows at her court martial.[135]

Assange arrested at the embassy April, 2019

After almost 7 years at the Ecuadorien embassy, Julian Assange finally leaves the embassy and is arrested.

While he was immediately indicted on 17 counts of violating the Espionage Act by the U.S.[136] his release was news for the Swedish prosecutors. Nevertheless the Swedish investigation was soon reopened[137] as well.

Confusingly he was actually arrested twice. First for skipping a U.K. court warrant[157] and a second time at the request of the U.S. seeking his extradition[158].

The rape investigation is dropped November, 2019

A few months later, the Swedish prosecutor once again dropped their investigation against Assange, citing the long period of time since the alleged crime as the reason.[138]

When Assange first sought asylum many people said it was only to avoid the Swedish charges and he used fears of the U.S. as a pretext, but in hindsight the fears might have been real.

Observers are denied entry to the Assange hearings September, 2020

During Assange's extradition hearing, where the U.K. will rule on extradition to the U.S., Amnesty International were blocked from observing the hearings.[139] They claim the hearings were intentionally locked down:

> The judge wrote back expressing her "regret" at her decision and saying: "I fully recognise that justice should be administered in public". Despite her regret and her recognition that scrutiny is a vital component of open justice, the judge did not change her mind.
>
> [...]
>
> Amnesty International have monitored trials from Guantanamo Bay to Bahrain, Ecuador to Turkey. For our observer to be denied access profoundly undermines open justice.

A farcical extradition hearing September, 2020

The human rights activist, Craig Murray, was allowed to observe and he's been documenting the hearing on his blog[140], and it's not an exaggeration to call the hearing a farce.

Witnesses were prevented from taking the stand because the U.S. managed to block any reference to the torture at Guantánamo (which we know is true):

> The next witness, Andy Worthington, was at court and ready to give evidence, but was prevented from doing so. The United States government objected to his evidence, about his work on the Guantanamo Detainee files, being heard because it contained allegations of inmates being tortured at Guantanamo.
>
> Craig Murray, Assange Hearing Day 14[141]

In another instance, the prosecution—with the cooperation of the judge— tries to hide the fact that Assange was caught with a razor in the cell, which would imply that Assange is thinking of suicide:

> For Baraitser [the judge] to try to protect both Lewis and the prosecution by pretending the existence of the blade is dependent on the outcome of the subsequent charge, when all three people in the cell at the time of the search agreed to its existence, including Assange, is perhaps Baraitser's most remarkable abuse of legal procedure yet.
>
> [...]
>
> The existence of the blade was not in doubt. Julian Assange had attested to it and two prison warders had attested to it. *Baraitser said that she could only base her view on the decision of the Prison Governor.*
>
> [...]
>
> The Governor's decision was at paragraph 19. Baraitser told Fitzgerald she could not accept the document as it was new evidence. Fitzgerald told her *she had herself asked for the outcome of the charge.* He said the document contained very interesting information. Baraitser said that the Governor's decision was at paragraph 19, that was all she had asked for, and *she would refuse to take the rest of the document into consideration.*
>
> (Emphasis mine)
>
> Craig Murray, Assange Hearing Day 17[142]

The hearing is full of problems like these. The prosecution changed their accusations hours before and the defense not getting enough time to prepare, that the defense was prevented from questioning key witnesses and that there will be no closing speeches in the hearing.

Nevertheless, in January 2021 the judge blocked Assange's extradition to the U.S.[143]

Not because she disagreed with the prosecution, but because Assange would face barbaric prison treatment in the U.S., and thus it would be "unjust or oppressive to extradite him".

As of March 2021, the judgement may still be overturned by appeals.

Hiding skeletons in the closet

There's another theme in the WikiLeaks story: How the U.S. government instead of admitting these horrible events, punishing the responsible and making sure they never happen again, seem to do everything to cover them up.

This idea that American soldiers are unconditionally heroes, regardless of what they've done, makes me both angry and sad. Donald Trump has for example expressed concerns over soldiers being prosecuted for war crimes, and considered pardoning them[144]. This includes a Navy Seals soldier who (allegedly) killed a 15-year old defenseless kid with his hunting knife and shot unarmed civilians[145].

Those aren't the actions of a hero.

The serious charges against the Navy Seal solder were later dismissed and he was "only" convicted for posing for a picture with the dead body of the 15-year old.[160]

Trump continued his support as he announced he was rescinding awards given to some of the Navy prosecutors who brought up the case.

Of course, covering up or rationalizing events isn't a U.S. only phenomena. Here are other examples:

- As previously mentioned the Chinese cover up of the Tiananmen Square Massacre.

- How Genghis Khan is looked up to.

  Maybe you've heard that 1 of 200 people of all people alive today are related to Genghis Khan? That's because he raped young girls wherever he went.

- In Scandinavian countries we talk about Vikings with pride.

  But the word Viking originally refers to actions of a group: "to viking", "to pirate" or "to pillage". And pillaging means killing, stealing, raping and taking people as slaves. Not unlike the actions of the U.S. soldiers who executed children—which we find so revolting.

- How leaders like Ceasar and Kim Jong-il were glorified.

  It was even forbidden to talk about them negatively.

- How the Soviet Union tried to cover up the Chernobyl nuclear disaster.

Dan Carlin, creator of the excellent *Hardcore History* podcast, brought up an interesting question:

How long will it take for people to celebrate Hitler?

It seems absurd to us now, but Genghis Khan did similarly awful things yet there's a song in the 1979 Eurovision Song Contest about him and how "all women fell for him".[159]

I recently finished watching the *Chernobyl* TV-series and I think it lives up to the hype. Among other things it captures the feeling of the cover-ups very well.

Unfortunately it seems like a human thing to try to hide your misdeeds instead of coming clean, even when they're exposed.

No mom, it wasn't me!

A fidgeting child

Burying the truth will allow it to continue

… if all records told the same tale—then the lie passed into history and became truth. 'Who controls the past,' ran the Party slogan, 'controls the future: who controls the present controls the past.' … 'Reality control', they called it: in Newspeak, 'doublethink'.

George Orwell, *1984*[Orw49]

I know what some of you might say and others might feel: you don't want to know about these horrible things. It's true that you'll feel better if you're unaware and you'll probably personally be better off if you act like these never happened.

But if we practice collective 'forgettance', where we all pretend these never happened, they will continue to happen. This is why what Chelsea Manning and WikiLeaks revealed about the Iraq war is so important: we're forced to confront the truth.

I'm not so naive to say the leaks will prevent future atrocities—they won't. But knowledge of what actually happens is a necessary first step for change to be possible at all.

Cryptocurrency donations cannot be prevented

While the U.S. government was able to coerce payment processors and banks to drop WikiLeaks, they could never prevent Bitcoin donations. Even China, with the world's largest internet censorship, cannot censor cryptocurrency transactions. The best they can do is force some exchanges to cooperate—but that can be worked around, for example by selling bitcoins in person for cash or by avoiding fiat altogether.

China does have most of the Bitcoin hashrate inside their country. They could theoretically take majority control of Bitcoin's hashrate and censor transactions that way (this is the worst attack possible against a cryptocurrency, called a *51% attack* (p.22)). If successful this would also completely break Bitcoin's security, making it pointless.

In this scenario the Bitcoin community would most likely recognize it as an attack and a chain split would happen, making existing miners worthless.

It doesn't matter who you are or where you are, you can always accept donations digitally via cryptocurrencies. Even the most powerful nations in the world cannot prevent them, which is something unique for cryptocurrencies.

Chapter 10

For the unbanked
Digital payments for those without a bank account

A growing body of research reveals many potential development benefits from financial inclusion—especially from the use of digital financial services, including mobile money services, payment cards, and other financial technology (or fintech) applications.

Global Findex database, 2017

In the previous chapters we've looked at some problems with having to get permission to accept digital payments, and what happens when we don't. This time we'll look at the reverse problem: when you can't make digital payments.

To make digital payments, you typically need a bank account and those without one are often called *unbanked*. Paying bills digitally, using credit cards and even mobile payments all require a bank account. If you don't have a bank account, you're essentially shut-out from the digital economy.

The problems the unbanked face are difficult to solve, and cryptocurrencies won't magically solve them all, but if adopted they can be helpful.

Maybe there's a way to work around the bank requirement, possibly by using in-game currencies, but they're severely limited compared to the digital payments we usually think about. In practice you need a bank account for useful digital payments.

Who are the unbanked?

There are **1.7 billion adults** without a bank account in the world. To get a sense for what countries they come from, take a look at this world map:

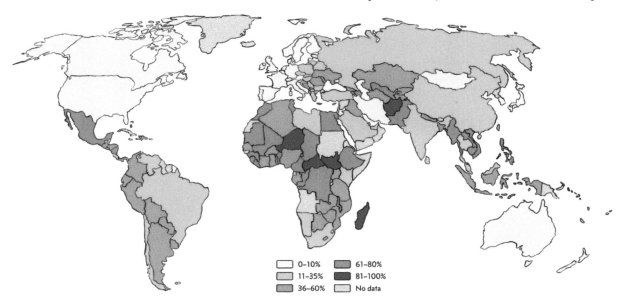

☐ 0–10%	☐ 61–80%
☐ 11–35%	☐ 81–100%
☐ 36–60%	☐ No data

Adults without a bank account, 2017.

Unless stated otherwise, all statistics and references are taken from Global Findex Database (2017) *Measuring Financial Inclusion and the Fintech Revolution*.[164]

This map helps us identify countries with a high fraction of unbanked and we can for example see that it's common to be unbanked in Africa and in South America but uncommon in western Europe and the Nordic countries.

The unbanked are in general less educated, where 62% of unbanked only have a primary education or less, compared to around half overall in developing economies. Twice as many unbanked people live in the poorest households as in the richest ones and 56% of all unbanked are women.

Another way to look at the world is to visualize the raw number of unbanked in every country, which shows us where the 1.7 billion unbanked come from:

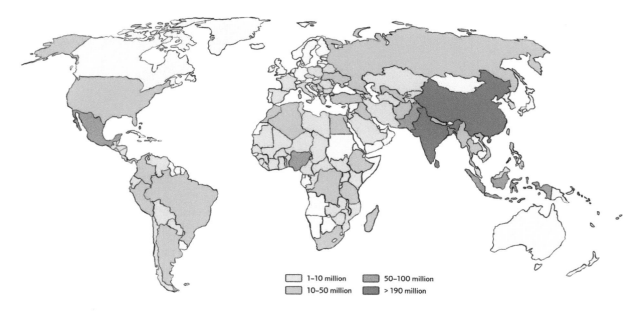

The number of adults without a bank account, 2017.

Almost half of all unbanked people live in just seven countries: China, India, Indonesia, Mexico, Nigeria, Pakistan and Bangladesh. In fact China (224 million) and India (191 million) alone make up nearly a quarter of all unbanked in the world.

While the fraction of unbanked adults are high in the developing countries with poor access to electricity and internet, a surprisingly large number of unbanked also live in developed countries. For example USA has 18 million unbanked and in France there are 3 million unbanked.

If this is interesting to you I suggest you give the report a read. There are tons of different statistics and I only refer to a fraction of the data available.

Why are they unbanked?

The Global Findex database also tried to examine why people stay unbanked:

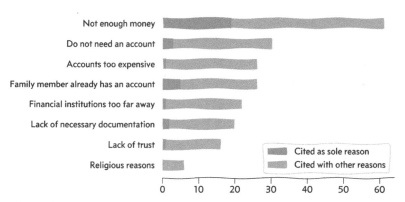

Reported reason for adults not having a bank account, 2017. More than one reason could be given. Source Global Findex database.

The most commonly cited barrier was not having enough money. Around 60% said they had too little money to use a bank account, with almost 20% citing it as the sole reason.

Most cite several different reasons, making it hard to rank the issues in importance. For example many say they don't need an account, but if the other barriers were to disappear they might find accounts useful if only they had access to them. At least this gives a sense of what issues are present.

Unbanked with internet

The question "But how do the unbanked pay for internet?" is always asked when discussing the unbanked. The report has this to say:

> How many unbanked adults have a mobile phone? Globally, about 1.1 billion—or about two-thirds of all unbanked adults. In India and Mexico more than 50 per-cent of the unbanked have a mobile phone; in China 82 percent do.

> Fewer unbanked adults have both a mobile phone and access to the internet in some form—whether through a smartphone, a home computer, an internet café, or some other way. Globally, the share is about a quarter.

Global Findex database, 2017

I assume it might mean poor people who might not have any savings but live day to day. But it's not clear where to draw the line between having too little money, accounts being too expensive and not having a use for an account. I feel these issues would go together to some extent.

So about **420 million** do have access to internet while being unbanked. I don't know if that's true or not, but anecdotally it seems almost all homeless people I've seen own a smartphone of some sort. You can even get internet in Venezuela, despite an unreliable power grid. And consider that even rich and successful people can become temporarily unbanked (p.55), for example if banks arbitrarily decide porn stars and marijuana supporters aren't something they want to be associated with.

What's the problem?

There are two big problems with being unbanked related to digital payments as I see it, one on a country level and one for individuals:

1   Countries miss out on economic growth.

2   Individuals may be shut-out from society.

Economic growth

Continuing the quote from the beginning of the chapter:

> The benefits from financial inclusion can be wide ranging. For example, studies have shown that mobile money services—which allow users to store and transfer funds through a mobile phone—can help improve people's income earning potential and thus reduce poverty.

> A study in Kenya found that access to mobile money services delivered big benefits, especially for women. It enabled women-headed households to increase their savings by more than a fifth; allowed 185,000 women to leave farming and develop business or retail activities; and helped reduce extreme poverty among women-headed households by 22 percent.

> Global Findex database, 2017

One of the best ways to fight poverty is economic growth.[161] This is fairly undisputed, although the link may be indirect. As I see it, convenient digital payments contribute to economic growth in two ways:

Reportedly Venezuela has one of the worst internet speeds in the world. Yet they still use social media actively[165] and interestingly they also mine Bitcoin[166].

Here in Sweden I had a fascinating encounter with Handelsbanken, one of the largest banks here. I asked if I could open an account there (because I wanted to try out their internet bank) but I couldn't get one unless I moved over all my accounts and used them to receive my salary.

I did finally get an account there when we took a mortgage with them, but I still don't use them as my main bank.

1   Increased economic efficiency.

Since digital payments allow for more convenient payments, especially over longer distances, they increase the efficiency in the economy leading to economic growth.

2   A cornerstone for inclusion into the ever-more digitalized world.

Globalization, or how the world has become more interconnected, has been a theme in the last century or two. It has never been easier to travel to the other side of the world, to talk to them over the internet or have them ship goods to you for very low fees.

If people don't have access to digital payments the country risks becoming more isolated and might miss out on the economic growth caused by globalization[162]. (Of course there are downsides with globalization as well, just look at the trade war between the U.S. and China[163]).

Shut-out from society

It might be relatively fine for you to live in a country without a bank account—as long as others don't use one either. But what if you live in a country where digital payments are an integral part of society?

For example here in Sweden almost everyone and everything uses digital payments. It would be **extremely** difficult for you to live here without a credit card or a bank to pay your bills.

One time when I went on a small business trip to the middle parts of Sweden, I accidentally forgot my wallet, including my credit cards and identification card. I borrowed some cash from a friend, thinking I could use them to pay for lunch and dinner, but surprisingly most restaurants didn't accept cash. So, I still had to ask my co-workers to pay for me...

I don't really know how people without a bank account manage in Sweden or what tourists will do if their credit card stops working? With the current development, they might not even be able to use public bathrooms!

In China, mobile payments are growing like mad. If you're a tourist, you should get them, otherwise you'll have a tough time. This in combination with China's *social credit*, which ranks people's behaviors to make sure they're in line with the party, is a recipe for disaster. If you score badly, you might not be allowed to fly and maybe you'll lose the privilege of using digital payments.

For an interesting angle on how globalization effected the world economy I recommend *The Box* by Marc Levinson[Box16].

A historical example is when China decided to isolate itself from the rest of the world.[167] They had all they needed and were ahead the rest of the world in many areas, but after they isolated themselves the rest of the world caught up.

A similar story of a co-worker who moved to Sweden. There was a delay for him to get his social security number, and thus his bank account, so he had to be taken care of by people at work until it got sorted out.

In fact when I last visited a public bathroom in a shopping mall they had a new payment system there. Instead of inserting a coin to get the door open—you guessed it—you had to pay with a credit card or with Swish (a mobile payment app, connected to your bank account). I guess the kids or tourists, who don't have a credit card or Swish, have to hold it in.

What might cryptocurrencies help the unbanked with?

Of course "just use cryptocurrencies" isn't the answer to all problems for the unbanked. Cryptocurrencies won't magically give poor people money, make them educated and they can't even completely replace banks. But it is a helpful tool which, as adoption grow, might be helpful for many without bank access.

There are a number of benefits cryptocurrencies have:

- Cryptocurrencies are for everyone.

  Cryptocurrencies are *permissionless*: you don't need permission from anyone to use them (p.6). It doesn't matter if you're homeless, a porn star or a tourist—you can always have access to digital payments and you cannot be shut-out.

- There is no KYC process.

  Because cryptocurrencies are permissionless there's no *Know your customer (KYC)* process, which banks are required to perform. That's good for people who might not have proper documentation such as ID-cards or birth certificates.

- The fees are low (p.49).

  There are no fees for opening or having an account—like with traditional banks—and there are no KYC associated costs. There is only a small transaction cost you pay when using a cryptocurrency.

- You don't need to trust a third-party with your money (p.6).

  In countries with high corruption you might not trust your local bank enough to handle your money. With cryptocurrencies you can hold your money yourself and there's no need for a third-party to use it (such as a bank making the payment for you).

- There's no need to visit a financial institution.

  As long as you have internet access you always have access to your money and can make payments. Getting started is as simple as installing an app on your phone.

These are directly related to the reasons why people stay unbanked (p.76), many of which cryptocurrencies might help solve. For example, the 30% who say bank accounts are too expensive and the 20% who say they lack documentation, may find cryptocurrencies a viable alternative as it is much cheaper than bank accounts and they don't require any documentation. Cryptocurrencies also remove the requirement of having to trust a bank, which 15% of the unbanked cited as a reason for not having an account.

These benefits makes it possible for the 420 million unbanked who have internet access to use cryptocurrencies and gain access to the global economy (p.119).

"Banking the unbanked" is a term cryptocurrency advocates like to use, and I even used it as the title of this chapter during the initial planning phase. But it's misleading as banks do things cryptocurrencies don't, for instance:

1. Extend loans.
2. Safeguard your money (while you can hold cryptocurrencies yourself, it makes sense for many to let others hold them for you).

Part IV

A better currency

Magic internet money

Let me issue and control a nation's money and I care not who writes the laws.

Mayer Amschel Rothschild

Our focus during the last part was on the use of cryptocurrencies as a payment system. But in fact Bitcoin wasn't invented to be just an improved PayPal—it was made to be something more, with much larger consequences: a completely new form of money.

In this part, we'll focus on the benefits of using cryptocurrencies as money and compare it to what we use today. We'll begin by highlighting flaws with the current financial system, flaws that originate from our use of unsound money. It's a system full of broken incentives that relies on being able to predict the unpredictable and that tries to solve all problems by printing more money, which has various negative side-effects.

Even though privacy is a human right, the digital money we use today is very bad for privacy as all our financial information is tracked, stored and sold to private companies. Privacy is important because it helps you stay who you are and it increases the personal security for yourself and others.

Cryptocurrencies mitigate all these problems, and they're also truly global, unhampered by borders, disputes and local monetary policy.

Remember that the term *money* refers to an intangible concept and *currency* is the actual thing used as money.

For example, cryptocurrencies are money— you cannot pay me with "3 cryptocurrency". And Bitcoin (BTC) is a currency because you can send 3 BTC to me.

Many of my arguments in this part will apply to gold or gold-backed fiat, as well as cryptocurrencies. See the comparision of properties between different forms of money (p.43) for more details on the pros and cons of different forms of money.

Chapter 11

The financial crisis, bad loans and bailouts

The doomsday, broken incentives and moral hazard

Give a man a gun and he can rob a bank, but give a man a bank, and he can rob the world.

Tyrell Wellick, *Mr. Robot (2015)*

During 2007–2008, the world experienced the biggest financial crisis since the 1930s Great Depression, often referred to as the 2008 financial crisis. What was so crazy about the crisis? And is there a relationship to *sound money*?

Sound money is not prone to sudden changes in long term purchasing power, and the value is determined by the free market.

What caused the 2008 financial crisis?

The financial crisis was caused by too many people borrowing too much money. The banks were happy to help and repackaged the bad loans and sold them to someone else, for a nice profit. When there weren't enough loans the clever banks conjured new ones, keeping the money machine rolling. This eventually blew up and brought the global economy to it's knees.

This explanation is naturally very simplified. There were for example two bubbles that popped: the housing bubble and the much bigger bond bubble (based in large part on mortgage loans). The complex financial products (for example the mortgage bonds or the CDOs nobody really understood) appeared to be low-risk but were high-risk. And of course the "heads I win, tails you lose" incentives at play all the way from top to bottom in the system.

It's not important to understand exactly how the complex financial products, such as CDOs, work; the important thing to know is that experts didn't understand them either.

A lot of ink has been spent on articles, books and movies explaining the events better and in far more detail than I could hope to do. I particularly like the explanations given in the Oscar-winning movie *The Big Short (2016)*. Just look at how they describe subprime mortgages and CDOs:

> Basically, Lewis Ranieri's mortgage bonds were amazingly profitable for the big banks. They made billions and billions on their 2% fee they got for selling each of these bonds. But then, they started running out of mortgages to put in them. After all, there are only so many homes and so many people with good enough jobs to buy them, right?
>
> So, the banks started filling these bonds with riskier and riskier mortgages. That way, they can keep that profit machine churning, alright? By the way, these risky mortgages are called "subprime." So, whenever you hear the word "subprime," think "shit."

Margot Robbie, *The Big Short (2016)*

It might sound strange, but you can resell loans. For example when you take a loan at the bank, the bank now earns a small fee for the loan in return for the risk that you might not pay them back. The bank can decide to sell this loan to others, so they take the risk but earn the fees. Many such loans can be combined into bonds and sold or even insured.

In *After the Music Stopped* Alan S. Blinder identifies seven villains responsible for the crisis:[Mus13]

1. Housing bubble
2. Bond bubble
3. Regulatory shortfalls
4. Subprime lending disgraceful practices
5. Complexity run amok
6. Overrated rating agencies
7. Crazy compensation schemes

He does a good job describing the background of the crisis, although he's been criticized as being too positive towards the actions of the Federal Reserve and the politicians.

OK, I'm a chef on a Sunday afternoon, setting the menu at a big restaurant. I ordered my fish on Friday, which is the mortgage bond that Michael Burry shorted. But some of the fresh fish doesn't sell. I don't know why. Maybe it just came out halibut has the intelligence of a dolphin.

So, what am I going to do? Throw all this unsold fish, which is the BBB level of the bond, in the garbage, and take the loss? No way. Being the crafty and morally onerous chef that I am, whatever crappy levels of the bond I don't sell, I throw into a seafood stew. See, it's not old fish. It's a whole new thing! And the best part is, they're eating 3-day-old halibut. *That* is a CDO.

Anthony Bourdain, The Big Short (2016)

A pitch of humor sure makes for memorable explanations. But if it's too much Hollywood for your taste I recommend the book the movie is based on: *The Big Short: Inside the Doomsday Machine* by Michael Lewis[Big10]. Or if you're short on time maybe the 11 minute video *The Crisis of Credit Visualized*[168] might suffice.

The effects of the crisis

The crisis began with the collapse of the bank Lehman Brothers, marking the start of the Great Recession. In the U.S. alone the crisis meant $18 trillion disappeared, millions of jobs were lost and more than a million people lost their homes.[Mus13]

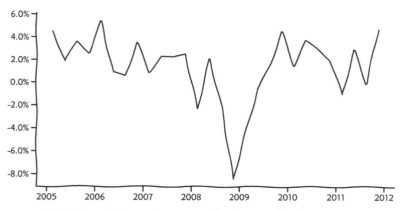

United States GDP growth rate surrounding the years of the financial crisis. It bottomed out at -8.4% the fourth quarter of 2008.[169]

Although the crisis originated in the U.S., the crisis spread globally. For example, in only the first quarter of 2009 the GDP rate was -4.7% in Germany[170], -4.8% in Japan[171] and -3% in the Euro area[172]. There are many details to dig into here, such as the unemployment rate or stock market valuations, but I'm content with just noting that the crisis was indeed a global disaster.

The bailouts

Although bad, the crisis could have been much worse. The U.S. came close to a complete financial meltdown, but without crossing the line. Partly thanks to the bailouts, where the Federal Reserve bailed out banks and other private companies. The extremely risky assets—too risky for anyone else to touch—were bought up to rescue the banks which were "too big to fail".[Mus13]

The bailouts started when the government guaranteed assets of the investment bank Bear Stearns and encouraged J.P. Morgan to buy them for a knockdown price. Then the mortgage lenders Fannie Mae and Freddie Mac collapsed, promptly rescued by being nationalized coupled with a $200 billion government investment.

While the investment bank Bear Stearns was saved, the investment bank Lehman Brothers was allowed to go bankrupt. At first the Treasury and Federal Reserve claimed they allowed Lehman to fail to send the signal that recklessly managed Wall Street firms did not all come with government guarantees. But when they saw the fatal effects the bank's collapse had on the economy they changed their tune and claimed they lacked the legal authority to do so.[Big10]

Then followed massive new efforts to bailout banks and other private companies. The Federal Reserve, for the first time in history, took control over the private company American Investment Group (AIG) while giving them a $182 billion loan. The laws allowing them to do this, but not bailout Lehman Brothers, must be very interesting. (Lehman Brothers was an *investment* bank, which isn't a real bank. Other investment banks later converted to "commercial banks" in order to receive bailouts.)[Mus13]

In September 2008, U.S. Treasury Secretary Henry Paulson persuaded the U.S. Congress for $700 billion to buy subprime mortgage assets from banks. Once handed the money they abandoned the promised strategy and instead essentially gave away billions of dollars to Citigroup, Morgan Stanley, Goldman Sachs and others. For instance the $13 billion AIG owed to Goldman Sachs was paid off in full by the U.S. government.[Big10]

The government guaranteed $306 billion of Citigroup's assets. They didn't ask for a piece of the action, change in management or anything

The crisis was able to spread because bankers all over the world bought these shitty assets that later collapsed to nothing. Banks were simply too interconnected and had too much risk, and when some banks started having trouble they all were in trouble.

Or perhaps a better term would be "too interconnected to fail". The biggest fear of a big bank going bankrupt is if it brings down the rest of the economy with it, which to an extent happened when Lehman Brothers failed.

The Federal Reserve is supposed to be completely politically independent. But with their actions during the crisis, can they still claim to be independent?

This is known as the Troubled Asset Relief Program, or TARP.

of importance. The $306 billion guarantee—nearly 2% of U.S. GDP, and roughly the combined budgets of the departments of Agriculture, Education, Energy, Homeland Security, Housing and Urban Development and Transportation—was presented undisguised, as a gift. No explanation was given, just that the action was taken in response to Citigroup's "declining stock price."

When it was clear the money wasn't enough, the Federal Reserve started buying bad subprime mortgages directly from the banks. By early 2009 the tax payers were stuck with more than a trillion dollars of risky assets and, if things went sideways, would end up eating a huge loss while the banks were in the clear.

For the taxpayers, it's like betting all on red on a roulette wheel—you risk a very big loss. In this case American taxpayers got a good outcome, they even made money on the bailouts[173], but the Irish taxpayers for example weren't so lucky[174].

A message from Satoshi

After having released the Bitcoin white paper (p.189) in 2008, Satoshi mined the first bitcoins and launched the Bitcoin network January 2009, just after the financial crisis. Little is known of the ideals of Bitcoin's creator, but Satoshi did leave a message in the first ever Bitcoin block (p.156):

> The Times 03/Jan/2009 Chancellor on brink of second bailout for banks
>
> Satoshi, Coinbase parameter for block 0[175]

Satoshi refers to The Times issued the 3rd of January, 2009 with the title "Chancellor on brink of second bailout for banks" and the subtitle "Billions may be needed as lending squeeze tightens".[176]

Which you might see as a sign that Satoshi wasn't a fan of bailing out the banks (if developing an alternative to the banking system wasn't enough of a hint).

There are many important problems a nation need to handle; health care, poverty, education, infrastructure, security and immigration; but with too little money to solve them. Yet there's almost an infinite money for the banks. I find it fascinating and incredibly frustrating.

Investments come with a risk–reward trade-off. If you want the potential for higher return then you need to take a larger risk and if you want lower risk you'll sacrifice potential gains. In this case the bailouts forced a very large risk on the taxpayers, with questionable upside.

You can read the issue online[184], although the title is different compared to the printed copy.

Life is unfair

> In medieval Europe, a banker who couldn't pay depositors was hanged. Today, that same banker would get bailed out, paid bonuses and enjoy some tax benefits, too.

> *Bitcoin the end of money as we know it (2015)*

After the dust settled, it's easy to think the guilty got punished—after all the U.S. loves to dish out harsh punishments—and the system was reworked to prevent a similar crisis from ever happening again. The reality is often disappointing.

Iceland is the only nation that actually put top finance executives behind bars after the 2008 crisis.[185]

The bankers weren't punished for their unregulated gambling or outright fraud. In fact only a single U.S. banker went to jail[177]. Instead they got bonuses and in 2010 the banks were enjoying massive profits—while regular people were still struggling without jobs and houses.[Big10]

Remember the $182 billion AIG bailout? Shortly after accepting the bailout they paid out **$165 million in bonuses** to their executives, those responsible for the biggest corporate loss in history[178]. As president Obama asks: "how do they justify this outrage to the taxpayers who are keeping the company afloat?"[179]. One can't help but wonder...

Just for context, $10 million is many times more than enough for me and my family to live on for the rest of our lives. Even if we start going on vacation several times a year.

Then, there's the case of Howie Hubler[180], which to me exemplifies the mindbogglingly stupid bonuses oh so well. He was responsible for the biggest loss of a single trade in history—a staggering *$9 billion*—yet when asked to resign (a friendly way to get fired) he received $10 million.

I can't help but regret my life choices here. Bankers seem to have a pretty sweet deal— you'll get rich even if you have no idea what you're doing! As long as you can sell shit to unsuspecting customers with a straight face...

Well, I can try to take comfort that I didn't sell out my morality.

How about the other traders and the "CDO managers" who sold junk disguised as safe assets to their customers? They became rich too.

It's all about incentives

> Never, ever, think about something else when you should be thinking about the power of incentives.

> Charlie Munger, *The Psychology of Human Misjudegement*, 1995[181]

What *really* caused the financial crisis, and made the crisis so large? It's easy to point the finger at people who borrowed money they couldn't afford, at the bankers who helped them (or tricked them) and at the rating agencies who didn't really know what they were rating. But the greed of Wall Street shouldn't be surprising—it should be expected.

The blame should be placed on the incentives that enabled the greed to flourish. They made the rating agencies not look too closely at the assets they were rating—otherwise the bankers would go to another rating agency and take their money with them. The people taking loans were incentivized to loan more since the house prices kept rising, making them more money. And the people giving out loans were encouraged to give out as many loans as possible, because they would get a cut of every loan they gave out.

> What are the odds that people will make smart decisions about money if they don't need to make smart decisions—if they can get rich making dumb decisions?

Michael Lewis, *The Big Short: Inside the Doomsday Machine*[Big10]

If you exploit and gamble, but instead of a prison sentence you're rewarded with a fat bonus check, you will not change your actions. In fact you'll be more likely to continue. It's exactly like a child who wants candy: if he screams and cries until he gets candy, what will he learn? He'll learn that you get candy when you cry—so now he'll cry to get the candy.

Indeed, as investor extraordinaire Charlie Munger says: if you want to predict how people will behave, you only have to look at their incentives. This is why the bailouts, while helpful in the short run (the child stopped crying), made the fundamental problem that enabled the crisis worse (the child will cry more in the future). Bad behaviour by banks and the people working at banks are even more likely now since they've learned that if they fail they will just get bailed out, and keep their bonuses. They even passed laws to make it even easier for the Federal Reserve to step in and rescue whatever they deem "too big to fail", without the *unnecessary* overhead of going through congress.

I find it interesting to compare the incentives for banks with the incentives for cryptocurrency miners (p.22). While banks are incentivized to gamble, exploit and cheat as much they can get away with, the incentives for miners are to work in the network's best interest. While incentives makes the financial industry unstable, it's what makes cryptocurrencies secure.

Will history repeat itself?

The 2008 financial crisis was a combination of a number of different factors working together. If only one were removed, for example if bankers didn't give out loans to everyone and their pets or if the rating agencies would rate the assets correctly, then the crisis would never have grown so big. And there were changes to the financial system after the crisis which should prevent a repeat of the crisis.

But as I wrote previously, the core incentives problem is unsolved and even made worse. There won't be an exact repeat of the 2008 crisis, but

Strawberry pickers were given out million dollar loans despite having a tiny income, and without posting any collateral. Las Vegas strippers owned multiple houses and people were getting loans by writing their pet's name on the loan.

The term *moral hazard* is often used to describe the bailouts. It refers to someone taking risks that others will pay for.

"Heads I win, tails I get bailed out."

Instead of bailouts banks can be rescued by *bail-ins*[186]. Instead of using money from taxpayers it uses the money from unsecured creditors, depositors and bondholders. In English it means the banks can take money from their customers to save themselves. The banks can also be placed under direct federal control.

This should in theory protect taxpayers, which is great, but it doesn't change the incentives. The banks can still play fast and loose and be saved by someone else.

we might see similar problems resurface in the future. It's like "curing" fever by lowering your body temperature, while leaving the virus infection intact.

For example in 2015, several banks began selling billions in something called a "bespoke tranche opportunity"—which is just another name for a CDO (the 3-day old halibut)[182]. The banks are also warming up to the same mortgage bonds that burned them in 2008[183], while housing prices are going through the roof and people are borrowing like mad.

History doesn't repeat itself, but it rhymes awfully well.

What if we used sound money?

With *sound money* nobody can manipulate the money supply. For example fiat backed by gold (as long as we trust the backers), actual gold coins or cryptocurrencies. The question is: could the financial crisis have been prevented if we used sound money?

Unfortunately, probably not. The housing and bond bubble might still have happened as the banks can still create mortgage backed securities, CDOs and other complex derivatives. Sound money cannot prevent anyone from creating and selling junk.

But the incentives would be different. Banks can still use *fractional banking* (create IOUs and inflate the money supply) (p.100), but if they fail there's nobody to print money for them to bail them out. The bailouts in 2008–2009 were only possible because the Federal Reserve has the ability to print as much money as they want. There's no upper limit to the size of the bailout—they can always conjure enough. Not so with sound money.

Therefore the unhealthy "heads I win, tails I get bailed out" incentives would return to the normal "heads I win, tails I lose" incentives we see in any healthy gamble. This seemingly small but important change would force banks to be more careful with their risk-taking, and if they overstep their bounds they will fail. This might have bad effects in the short-term, but would lead to a more robust and healthy risk management in the long-term. The virus infection would be cured, but the fever might worsen temporarily.

With a feeling of déjà vu the house prices have been rising globally, especially in cities, for many years now. Here in Sweden it's almost impossible for young adults to buy their first house or apartment in a city unless they get help from their parents or work for years saving up for the down-payment.

Of course, they don't actually print physical bills worth billions of dollars, they just move digital numbers in some spreadsheets. The effect is the same.

Chapter 12
The blind leading the blind
We don't understand, and neither do the experts

It's almost been worth this depression to find out how little our big men know.

Will Rogers, 1930s

Even though *sound money*—like cryptocurrencies or money backed by gold—might fix the bad incentives at the heart of the 2008 finanical crisis (p.83), there are many arguments against it. One of the most common is that we lose the ability to influence and react to the market. For example if the economy crashes, or we think it will crash, the modern central banks might try to print money and buy things to soften the crash. This isn't possible with cryptocurrencies or gold, since they cannot be created freely.

But there's a fatal flaw with this argument: it relies on being able to predict the market and to know what actions to take to move it in the direction you want. With how intricate and complex the economy is, it's an absurd assumption.

Elasticity is a nice word *fractional banking* (p.100) proponents have used to describe this ability. In plain English it means the ability to inflate and deflate the money supply freely.

How to become an expert

To become an expert in a field you need a lot of dedication, effort and maybe a bit of talent, but as Daniel Kahneman points out in his book *Thinking, Fast and Slow* you also need the right environment to develop expertise:

- An environment that is sufficiently regular to be predictable.
- An opportunity to learn these regularities through prolonged practice.

For example picking stock is notoriously difficult, so difficult that in general you'll be better off investing in a passive index fund than picking stock yourself[187]. This may not be surprising but it also applies to professional investors, most of whom under-perform compared to the index! This is because the stock market isn't regular enough to be predictable.[Thi11]

In contrast learning how to drive a car provides an ideal learning environment. You'll get instant feedback whenever you break or use the gas pedal, when you turn the steering-wheel the car turns and you'll quickly find out if you changed gears correctly. While similar, learning how to maneuver a large ship is more difficult because of the delayed feedback.[Thi11]

The problem with planning the economy

In *economic planning* central governments make, or influence, economic decisions[188]. There's nothing inherently bad about this and all governments do it, for example large infrastructure projects are often created by the government. The Soviet Union took this concept further by letting the government decide what goods to produce, how much and when[189].

This didn't go so well, with huge queues outside almost empty stores and people having to resort to the black market for necessities. The inability to predict the market, and control the economy, is one of the reasons the Soviet Union collapsed[190].

Because the economy is made up of millions or even billions of people, with different motivations and imperfect knowledge, it's **extremely** hard to predict all the needs of the market. For example you need to predict larger demand for butter closer to Christmas, because people are more likely to bake. Or that the demand for fluffy toys will skyrocket, because a game called Pokémon will become unreasonably popular. You think picking stock is difficult? This is much harder.

There's a misunderstood myth that you only need to put in 10,000 hours, and then you become an expert. But that's not the truth; with the right environment and deliberate practice you can become an expert much faster, and if you don't use your time efficiently you may never become one.

To learn more about this fascinating subject I highly recommend the book *Peak: Secrets from the New Science of Expertise* [Pea16].

There's also a "wicked" environment where you're likely to learn the wrong lesson from your experience. The example given is of a physician who tried to tried to confirm his hypothesis for who might develop typhoid. Unfortunately he tested his hunch by palpating the patient's tongue, without washing his hands, making him draw the wrong conclusion.

You also need to predict a larger demand for milk, because there are people like me who only drink milk with gingerbread.

I do think it's an impossible task. You need to accurately predict small events that can have large effects, known as the *Butterfly effect*.

Not to mention *Black Swan* events which are by definition unpredictable.[Bla08] The rise of Bitcoin is one example (currently valued at above $50,000).

Our leaders are blind

> When the music stops, in terms of liquidity, things will be complicated. But as long as the music is playing, you've got to get up and dance. We're still dancing.

Citigroup CEO Chuck Prince, 2007

It's not just the Soviet Union that has problems predicting and adapting to the whims of the global economy. The financial crisis in 2008, as we discussed in the previous chapter (p.83), should have been obvious yet took almost everyone by surprise. Here's what the Federal Reserve had to say, merely a month before the financial meltdown:

> Financial markets have been volatile in recent weeks, credit conditions have become tighter for some households and businesses, and the housing correction is ongoing.

> Nevertheless, the economy seems likely to continue to expand at a moderate pace over coming quarters, supported by solid growth in employment and incomes and a robust global economy.

The Federal Reserve, August, 2007[191]

The Federal Reserve, calling the global economy "robust", fanned the flames of the housing bubble by focusing on inflation and keeping the rate low, all the way up to the crash. They also let Lehman Brothers fail, not realizing the disaster it would create.[Mus13]

Maybe you feel like I'm focusing too much on the 2008 financial crisis? Then how about their actions around the Great Depression (which were critiqued as worsening the crisis), of which the Federal Reserve chairman had this to say:

> Let me end my talk by abusing slightly my status as an official representative of the Federal Reserve. I would like to say to Milton and Anna: Regarding the Great Depression, you're right. We did it. We're very sorry. But thanks to you, we won't do it again.

Oops!... you did it again.

Ben S. Bernanke, chairman of the Federal Reserve, 2002[192]

This shouldn't be that surprising when you consider that the national and global economy is too irregular to be predictable, and the feedback loop is extremely long—if it even exists. If for example the central bank lowers the interest rate, how long do we have to wait to see the effect? Days, months and maybe even years. And how do we know the economy reacted this way because of the changes to the interest rate, and not because of the trade war between the U.S. and China, Brexit or a million other reasons?

These people aren't experts, simply because the environment doesn't lend itself to creating experts. The worst thing isn't that they're clueless; the worst thing is that they don't know their limitations:

What do you do then? You use complicated models, based on historical data, to predict the effects on the economy.

How do you know the models are correct? You don't.

Well, the actual worst thing is that the economic system is built upon these "experts" predicting and reacting to events.

> Although the experience with negative nominal interest rates is limited, we tentatively conclude that overall, they help deliver additional monetary stimulus and easier financial conditions, which support demand and price stability.

> IMF financial advisor Jose Viñals, 2016[193]

While the article itself is more nuanced, you can't conclude anything with such a small sample size, with such a short timespan and in an irregular environment.

We are blind

> It is well enough that people of the nation do not understand our banking and monetary system, for if they did, I believe there would be a revolution before tomorrow morning.

> Henry Ford

I could argue that we're blind because we collectively don't understand the banking system, the modern monetary system or the financial system—which would largely be true. But there's another, more sinister, cause of our blindness: the Federal Reserve.

Do the people know that the least accountable operation in the U.S. government isn't the FBI, CIA or the NSA—which are all accountable to congressional supervision—but the Federal Reserve? The central bank of the United States, the largest economy in the world, isn't accountable to anyone, has no budget and nobody has insight into it's operations.[Fed94]

The Fed isn't a government agency. It's a private entity and its shareholders are banks which earn a dividend—at 6%, often tax-free.[194] (Which banks? It's a secret.) Nobody knows how much banks are printing to pad their own pockets and nobody knows how many dollars exist.

An easy thing to criticize is how the banks got bailed out in the 2008 financial crisis, and were given money with almost no strings attached and paid out ridiculous salaries and bonuses (p.83). Conflict of interest much?

It's worse than us not understanding how the system works. We simply don't have the ability to understand because the Federal Reserve makes us all blind. But this is often promoted as a benefit, not a drawback:

> The temptation is to step on the monetary accelerator or at least to avoid the monetary break until after the next election... Giving in to such temptations is likely to impart an inflationary bias to the economy and could lead to instability, recession and economic stagnation.
>
> Alan Greenspan, Chairmain of the Federal Reserve

The resistance isn't just regarding control. It's also about transparency—they don't want us to see what's going on.

This argument could be made against almost everything. For example megaprojects often fail (vastly overruns their cost or timetable) because politicians make them their pet project, pushing them through against all odds... And leave it to other people to pick up the pieces after the next election.[195]

My favorite example of failing megaprojects is the Olympics, which have vastly overrun their initial projected cost every single time.

Proponents will say that money is more important than other issues—too important to leave it to the whims of the politicians—and therefore the Federal Reserve must remain independent. I believe it's much too important to be handled in the dark, by a private entity.

A new hope

Cryptocurrencies are interesting because they allow anyone to verify the number of coins in circulation—with certainty. No money in history has had this valuable property. There's always been the need to trust the word of someone, that the amount of money is what they say it is. Even with gold coins there's trust involved; you have to trust the issuer to include the right amount of gold, otherwise the trust—and the currency—will collapse in value.

You can also predict how many coins will be created and when, it's coded into the rules of the cryptocurrency after all. While Bitcoin mimics the rate that gold is mined (p.8), there's no risk of counterfeit bitcoin or a meteor made of bitcoin crashing on earth to disrupt the supply, like with gold or other precious materials.

Finally, cryptocurrencies don't rely on "experts", who are supposed to avoid crashes by predicting what cannot be predicted. There's nobody in control so nobody can push the wrong button or pull the wrong lever to cause economic chaos.

Therefore, cryptocurrencies are a more transparent and robust alternative, which avoids many of the problems inherent to the modern financial system.

> An elegant weapon for a more civilized age.
>
> Obi-Wan Kenobi, *Star Wars: Episode IV - A New Hope (1977)*

Ever wonder why there are portraits on coins? Because they make them recognizable so you can decide to trust them or not. "I'll gladly accept emperor Augustus' coins" or "we don't accept that usurper's coins here."

With cryptocurrencies there's instead a risk of bugs in the code which may allow hackers to print coins.

This is a half-truth. Yes there's nobody who can create coins out of thin air, but there are developers, miners, exchanges and users of a cryptocurrency who can influence its development. After all it's "just code" (and a lot of people agreeing with the rules of the code).

Chapter 13
A defective system
There is something terribly wrong with this system, isn't there?

So you think that money is the root of all evil. Have you ever asked what is the root of all money?

Ayn Rand

In the chapter *What is money?* (p.31), we saw some historical examples of money and some properties that good money should have. Unfortunately looking at money through history, and what properties money should have, is not enough to understand the current economic system, which is a completely different beast.

As we saw in the previous chapter (p.91), a big problem is that our leaders don't know how to steer this financial beast. But there are more problems to the modern system, again related to being based on *unsound money* where a flexible money supply breaks the properties of good money. This has far-reaching negative consequences and it means the economic system we use today is broken, on a fundamental level.

Economic effects of counterfeiting

Imagine a counterfeiter, who has the ability to print money from thin air. What would he do with all the money? What would *you* do?

Personally, I would probably pay off my loans, renovate our house, go on vacation and buy a bunch of LEGO®. If I was smart I would also invest it; buy some stocks, some gold, maybe a house or two and rent them out. In short I would buy a bunch of stuff—and I think most would do the same.

If I did print money—a **lot** of money—and spent it like this, what would the effect on the economy be?

For starters, if I just kept the money without spending it, nothing would change:

The counterfeit money is colored yellow and the real money is green.

Then if I decided to buy a bunch of LEGO®, the store would get some of my money:

After a while the store would use the counterfeited money to pay their supplier:

Who in turn will use it to buy other stuff, and in this way the counterfeited money slowly trickles out into the rest of the economy.

This extra money has two important effects:

1   Higher prices.

     Because there's more money going around, with the same amount of goods, the prices will rise. For instance if all the money in the world would double overnight, then naturally all prices would double too. Yesterday's $100 bill would today only get you $50 worth of stuff.

     When prices rise and the same amount of money buys you less stuff, we call it *inflation*. It's how my grandmother could buy candy for one cent (0.01 SEK) when she was a child, while today our smallest coin is 1 SEK.

2   Redistribution of wealth.

     Notice how in our previous example the counterfeited money isn't divided equally. The counterfeiter suddenly became much richer than everyone else, and some received a bit more than others. Notice that the poor guy to the right in the example—who had very little to start with—didn't receive any money and became even poorer, relatively speaking.

Counterfeiting means everyone's savings—the "old" money—will lose value. This is why you shouldn't just store all your money as cash under the mattress or in a bank account—the value will be eaten up by inflation.

The opposite is *deflation*, when money increases in value and buys you more stuff.

While it may sound strange, technology has been deflating in price forever. When computers were just introduced they were *extremely* expensive, but now everyone and their mother literally has one in their pocket, and probably several at home. Some even have one on their wrist.

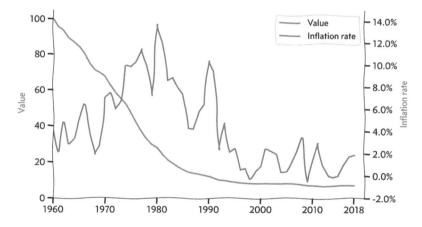

How the inflation in Sweden has caused the actual value of money to decrease. [196]

The graph shows an inflation adjusted index, starting from 1960. You can think of it what 100 SEK of goods in a given year would be worth in 1960's money. For example 100 SEK from 2018 would only buy 7 SEK worth of stuff in 1960—a 93% drop in value.

You can also compare two years with each other. For example the index in 1976 was around 40, and in 1982 around 20, which means money lost 50% of its value between 1976 and 1982.

The Money Project has a cool visualization of the expanding money supply and what $1 could buy. [211]

Why pick out Sweden as an example? No particular reason really, the graph would look similar if I picked the United States or some other well-functioning country. At first I was going to exemplify both Sweden and the United States, but the differences were so small I didn't see the point.

Counterfeiting redistributes wealth from everyone to the counterfeiter (and to a lesser extent people the counterfeiter buys from) at the same rate as the inflation eats up the value of money. Even though nobody's stealing your money, the effect is the same: your wealth relative to others will decrease.

Legal counterfeiting

While I think most will agree counterfeiting shouldn't be allowed, the modern economic system is built upon legal counterfeiting. There are entities who have the legal right to print money—with the same negative consequences on the economy that counterfeiting has. As noted earlier the central banks have this right, but regular banks can increase the money supply as well.

If the central banks want to increase the money supply, it's inefficient to print physical money. Instead they buy assets from banks who in turn can use the money as reserves while increasing the money supply. This is called *quantitive easing*, but it's unknown how well it actually works.

The central banks—the Federal Reserve (Fed) in the U.S. or the European Central Bank (ECB) in the EU—are the only ones allowed to print physical money. Which they have to do, if only to replace old bills. They also have an inflation target, usually 2% or 3%, meaning the goal is to devalue the money. The rationale is it drives economic growth because shoppers will buy now to avoid higher prices later[197].

Although the central banks are ultimately responsible, it's the regular banks who expand the money supply the most. It's done via *fractional banking* which works like this:

I always found the argument of inflation pushing people to spend weird. Most people I know don't even know about the effects inflation has, even less so when the inflation and the rising prices are so small you don't really notice them.

1   In the beginning John has 1 000 SEK, with nothing strange going on. This is the balance sheet for John and the bank:

John	Bank
1 000 SEK	

2   John lends the money to the bank, and receives money promises from the bank (let's call them IOUs):

John	Bank
1 000 IOU	1 000 SEK

3   The bank can issue more IOUs if they want, here they lend out IOUs to Jane:

John	Bank	Jane
1 000 IOU	1 000 SEK	9 000 IOU

There is now 11 000 money circulating the system. Because an IOU is treated like a SEK for all intents and purposes we can even say that there's 11 000 SEK now after we started with only 1 000 SEK. The bank printed 10 000 SEK from thin air and has only 1 000 SEK to back them up. The ratio of SEK to IOU, in this example 10%, is called the reserve.

> That's as good as money, sir. Those are I.O.U.s.
>
> Lloyd Christmas, *Dumb and Dumber (1994)*

We might wonder why stop at only printing 10 000 SEK? Why not 100 000 SEK? Or more? When the bank gives out IOUs they do need to repay them, otherwise they'll fail and become bankrupt. In the example above if Jane would withdraw 2 000 SEK the bank would fail, because it can only repay 1 000 SEK.

The system works as long as people just keep their money at the bank, and only occasionally withdraw their money. But if people start withdrawing a lot of money at the same time, a bank run may cause the bank to fail. To reduce this risk, banks have requirements on their reserves.

My example is simplified and banks aren't always required to have the reserves in cash. They can have them in other assets, which they can convert to cash if needed. See for example the "Capital requirements for the Swedish banks, second quarter 2019"[212].

The reserve requirements can also be fluid, see the ECB's "minimum reserve requirements"[213] for example.

Lender of last resort

As money printers, the central banks play an important role—as the "lender of last resort". This means when all else fails, for example if the banks are about to go bankrupt because they have too little reserves or if the economy is going bad, then central banks can step in and save them. As we saw in an earlier chapter this is exactly what happened during the 2008 financial crisis, where banks and other institutions messed up in a major way but were bailed out and made whole again (p.83).

This means the real check against fractional banking (the risk of going bankrupt) is thrown away and replaced with regulation that's supposed to keep the banks in check, while making the banks more robust against failure. While fine in theory, in practice it means banks are now incentivized to push the limits any way they can, to maximize their profits.

I don't think there's a better example of the hazards the lender of last resort creates than the 2008 financial crisis. I feel the term *moral hazard*, to describe someone taking risks others will pay for, is too soft to describe the situation.

Perhaps the words *deceit, scam, fraud* or *swindle* comes closer to describe my feelings.

A crucial part of being the lender of last resort is to act as an overseer and to keep the banks in check. But as Fed whistleblowers show, the Fed acts less like an enforcer and more like a kind grandpa, silencing examiners to help the banks look good:

> In a tense, 40-minute meeting recorded the week before she was fired, Segarra's boss repeatedly tries to persuade her to change her conclusion that Goldman was missing a policy to handle conflicts of interest. Segarra offered to review her evidence with higher-ups and told her boss she would accept being overruled once her findings were submitted. It wasn't enough.

Jake Bernstein, Inside the New York Fed: Secret Recordings and a Culture Clash[198]

Reason behind the madness

If you've followed along this far, you might get the feeling that the economic system is completely corrupt and wonder why anyone would ever get along with it? But not so fast—there's a reason things are the way the are, and a big part can be traced the Great Depression in the 1930s.

The Great Depression was a huge economic crisis, the worst in modern history, that dwarfed the 2008 financial crisis. Experts debate the causes of this decade long crisis to this day, with explanations ranging from governments spending too little, printing too little money, printing too much money or the gold standard.

There's more to these theories than my attempt to simplify them suggests, and there's probably not a single cause. For instance the global gold standard probably helped the crisis to spread, even if it might not have caused the crisis. There are also more theories than I list here.

While it's difficult to point out causes, and it's even debatable why we got out of it, it's fairly easy to point out some big changes introduced when combating the crisis:

1 Abondoned the gold standard

After briefly dropping the gold standard to pay for World War I, all countries left the gold standard during the depression.

Because the government ran out of gold, in 1933 private ownership of larger amounts of gold was made illegal[214]. It was forbidden until 1974.

2 Proactive governments

In the New Deal the United States tried to stimulate the economy by for example building infrastructure, building houses, paying farmers to plant crops, producing power and insuring loans.[199]

3 Debt fueled investments

To pay for these investments the United States greatly increased their debt from $22 billion to $40 billion.[200]

Still, they were comparatively conservative with increasing the debt[215]. To pay for World War II the debt rose to $241 billion in 1946[216].

These align with the ideas of *Keynesian Economics* (also developed in the 1930s) where governments should stimulate the economy during recessions, and compensate by pulling back when the economy's expanding[201]. The rationale is that the *velocity of money* (how fast companies and people spend money) will slow down during a recession, making it worse. Therefore the government should increase their spending—increasing the velocity of money—to help dampen the recession[202].

Seen through this lens, it all makes sense. To help the government spend money it doesn't have, being able to print money is a huge help. When the government goes deeper into debt, again it helps to be able to print money. And the interaction between central banks and banks is a fairly efficient way to setup a money-printing machine.

A mountain of debt

While taking out debt to fuel investments was only supposed to be a temporary measure, to help the economy during downturns, today we massively increase the debt all the time. For example we've seen a record bull run in 2009–2019, yet the U.S. debt doubled from $11 trillion to $22 trillion during the same period.

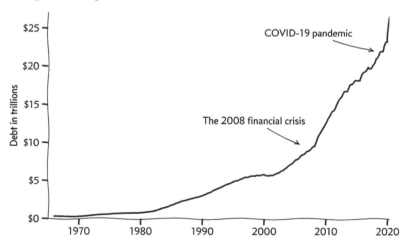

The federal debt of the United States, measure in trillions of dollars, since 1966.[203]
After the 2008 financial crisis the amount of debt skyrocketed, signifying a shift in economic policy. During the COVID-19 pandemic the debt explosively increased at a pace unseen before.

Taking out a loan essentially borrows money from the future you, since you have to pay it back with interest. And the U.S. is paying for that now: in the 2020 budget 10.1% is spent on only the interest rate, and it's expected to take up 12.9% in 2026, making it the fastest rising expense in the budget[204].

After World War II the United States went back to the gold standard, a little half-heartedly. They only allowed foreign nations to redeem dollars for gold, which took an abrupt end in 1971[217].

Donald Trump promised to eliminate the nation's debt in eight years[218], and instead he greatly increased it. Let's just add that to the list of president Trump's list of broken promises.

Most of the debt is public debt (debt to people, companies or other governments), so refusing to pay would have disastrous consequences.

> Compound interest is the eighth wonder of the world. He who understands it, earns it... he who doesn't... pays it.

> Albert Einstein

This isn't a situation unique to the United States, but a global phenomena[205]. While the U.S. has a national debt at 104% of *GDP* (a way to compare relative debts between countries), Sweden has a debt of 38%, Germany 61%, Italy 132%, Greece 181% and Japan a staggering 235%.

There are different ways to measure national debt, each with pros and cons. Percentage of GDP seems to be the common way to do it.

It seems like we're moving away from the original Keynesian ideas to something else, where paying off national debt matters less as we can just print more money.

Growing inequality

> It doesn't matter if you're black or white... the only color that really matters is green.

> *Family Guy*

There's a worrying trend in the world: global inequality is rising. The rich get richer and the poor get... poorer.[206]

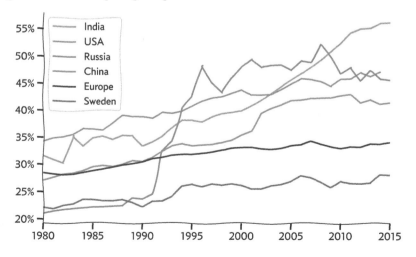

Top 10% income share between 1980 and 2015. (World Inequality Database)

The inequality is on the rise in nearly every country. If we take a closer look at the United States, it paints a gloomy picture:

The following graphs are based on the *World Inequality Database*.[219]

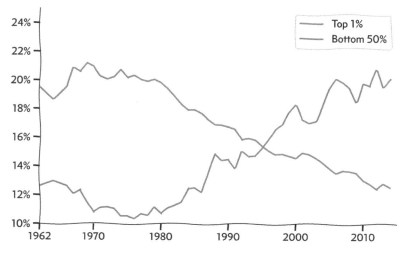

Income share in the United States between 1962 and 2014. (World Inequality Database)

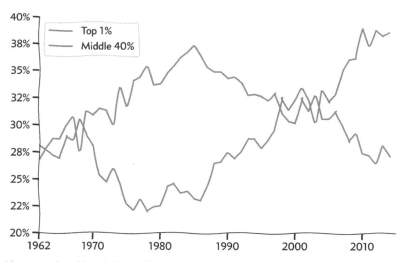

Net personal wealth in the United States between 1962 and 2014. (World Inequality Database)

While the money-making machine isn't the only cause of the inequality, it's a pretty difficult situation to reverse when even the national economy works against you. Printing money to solve problems will, in line with the previous counterfeiting example (p.98), only fan the flames and make the situation worse.

Some will argue that the trickle-down effect makes inflation affect everyone equally. Unfortunately that's not the case, as the rich will both receive the money first (via the banks) and they have better access to financial tools to hedge against inflation (investing in gold, real estate or offshore banking).

No tools left

We want to pull back on stimulation when the economy is booming, so we're prepared with all our tools when the economy is crashing. Unfortunately after a decade of economic boom, we've done the opposite:

- The national debt has skyrocketed

  The larger the debt, the more expenses must be devoted to repaying the debt, leaving less for other more useful things.

- The central bank interest rates are already low

  A low rate means banks, and in extension we, can get cheaper loans which stimulates the economy. It's difficult to lower it more when it's almost zero, or even negative, already.

- We're continually printing money

  The Federal Reserve is pouring money into the financial system. Printing an unlimited amount of money isn't great, not only because of the erosion of wealth, but rampant inflation can quickly destroy the economy.

To be fair, the Federal Reserve knows this isn't an ideal situation, so they tried to raise interest rates. Unfortunately, the stock market reacted poorly—many people got angry—and now they've backtracked and lowered them again. When problems arise, they use the financial equivalent of taking a sledgehammer to squash a bug.[207]

So, we're stuck in a situation where we don't have the tools to defend against a recession—tools the economic theory the system is built on needs. Tools that have been used up, because that's what the theory says we should do.

It seems to me if (or when) a recession comes we'll get caught with our pants down. And things have been looking pretty shaky a while now.

In Sweden we've had a negative repo rate since 2015[220]. Denmark's Jyske Bank also give depositors a negative rate[221], meaning you have to pay to loan out money to the bank. These are strange times.

An interesting case is how hyperinflation took hold in ancient Rome[222]. Centuries of debasing the currency was followed by a sudden loss of trust and the collapse into hyperinflation. A lesson here is that rapid inflation can quickly throw the economy into chaos.

It may sound like I'm referring to a single economic theory, which all governments and central banks follow. But that's not the case—there are many different theories, with slight differences, but I think it's a fair generalization to say that they mostly follow the push-pull idea of stimulating the economy.

Maybe a more correct thing to say is that many are just winging it, and making up rules as they go.

The stock market magic trick

When the world locked down during the COVID-19 pandemic the economy predictably crashed. Many people (including me) thought that the big recession was finally here and we'd be looking at several years of tough times.

But then something weird happened. Despite entire cities and countries locking down; the number of unemployed reached record numbers and many smaller companies closed their doors for good, the recession didn't come. Instead the stock market recovered very quickly, as if closing down the world economy was just a minor speed bump.

One might wonder, what the hell happened?

The Federal Reserve followed the script and printed trillions of dollars and used it to prop up the stock market. As seen in the M2 graph this was an extreme amount of money in a very short period of time:

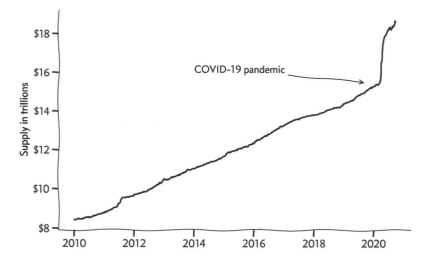

The M2 money stock of the United States between 2010 and mid 2020.[208]

M2 is a measure of money supply that includes cash, checking deposits, savings deposits, money market securities, mutual funds and other time deposits.

Unfortunately the money printing didn't help the businesses that went out of business or the people who became unemployed. The money was instead funneled to the big companies who used it to artificially increase their valuation with *stock buybacks* or just placed the money in their reserves. The money didn't trickle down to the masses; it got stuck driving up the stock price.

This is also why the inflation hasn't shot up (yet).

Nothing fundamentally changed. The deep-rooted economic problems are still there, festering.

Where do we go from here?

Since the financial crisis in 2008 we're in uncharted territory, and we actually don't know what we should do. Therefore new economic theories, like the *Modern Money Theory (MMT)*, are developed. MMT basically says the government can pay its bills by just printing all the money it needs, checked only by inflation. It's reasonable to ask if MMT is a sound economic theory, or if it's just describing what's already happening[209].

While "printing more money" is a popular solution, *sound money* (with a stable money supply) might represent a compelling alternative for critics of the modern economic policies. For example fiat backed by gold, actual gold coins or cryptocurrencies.

It's not easy to see how a switch to sound money would occur and such a switch may likely introduce more problems than it solved. However, it would mean that manipulation of the money supply would disappear; that we wouldn't accumulate a mountain of debt; that we wouldn't devalue our savings while increasing the wealth inequality; and that we wouldn't cling to the broken and defective economic theories in use today.

The state that creates gold coins can still inflate the money supply by decreasing the amount of gold in the coins. This is called *debasement* and has been quite common historically.[223]

With cryptocurrencies debasement isn't possible, which is one reason they're better money than gold (p.41).

Chapter 14
Private money
Reclaim your financial privacy with cryptocurrencies

Arguing that you don't care about the right to privacy because you have nothing to hide is no different than saying you don't care about free speech because you have nothing to say.

Edward Snowden, May 21, 2015[224]

The erosion of personal privacy is one of the many important issues in today's society. Everything we do digitally is tracked—what sites we visit, how long and what we do there. This data is then packaged and stored, waiting to be used to convince us to buy stuff or used to attack us. Even what we do with our own money is tracked and used to figure out how to separate it from us.

One of the very good things about cash—physical coins or bills—is that there's very little tracking on them. You can buy things with them, or give them to someone, and nobody else needs to know about it. Unfortunately people aren't using cash as much anymore, some have even stopped accepting cash, and all commonly used alternatives come with the privacy trade-off.

Cryptocurrencies can help us with this—they're digital and just like cash they can be used privately.

For instance if you want to purchase a VPN, a domain or a VPS anonymously it's probably a good idea to use cryptocurrencies.

But remember that most cryptocurrencies, Bitcoin included, are only *pseudo-anonymous* and it's easy to make a mistake and break your anonymity (p.193).

What is privacy and anonymity?

It's easy to mix-up the terms "privacy" and "anonymity" (which I've done many times myself writing this chapter). They're related, but different:

Privacy

Concerns content, for example text in messages you send to your friends.

Anonymity

Refers to identity, for example that I, Jonas, received a text message.

In practice they often overlap. For example if all my emails were available online for anyone to read, it would be a breach of my privacy. But it would also affect my anonymity, since my name is included in the emails.

Why privacy matters

Privacy and anonymity are important issues in the modern world and there are examples of privacy violations everywhere. Before we get to some of them we first need to address why privacy matter, because today government officials, company owners, the news and regular people all ask the same questions:

Why would you want privacy? What are you hiding? Are you criminal?

It's natural to seek privacy

When people are alone and relaxed, they do things they otherwise wouldn't. Maybe you like to dance when you're alone, sing in the shower or scratch yourself somewhere... nice. If you're caught in the act you immediately stop what you're doing and feel embarrassed.

If you don't recognize the situation please watch the scene where Hugh Grant plays the dancing prime minister in *Love Actually (2003)*. Even if you do recognize the situation, the scene's so good you should watch it anyway.

What's better than dancing naked, singing your favorite song, without a care in the world? And what's worse than having someone catching you in the act?

I have a two year old child, and even he wants privacy sometimes. He likes to build a cabin made of pillows and hide in it, and if I disturb him he pushes me and shouts "Go away!". After we recently renovated his room he was *so happy* that he had a room of his own again, which he likes to be alone in when he's pooping (in his diaper thank god).

Privacy discussions can often be summarized as:

- Why do I need privacy? I have nothing to hide.
- Then pull your pants down, send me a dick pick, your email password and your credit card number.

I can't promise I'll do better, but I'll try.

It's really quite fascinating. Sometimes I can hug him while he's playing, but other times I'm not even allowed to be in the same room. I guess he just wants to be alone from time to time.

People may say privacy don't matter, yet their actions tell a different story. For example Facebook's founder Mark Zuckerberg has said that "privacy is no longer a social norm"[225], but then he buys up four homes surrounding his home because he wants privacy[226].

After all, we don't have curtains or blinders on our windows because we do something illegal, it's because we want control over our privacy.

Personal security

Caring about privacy is a natural instinct—for good reason. It's not just about avoiding embarrassment; it's also for your own personal safety. In fact privacy is closely related to security. Your passwords and credit card numbers are obvious examples, but there are more:

- Identity theft can ruin your life

  When someone assumes your identity, and use it to issue credit cards or promote scams, it can ruin your credit score, cost you millions, and force you to abandon your job and your house. Using only your private information people can literally take over your life[227].

- Criminals target rich people

  The most important advice if you win the lottery is to not tell anyone—people will target you like vultures[228]. The same advice is given to people who want to invest in physical gold, for similar reasons.

  The best way to get targeted by criminals is to let them know how rich you are. And conversely the best way to avoid getting targeted is to hide your wealth.

- Crime of opportunity

  Many crimes aren't carried out by super-criminals with a master plan. Often they're done in the heat of the moment, when an opportunity arose. For example if everyone knows you're away for a week, the risk for a burglary rises. Or if you tell everyone that you're carrying $10,000 in your wallet, the risk of getting mugged increases.

Others have important things to hide

Even if you don't think you have anything to hide, others do. Here are some examples where lack of economic privacy is harmful:

- Unwanted pregnancies

  There was a story that went viral years ago on how Target predicted a teenage pregnancy and exposed it to her father[229]. In a normal western household it might not be that big of a deal, but thousands of women are killed each year for family "honor"[230]—often for much less than a teenage pregnancy, such as not getting paid enough for marrying the bride[231].

I'm a problem solver, and I do wonder how everyday problems are solved. For example how milk ends up in the milk packages or how you paint a heart in the sky with an airplane. Not because I need to solve them—and I don't even want to know the right answer—I just need to let my mind work on something.

Sometimes the questions are darker, like what's the most effective way to destroy someone's life. Stealing their identity have to be one of the top candidates.

I focus on the economic side of privacy here, because that's related to cryptocurrencies, but it should be easy to find examples in other areas.

I read a story long ago, but I can't remember if it was real or made up.

It was about a couple and their son who liked to play with their neighbours. They were happy to let him, the neighbours were really friendly, and they liked to spend time with them too. But one day they found an amateur porn DVD—the neighbours apparently liked to create porn.

The DVD never harmed them, and their son didn't know about it, but they never allowed their son to visit the neighbours anymore, and the couple stopped spending time with them because it "felt weird".

I guess the point of the story is that some things are best left unknown.

- Sexual preference

  While homosexuality is becoming more accepted, it's still illegal in some countries where you might face execution. Similar to the story of the girl's pregnancy above, having a history of your purchases might expose you. (Why did you visit this gay bar?)

  There's also nothing wrong with having a fetish and engaging in strange sexual fantasies in your own home, but maybe you don't want your neighbourhood to know you bought a vibrating horse dildo.

- A cause for oppression

  In China if you're end up on the wrong side of their social credit system, you're banned from spending on "luxuries". If prospective business partners or customers discovers your status as a "deadbeat", you might get shunned and your hope of climbing out of your situation disappear.[232]

As Snowden's quote in the beginning of the chapter says: just because you choose not to exercise your right, why should you remove the right for others? Privacy should be a *choice*—not something that's chosen for you.

Privacy is a human right

That privacy is important is widely acknowledged. It's for example recognized as a human right by the United Nations, along with the right to food, clothing and medical care:

> No one shall be subjected to arbitrary interference with his privacy, family, home or correspondence, nor to attacks upon his honour and reputation. Everyone has the right to the protection of the law against such interference or attacks.

> Universal Declaration of Human Rights

I was going to quote the grown-up version of the children's rights, but they use a muddy language that's difficult to read.

Children's right to privacy is also acknowledged by UNICEF:

> Every child has the right to privacy. The law must protect children's privacy, family, home, communications and reputation (or good name) from any attack.

> Convention on the Rights of the Child: The children's version

Even the constitution of the United States—written more than a hundred years before the first computer—intends to protect our privacy:

> The right of the people to be secure in their persons, houses, papers, and effects, against unreasonable searches and seizures, shall not be violated, and no Warrants shall issue, but upon probable cause, supported by Oath or affirmation, and particularly describing the place to be searched, and the persons or things to be seized.

Fourth Amendment, United States Constitution

We're living in a Stasi fantasy

The Stasi, the secret police of East Germany, has been described as one of the most repressive organizations in the world[233]. One of their purposes was to find and imprison political enemies, which basically meant anyone critical of the government.

They used 100,000 employees and between 500,000 to 2,000,000 snitches to maintain files on more than one-third of the population. There were always spies in the bars and libraries who listened to your conversations and they encouraged (or threatened) people to snitch on their co-workers, neighbours and family.

People could be placed in prison and tortured by isolation or sleep deprivation in the hopes of getting them to snitch on others.

> In an authoritative state, rights derive from the state and are granted to people. In a free state, rights derive from people and are granted to the state.

Edward Snowden, Permanent Record[Per19]

The goal of the Stasi was to imprison everyone critical of the regime. To do that they tried to map out the lives of everyone—where they went, what they did, what they said and who they talked to. This was painstakingly difficult and required tremendous resources.

Today we live in a society the Stasi couldn't even dream of. There's no need for a shady person to follow us around, because we already have a surveillance device in our pocket. All information they could ever want is already available, they just have reach out and grab it.

Our smartphone really do everything the Stasi spies tried to do. It tracks your location, it listens to your conversations and it follows you everywhere. And it always keeps a perfect record.

Back in 2013 Edward Snowden revealed that governments were doing just this.

Here are just some of the things he leaked:

- **All phone calls are recorded**[234]

  The N.S.A. (the U.S. intelligence service) collect all U.S. phone calls and text messages. They also collect foreign phone calls, including those of foreign leaders such as Angela Merkel[235].

- **Remotely controlled phones**[236]

  The GCHQ (the british intelligence service) can remotely control your phone. They can for example turn it on remotely and use the microphone to record you.

- **Big tech data isn't private**[237]

  The government can ask for (or rather demand) data from the big tech companies like Facebook, Google or Apple. If they refuse they can just hack them and steal the data anyway[238].

- **A search for you**

  There's an internal search engine where N.S.A. employees can search through your emails, pictures, medical records and private Facebook messages. Like Google, but with the contents of your online life.

  Snowden writes in *Permanent Record* that it was common for N.S.A. employees to abuse this to spy on their girlfriends, ex-girlfriends or girls they were interested in. This includes sharing nude photos with their co-workers, which the girls either took themselves or photos the N.S.A. took by hacking their webcam. [Per19] (Quite literally a stalker's wet dream.)

As is praxis for authoritative regimes, this capability isn't used to protect the people of the state, but the state itself. Snowden's leaks were to the benefit of the people, yet he and other whistleblowers like him are facing the full power of the U.S. aimed at them[239]. This despite the U.S. court finding that the mass surveillance program was illegal[240].

You see, all this data is stored *forever*, just waiting to be used to nail you for a crime. And let's be clear: everyone has committed a crime. For example how many have ever illegally downloaded a movie or music? Or driven too fast? Not to mention old ridiculous laws that are still in effect, such as the "Metropolitan Police Act of 1839" Section 54, which makes carrying a plank along a pavement illegal in the U.K.[241].

The N.S.A. has proved again and again that they stand above such trivial things as legality. For example James Clapper, the Director of National Intelligence, lied under oath to the Senate[248], without any consequence.

If I did that I'd be in prison for years.

This is a counterpoint to the argument that it's fine for the government or the police to have this data. The government or the police aren't full of only good people—there will always be bad ones somewhere.

It's not something wrong with being a Jew, so why would a record of all Jews living in a country be problematic?

The problem is when a group like the Nazis take control over the country (which only took a few years).

Once the ubiquity of collection was combined with the permanency of storage, all any government had to do was select a person or a group to scapegoat and go searching—as I'd gone searching through the agency's files—for evidence of a suitable crime.

Edward Snowden, *Permanent Record*[Per19]

Now, Snowden lives in exile in Russia, where the black bags of the U.S. cannot reach. He recently released his memoir *Permanent Record* which details his life leading up to the leaks. It's a great book, but the U.S. doesn't want you to read it. They even filed a lawsuit against him and seized the revenue of the book[242].

As in response to the lawsuit his book shot up to the Amazon bestseller list. Snowden concluded that "this is good for bitcoin".[249]

The *Streisand effect* strikes again.

Fear is the mind-killer

The road to hell is paved with good intentions.

Proverb

I think people often give up their privacy because of **fear**. Since the September 11 attacks we've been showered with fear-inducing news and propaganda, making our minds numb. This fear of terrorism (and murderers, pedophiles and other Bogeymen) has made us go to war, consent to torture (or "advanced interrogation") and give up our human rights.

Just to put the overreaction in perspective: 2,977 people died in the 9/11 terrorist attacks, but one million died because of the American retaliation.[Per19]

Terrorism is real and scary, there's no denying that. But our level of fear is irrational and would be better placed worrying about cars or unhealthy food—both of which kill more people than terrorism do. Yet fear is such a powerful emotion that it prevents us from thinking logically.

That's like sentencing a shoplifter to death— a completely disproportionate response.

For example people may be willing to give up their privacy, because it might make it easier to catch terrorists. But if we try to compromise everyone's privacy, we'll jeopardize the personal security of the innocent, yet the terrorists will still have access to privacy through strong encryption (with strong encryption it's impossible for *anyone* to read what you write or access your data). We may think we're more secure, but we're really not.

The security checks at airports are annoying, expensive and ineffective[250]. It's *security theater*.

If privacy is outlawed, only outlaws will have privacy.

Philip R. Zimmermann

You're the product

It's not just the governments of the world who are collecting our data and violating our privacy. Companies of all sort do this too, but they sell it for profit.

Alphabet Inc. (company name of Google) and Facebook are two of the most valuable, richest and powerful companies in the world. Yet their main services—search and social networking—are completely free for us to use. So where do they make their money? And where's the product they're selling?

The product they're selling is **you**.

They're selling knowledge about you. What you're searching for, what sites you visit, what products you buy, what places you visit, what friends you have and what you're talking about with your friends. With the combination of massive data collection and clever computer algorithms it's scary what they know about you.

For example they probably know if you're gay or if you're pregnant (and if you are, they'll know if it was an accident, if your parents know about it and who is the father). They might also predict—with high confidence—if you're religious, even if you don't want anyone to know. Or who you're going to vote for in the *next* election or how likely you are to commit a crime.

And it's not just a problem with Google and Facebook. An increasing number of companies are discovering how lucrative your data is. If you buy a Coca-Cola, the information that you bought it at this place and at this specific time might even be worth more than the Coca-Cola itself!

For example smart TVs come with a microphone that listens to everything you do[243], and the TV company then sell the recordings to the highest bidder[244]. Credit card companies have full records of all purchases you make—which they sell to someone else[245]. Even the banks, who we assume should work for us, sell our data to third parties[246].

What about your privacy? That's not something they care about, because they can sell it and make lot's of money.

It might be hard to come to terms with how the algorithms can predict your behavior. But it's really not that different from how Youtube, Netflix or Spotify recommends videos and songs to you.

Oh? He watched a video of a Japanese rock band? And he has listened to Raubtier? Then let's recommend Band-Maid, he'll love them! (I assume this is how YouTube decided to recommend me Band-Maid—the best rock band in the world.)

Pre-crime, like in the movie *Minority Report* (2002), is the idea that you can predict someone committing a crime and catching them before they do.

Thoughtcrime, as explored in the book *1984*, says that thoughts are criminal[Orw49]. Like entertaining a politically unacceptable thought.

While this is fiction, our technology is edging ever closer. Soon we might have killer robots going around streets enforcing laws on our predicted behaviour. (The U.S. already deploys killing drones, which kill civilians.)

Reclaiming our financial privacy

The *great man theory* of history says that most of history can be explained by the impact of great men[247]. Julius Caesar, Genghis Khan and Hitler are examples of "great men". (They don't have to be good or even be men, just people who cause large changes.) If Edward Snowden will be considered a great man depends on the effects of his leaks; they might mark a turning point for government surveillance, and change the course of history, or they might be forgotten as a side note in the history books.

It's still uncertain how much will really change, but either way Snowden is my hero.

While the great man theory is interesting, wouldn't it be better to describe modern history using a *great technology theory*? For example the printing press, the internal combustion engine, the atomic bomb, the transistor and the internet have had great impact on history—greater than any single person I can think of.

Proponents of the great man theory might say that these are inventions of a great person. To which I'd say that they weren't the result of a single person, but of many small improvements over existing tech, made by countless of people.

So instead of looking for a great man to solve our privacy problems, maybe technology is our solution? With strong encryption we can keep our messages private and our data safe, and with the great innovation called tape we can prevent our webcams from spying on us.

So far we've had to surrender our privacy to gain access to digital payments and even to our own money. But nobody needs to know how much cryptocurrencies we have or what we do with them. They can help us claw back some of that privacy—and isn't that pretty great?

Unfortunately Bitcoin is sometimes even worse for privacy than regular payments, because you have a permanent record of all transactions open for all to see. There are other cryptocurrencies that hides the transaction details. (p.193)

Chapter 15
A global currency
Money without borders

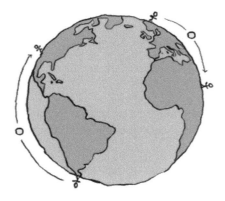

Cryptocurrencies don't have any borders. They allow you to send and receive money from anywhere in the world; to bypass sanctions and border control; opt-out of local monetary policies; and use a currency that's global to an extent we've never seen before.

Remittance

Sending money to other countries, called *remittance*, is one of the first promoted use-cases for cryptocurrencies. The benefits over existing solutions, such as Western Union, are numerous:

Why not make a comparison to bank transfers? Because the problem with remittance is transfers to countries far away, often poorer countries. There's no problem with transferring money from Sweden to Finland for example—bank transfers work great there.

But it's very difficult to make a bank transfer from Sweden to Zimbabwe; or impossible, if you don't have a bank account at all (p.73). With Western Union you can effectively send physical cash, to many parts of the world.

1   You can send to any country

    For example it's not possible to send money from Sweden to Venezuela or North Korea using Western Union (or any bank). With cryptocurrencies you can.

2   Cheaper

    The cost to use Western Union varies depending on the amount, the target country, your payment method and how the recipient should receive the money.

	United States (to bank)	Zimbabwe (cash pick up)
Credit Card	$27	$56.50
Debit Card	$15	$42
Bank Account	$0.99	$21

Western Union fees to various countries, using different payment methods, measured in USD. You can either send it to a bank account or as a cash pick up. It's cheaper to send it to a bank account, but it's not always available. I could only choose the cash pick up option for Zimbabwe. Fees are calculated from sending $400 using their homepage in 2019-11-15[251].

    This is expensive compared to cryptocurrency fees, which are **less than a cent** no matter the amount or receiving country (p.49).

3   Faster

    It can take between zero to six days for Western Union to process a payment to a bank account, and sometimes only minutes for a cash pickup. If you want a cash pickup you will of course have to visit a physical store, which can take some time especially as they're not always open.

    Cryptocurrencies are sent in seconds (and become irreversible in an hour) (p.52).

4   Send any amount

    Western Union also has limits on the amount you can send. I got a limit of $5,000 to Zimbabwe for example. It's a fairly high limit, but it cannot compare to cryptocurrencies where you can send any amount with a single transaction.

The big drawback with cryptocurrencies is that you're sending cryptocurrency coins, and if you wanted fiat money you need to find a way to exchange the coins for fiat, which might be difficult, slow or expensive.

Someone transferred 94,504 BTC—valued around 1 billion USD at the time—with a single transaction.[263]

Borderless charity

Venezuela is currently going through an economic crisis of extreme proportions[252]. It's much worse than for example the Great Depression in the 1930s and perhaps it's better to compare it to a country devastated by war. Millions of people have fled the country and those left struggle with unemployment, a collapsed health care system and starvation. Corruption and strict border control makes it difficult for Venezuelans to receive outside help.

There's an opportunity here for cryptocurrencies, which is demonstrated by the charity *eatBCH*, that use cryptocurrencies to help feed people in Venezuela. They receive donations in Bitcoin Cash from all over the world, which goes directly to volunteers inside the country, who then use them to buy food and water from local vendors and give them to people in need.

Venezuela also has their own "cryptocurrency", called *Petro*. But it's not decentralized—it's snake oil (p.27).

People often wonder how much cryptocurrencies are used in Venezuela. While there are heartwarming stories like how "Bitcoin Has Saved My Family"[264], it's still a niche.

But adoption is growing and enough merchants accept Bitcoin Cash directly to support eatBCH for example.

eatBCH converts donations from all over the world to food for people in Venezuela.
Image used with permission from eatBCH.

This kind of charity is only possible if you can cheaply transfer money to the heart of a very unstable and closed off country, bypassing sanctions and border control.

Capital flight

> "It's very unsettling here," said Ms. Fairhurst, who has lived in Hong Kong for 12 years. She said seeing videos of police using tear gas near her office have made her particularly nervous. "I don't know what's going to happen, but I know that I don't want my money trapped here."

> Worried Hong Kong Residents Are Moving Money Out as Protests Escalate
> Aug, 2019[253]

If you decided to leave Venezuela, but wanted to bring your wealth with you, what would you do? Sell your bolívar for U.S. dollars and cross the border? You might get searched and lose it all. Same with gold, jewelry or other valuable items you can think off—it's not easy to hide them from the search at the border. You also cannot send the money abroad digitally, because there are no banks and no Western Union to help you.

Fortunately cryptocurrencies may aid you here. You can store any amount on a piece of paper in your pocket, an encrypted key online or even on a dozen memorized words in your head, and there's not much the border search will reveal.

You don't have to physically leave the country to benefit from storing your wealth in a global currency. China is struggling with capital leaving the country[254] and it's one reason they've been trying to ban cryptocurrencies for years.

China banning cryptocurrencies has become a joke in the community. One week they're legal, the next they're illegal and then they make it legal again. Last I checked they made it all legal, but I'm sure they'll change their mind again.

1. I think this is what happens:
2. China wants to ban cryptocurrencies.
3. But banning them is very difficult.
4. Maybe it's better to embrace them?
5. Permissionless doesn't fit China's ideology.
6. And the cycle repeats.

The next logical step for China is to announce "ChinaCoin"—their own snake oil (p.27).

Hyperinflation is real

Cryptocurrency skeptics often ask why anyone would ever want to use money with such large volatility. They have a point—daily swings of 5% are almost expected and larger changes are common—but that's nothing in the face of *hyperinflation*.

Venezuela had a monthly inflation of 815,194%, in May 2019 alone. It's a huge number that causes prices to double in less than two days—all the time. This means if you could afford two chickens today, in two days you can only afford one. For those living through it they would prefer *anything* else over the local currency; be it gold, U.S. dollars, Bitcoin, clothes, food—you name it.

It's easy to think that hyperinflation is a thing of the past, or that it only affects poor countries far away. But according to the *Hanke-Krus hyperinflation table*[255] we've had 55 cases of hyperinflation since 1920, with 31 of them after 1990 (roughly half related to the collapase of the Soviet Union).

Hyperinflation is defined as a monthly inflation exceeding 50%.

For example:

Germay 1920s

In Germany after the first world war, when inflation was at its height, prices doubled in less than four days. It's not the worst case of hyperinflation, but it might be the most well-known, maybe because it happened to a powerful western nation and it's related to the world wars.

Hungary 1945–1946

The worst hyperinflation in history happened in Hungary[256], when they had to repay the cost of the second world war. There prices doubled in only 15 hours.

I'm always fascinated by the hyperinflation stories. In Hungary for example the government ran out of good paper to print the new money on.

Zimbabwe 2004–2009

The first example of hyperinflation in the 21th century is Zimbabwe. At its worst prices doubled in just over 24 hours. While things settled down, Zimbabwe is once again in trouble[257] and the International Monetary Fund projects an inflation of 319% for 2020[258].

Lebanon 2020–

After an inflation of 56.53% in May[259], Lebanon became the second country after Venezuela to experience hyperinflation in 2020.

In each case, hyperinflation is an economic disaster. Hoarding causes shortages, with even basic goods like clothes or food becoming hard to find. Importing goods become impossible and companies go out of business, causing mass unemployment. When tax revenue falls, government services fall with them.

Although hyperinflation is the extreme case, high inflation rates can still very be problematic with the same type of problems.

Always available

I used hyperinflation as an example of economic turmoil, but it could be anything really. Another good example is if banks in your country close, which happened recently in Lebanon when banks decided to shut down during heavy protests[260]. (This was before hyperinflation set in.)

> The most potent case for cryptocurrencies: banks are never there when you need them. And they are trying to bully the public so they avoid accountability and profit disbursements.
> Bankers are legal crooks.
> #bottomup #bitcoin
> #Lebanon

Nassim Nicholas Taleb, Twitter, 24 Oct 2019

Because of the decentralized nature of cryptocurrencies it's very difficult for them to "shut down". It doesn't matter if the computers of some people—or even whole countries—break down, the cryptocurrency network is unaffected.

Cryptocurrencies are so robust we might as well say they're always available, for anyone and anywhere (as long as they have internet access).

A currency for the world

The U.S. dollar is the closest we have to a world currency[261]. More than half of all U.S. dollar bills are used outside of the U.S.—often as hard currency. Almost 40% of all debt in the world is issued in U.S. dollars and the central banks of other countries hold a large part of their reserves in U.S. dollars (making it the most widely used *reserve currency*).

But the U.S. dollar isn't truly a world currency, it's just one country's currency that happen to be widely used. The U.S. government and the Federal Reserve still have full control of the currency—they can dabble with the money supply however they want—and the rest of the world can only hope they won't get shafted.

In contrast cryptocurrencies exist outside the control of any country. They're instead controlled by people all over the world, who come together and agree to the rules governing the currency.

What's more, cryptocurrencies are also easier to use on a global scale. It's hard to send U.S. dollars across the world—you'd have to rely on others to do so—but cryptocurrencies can be sent as easily to your neighbour as to someone on the other side of the world.

> I wanted to help someone in #Venezuela , so I'm tutoring a novice #JavaScript developer as he writes #opensource software. I pay him $100 per week. It's making a huge difference in his life. With #BitcoinCash we don't have to consider what governments or banks think about it.
>
> Chris Troutner, Twitter, 21 Jun 2019[262]

Instead of being just a currency used throughout the world, a cryptocurrency is a currency **for** the world.

Part V

Brave new world
The world is changing

We knew the world would not be the same. A few people laughed, a
few people cried. Most people were silent. I remembered the line from
the Hindu scripture, the Bhagavad Gita; Vishnu is trying to persuade
the Prince that he should do his duty and, to impress him, takes on his
multi-armed form and says, "Now I am become Death, the destroyer of
worlds." I suppose we all thought that, one way or another.

J. Robert Oppenheimer, 1965 TV Broadcast

In previous parts we've looked at how cryptocurrencies provide better digital payments (p.47) and why they might be better currencies (p.81).
This part focuses on some ways the world is changing, and what role cryptocurrencies may play.

Even if we'd collectively agree that the world would be better off without
cryptocurrencies, we cannot make them disappear. We cannot "uninvent"
them and they're extremely difficult to shut down. Therefore, like with
nuclear bombs, we're stuck with them and have to adapt to a new world.

There's an excellent *Hardcore History* episode
on the topic of nuclear weapons and how
humanity has been balancing on the edge of
destruction ever since their invention.[268]

Cryptocurrencies won't make the world a better place in all respects. For example untraceable digital money makes it easier for people to demand ransoms, such as *CryptoLocker* which locks down your computer and demands payment in order to unlock it[267].

Other things skirt the lines between legality and morality, such as the darknet markets that makes it easy to trade any type of goods. Or how cryptocurrencies allow you to store any amount of money, hidden from the watchful eyes of the tax collectors.

Governments can be our friend, but they can also be our foe as well.

While cryptocurrencies in some ways force the world to change, they can also protect us from the changing world. For instance the move towards a cashless society will spell disaster for everyone without access to digital money. But cryptocurrencies are for everyone, and they can shield us from tracking and seizures by the government.

And cryptocurrencies have the potential for something even bigger. For the first time in history there's the possibility to separate control of money from the state. This would be a historic shift that would cause massive change worldwide. Of course this is speculation on my part, and even if it were to happen it probably wouldn't be during our lifetime.

But one things seems clear to me. The Pandora's Box has been opened, and the world will never be the same again.

Chapter 16

Darknet markets
Global and digital markets for illegal goods

I wanted to empower people to be able to make choices in their lives, for themselves and to have privacy and anonymity.

Ross Ulbricht, creator of Silk Road

There's one thing that cryptocurrency proponents and skeptics can agree on: cryptocurrencies are excellent for illegal purposes. And is there a better example than darknet markets—websites where you can buy illegal goods vcurrencies?

Before cryptocurrencies, such sites would have trouble staying in business because payment processors would shut them down quickly. But nobody can block cryptocurrency transactions, and in 2012 the first darknet market "Silk Road" was created using Bitcoin. Since then there's been a bunch of different darknet markets, many with much larger volume than Silk Road[269].

I know I wrote in an early chapter that this book would describe legal use cases, but that's not really true. This book tries to describe *moral* use cases, which aren't always the same as legal ones. As we'll see later in this chapter, darknet markets might not even be moral, so I hope you'll forgive me.

As always where darknet markets fall on the universal scale of good and bad is subjective. But I hope to show that it's not a black-and-white issue.

Legality isn't morality

There's a concept we need to have in mind while looking at darknet markets: something being illegal doesn't make it immoral, and that everything legal doesn't have to be moral. Legality isn't equivalent to morality.

Here's a table to illustrate the problem:

	Legal	Illegal
Moral	Self defense Free speesh	Some types of sex Starving child steals food
Immoral	Mass surveillance Civil asset forfeiture	Slavery Murder

It's actually quite hard to classify things as legal or illegal and moral or immoral; they both change depending on the country, the time period and who you ask. For instance most would agree that slavery is immoral and should be illegal, but it was legal and viewed as normal for thousands of years. Similarly today in the western world we take free speech for granted, but that's not the case in all countries.

Mass surveillance, which we covered in the chapter *Private money* (p.109), is immoral yet legal. *Civil asset forfeiture*, which allows the police to outright take your stuff, is another example of an immora legal practice. (We'll explore civil asset forfeiture in the chapter *Protection against government confiscation* (p.145).)

It's easy to find examples of silly laws that make moral actions illegal (just search for "silly laws" or similar), but I think there are more interesting issues. For example stealing is illegal, but is it immoral for a starving child to steal food to survive? Or for the child to steal food for his starving little sister? And where on the moral scale would you place prostitution?

The issue of "right or wrong" isn't so easy to answer, and we cannot just rely on what's legal and what's not. Instead I think we should ask ourselves if it's moral or immoral, and let our internal moral compass guide us (morality is subjective as well).

You can argue that mass surveillance is illegal and the U.S. court did rule that the program that Snowden revealed was illegal.[275]

Black markets exist everywhere

Black markets refers to transactions outside government control. They're usually related to illegal behaviour in some way, like tax avoidance or the trade of illegal goods.

Black markets have existed as long as taxes have been collected, and it's not just for hardcore criminals. How many people do you know who've paid a craftsman off the book? Maybe paid a friend to paint the house, or paid a mechanic friend to fix the car? If it was paid in cash, and never officially registered the work, then they've engaged in a black market trade.

In countries with corruption or dysfunctional governments, black markets are huge. For example in the Soviet Union many people relied on black markets to get their food supply when the market economy failed them. Or in Greece during the economic breakdown in the 2010s, the black market was estimated at 20 to 25 percent of the GDP[270].

Black markets aren't inherently evil and sometimes they're even necessary for our survival. Instead they deal in both good and bad things, each of which should be considered on a case-by-case basis.

What can you buy on a darknet market?

Contrary to popular belief, you cannot buy *everything* on a darknet market. In theory it's possible, but in practice darknet markets operate with their own morality.

For instance it's very difficult, if not impossible, to hire a hitman on a darknet market[271]. This is a myth made popular by the false accusations against Ross Ulbricht, the creator of the first darknet market Silk Road[272]. The rumor was manufactured by corrupt federal agents (who got sentenced), yet their "evidence" was used by prosecutors and news media to make an example out of Ross.

Darknet market operators generally block things that are harmful to others. Murder harms others, so it's banned. Child porn is also harmful, so it's banned. Even very dangerous drugs, such as fentanyl, might be unavailable[273]. (But of course the ban isn't 100% effective, just as everywhere else in society.)

So if none of those things are available, what can you buy on a darknet market? You might be able to find books about banned topics that goes against the regime's propaganda, but usually you go to a darknet market to buy drugs or medicine. You can buy the same medicine elsewhere, but they might be much more expensive due to patents and other taxes.

Warming houses with geothermal heating is popular where we live. It works by drilling a large hole in the ground and transporting heat from the ground up into the house, and is a cost-effective way to heat houses. Many people drill the holes off the books, which can save you a lot of money.

We were quite tempted, but in the end we opted not to.

The sentence against Ross is yet another example of how the U.S. government tries to make an example out of people. It's good to keep in mind that the criminal justice system is a *legal* system, not a *justice* system.

A darknet story

The following example, based on a real-life story I read a few years ago, illustrates why darknet markets aren't purely evil.

Tom met the love of his life five years ago, when he went to get some of his teeth removed. Hardly the most romantic meeting, with her drilling into his aching teeth, but it was love at first sight.

Only a year later, they were married with a child on the way. They say love that burns hot quickly runs out, but that wasn't the case for Tom and Melinda. They bought a nice house in a nice suburb and settled down. They were planning a second child, and life was good.

But then Melinda got sick. It started with clumsiness, then some vertigo and she became more tired than usual. The doctor gave her some pills, which seemed to help, but when she got worse and when she started vomiting they knew something else was going on.

Melinda had cancer.

They went to see specialists, and she started chemotherapy. As luck would have it, she responded well, and the doctors gave her a good chance of recovery. But she was weak, and needed continuous treatment.

But Melinda's treatment was expensive—very expensive. Despite insurance, they would still have to come up with $600 a week—that's around $2,400 a month—just for her medicine.

While they both had decent jobs, and they were even a little frugal, it was very difficult to manage when their monthly expenses doubled, while their income dropped as Melinda couldn't work anymore. They took out a second mortgage, and a bunch of other loans, and starting selling the valuable stuff they had. But it wasn't enough, they were drowning.

Tom was desperate and was willing to try anything. He'd heard from a friend about "the darknet" where he might find Melinda's medicine for cheap, and while he was skeptical it couldn't hurt to try? After all he was running out of options.

He visited the darknet market his friend had suggested and searched for Melinda's medicine. To his surprise he found several sellers, who could deliver them right to his doorstep in just a few days. He decided to test it out and transferred some bitcoins to a seller. It was surprisingly easy, but he couldn't shake the feeling he had just been scammed.

But three days later a small package arrived in the mailbox, neatly wrapped in an unassuming box. It was Melinda's medicine, in fact exactly the same brand with the same packaging they used to buy, only now one week of medicine had cost them $30 instead of $600.

Tom couldn't understand how it could be so cheap. The medicine seemed real, it came in the same package and Tom even had it tested (can't be too careful, right?) Maybe it was stolen, and the thieves just wanted to sell it quickly? Or was it produced in India, for minimal cost?

But Tom didn't care. He had already placed his next order from the same seller. Tom only cared about Melinda.

While the story is made up, the situation is real. Medicine in the U.S. can be **extremely expensive**[274], and the cost isn't something all families can bear. The same medicine that will ruin you financially is often available for a fraction of the cost from darknet markets.

Yet we must always remember the dangers of buying medicine from darknet markets. It's entirely possible that you can get fake medicine, untested medicine or straight up dangerous medicine. You must be **very careful** when you buy from a completely unregulated market. Instead of the medicine saving your life, it might kill you.

Still, was it wrong to do what Tom did and buy the medicine from a darknet market? If it might save the love of your life, the mother of your child, would you do it? What if it was easy and the risk of getting caught was very small?

I'd imagine most would say yes, they would do anything to save her. While there is bad stuff on darknet markets—most of which is illegal—in this case cryptocurrencies and darknet markets helped save Tom's family, and I see that as a good thing.

It can be extremely expensive, even if you have insurance. The insurance companies try really hard to avoid paying the bills[276]. For example they might only cover certain "approved" medicines, doctors or treatments.

And even if they do cover it, sometimes it's still expensive. Even if you only pay 10% of the original cost, that's still $2,000 if the medicine was $20,000 originally.

Chapter 17

A Swiss bank account in your pocket

Unlimited and untraceable money on your smartphone

Of course I steal from the rich. They're the ones with all the money.

Gabriel Santiago, *Android Netrunner (2012)*

If you've seen spy movies, or maybe read *The Da Vinci Code*, you might be familiar with a private bank account. It's one where you don't need any identification other than the bank account number and a password to access, and you have access to all your money safely, securely and most importantly privately.

This is actually a great description of how cryptocurrencies work. You just need the account number (an *address* (p.206)) and the password (a *private key* (p.204)) to access your money, which you can do from anywhere in the world using the smartphone in your pocket.

Even the Gringotts Wizarding Bank in Harry Potter operates in a similar manner. But except for a password they use a physical key.

The myth of a Swiss bank account

This is how *Swiss bank accounts* are usually portrayed. While they can offer more privacy than other banks, it's just a myth that they offer truly private banking. Due to the additional privacy compared to the other banks, they also have tough anti-money-laundering laws that require more identification than other banks and they require proof of where the money comes from.

Recently Switzerland has begun sharing bank details of foreign account holders automatically with other countries[277]. At the time of writing they share data with more than 60 countries, and more will join[278]. I think it's fair to say that Swiss bank accounts don't live up to the private bank account dream.

Cryptocurrencies can fulfill the dream.

How private are cryptocurrencies really? Some are more private than others, see the discussion of the privacy challenge for more information (p.193).

Shell companies and offshore bank accounts

A common argument against truly private bank accounts is that they enable tax fraud and money laundering. And it's a valid point, but there's just one issue: it's already possible, and it's happening at a global scale.

The *Panama Papers*[279] was a gigantic leak that detailed the shady businesses of shell companies and how they're used to hide ownership of assets. It detailed how politicians, celebrities, drug dealers and the global elite obscured their wealth and in large part engaged in tax fraud and money laundering.

I can recommend the excellent documentary *The Panama Papers (2018)*.

There are other reports, such as the *Offshore Leaks*[280], the *Bahamas Leaks*[281] and the *Paradise Papers*[282], which all say that the use of shell companies and offshore bank accounts are used on a massive scale for tax fraud and money laundering. (In practice they're pretty close to the mythical Swiss bank account.)

They're not just for avoiding taxes. Look at celebrities for instance, they have tabloids dedicated to blow up any minor detail of their life into this huge scandal. It makes sense for them to try to keep their finances hidden, which is exactly what a spokesman for Emma Watson, who got named in the Panama Papers, claimed:

> Emma receives absolutely no tax or monetary advantages from this offshore company whatsoever, only privacy.

> Spokesman for Emma Watson[283]

It's up to you if you believe them or not. As the cynic that I am, I remain skeptical, but at the same time I sympathize with the privacy concern—I did after all dedicate the chapter *Private money* (p.109) to the topic. If you haven't read the chapter I suggest you do so now, as it tries to explain why it's important that financial privacy is available for everyone.

Absurd inequality

All animals are equal, but some animals are more equal than others

George Orwell, *Animal Farm*[Orw45]

While tax evasion through offshore banking is problematic, it pales to the problem that in practice there's another set of tax rules only for the super rich. Let's see what the previous president of the United States has to say about tax evasion:

Clinton: He didn't pay any federal income tax.
Trump: That makes me smart.

Trump debates with Clinton[284]

No, Mr. President, that makes you rich. You see, this kind of tax evasion is only available for the super rich. And it's not the top 1% we're talking about, more like the top 0.001%. We're talking about people who can afford private chefs and travel the world in private jets and yachts. (Alright, maybe it's not *only* for the super rich, you might be able to do it even if you're only very rich, but you have to have a very large amount of money to make tax evasion in this way feasible.)

This is why you don't see the names of normal people in the Panama Papers—no matter how smart they may be—but instead we find names like Lionel Messi, Donald Trump and Vladimir Putin.

Here, I use the term *tax evasion* instead *tax fraud* because, believe it or not, it's often legal! If you're rich enough you can hire tax experts who'll find the loopholes in the tax laws so you can avoid the taxes normal people have to pay[285]. And if you do happen to step on the wrong side of the law, you can hire the very best (and very expensive) lawyers to keep you out of prison. But you shouldn't worry about that too much, since the rich and powerful also lobby the law makers to make the laws beneficial for them and to keep the IRS starved for funds[286].

I'm personally worried about the potential problems that the lack of financial privacy may cause. In Sweden your tax records are public, and every year in the small community I live in there's discussion about the last year's "rich list"—a list of the people who earned the most taxable income in a year.

What would happen if cryptocurrencies sky-rocketed to the moon, and I suddenly became very rich? Everyone would probably know about it, and people wouldn't look at me the same way. Maybe I wouldn't even feel safe here anymore, as a target would be painted on my back?

And please don't gimme that crap about how all rich people are smart. It's just what rich people tell themselves, to make them feel smart. Most were born with a golden spoon in their mouth, and even the self-made super rich had a ton of luck and help.[289]

It's funny that you can find Trump's name in the Panama Papers 3,450 times, while Putin uses proxies to try and hide his involvement[290]. I wonder, does that make Putin smarter than Trump?

It's not just rich individuals that avoid taxes, it's big companies too. In 2018, 60 of the largest companies in the USA paid no taxes on pre-tax income of 79 billion dollars[291].

The three wealthiest people in the United States—Bill Gates, Jeff Bezos, and Warren Buffett—now own more wealth than the entire bottom half of the American population combined

Report: Billionaire Bonanza 2017[287]

The world is just extremely unfair, and if anything it should be the other way around. The poor should pay less taxes, while the rich should pay more. At least this would have a semblance of fairness.

The great leveller

In an ideal world everyone would pay their taxes as they should, while preserving their financial privacy. But this is sadly just a dream, and it's not possible in reality. So let's look at some hypothetical worlds, to find out what we'd like to move towards.

- It's fine the way it is

    I doubt anyone except the Trumps of the world, who are the ones who benefit the most, would say the ideal world is what we have today. The inequality is increasing[288] as the rich get richer while paying less taxes; it seems clear to me we have a serious problem that needs to be fixed.

- Everyone must use traceable money

    What if we forced everyone to use traceable money, where we can see where the money's coming from? And completely removed the possibility to hide money via shell companies and offshore bank accounts?

    At first glance this fixes our problem, but remember that this kind of tax evasion is already legal, and we'd first have to fix our laws for this to have any effect. And besides, completely removing our financial privacy comes with serious drawbacks, some which we'll explore in the next chapter about *The cashless dystopia* (p.139).

- Everyone can use untraceable money

    It's only recently, during the last decades, we've used truly traceable money. The rest of the time money has always been largely untraceable, where you don't know where the money comes from.

    If everyone would start using untraceable money, we would simply go back to how it used to be. With the upside that now everyone would have financial privacy, and not just the super rich as it is today.

Curiously enough, if everyone started to use a cryptocurrency like Bitcoin we would be pretty close to this world because all coins in Bitcoin can be traced. The only thing missing is tying addresses to identities, in which case we should use something like Facebook's Diem, which completely abandons all privacy.

If you view tax evasion as a problem, then making better laws is a necessary beginning. But we won't ever be able to get rid of tax fraud completely. This is especially true if there's a privileged elite that has access to tools to obfuscate their money, essentially making their finances private, which is out of reach for the rest of us.

We might try to force everyone to use traceable money, and thereby making tax collection equally fair for everyone. This is largely what society is moving towards, with the ever-more strict *Know Your Customer* and *Anti Money Laundering* laws. Besides the serious privacy and permission problems this creates, the problem is that if we outlaw privacy, only outlaws will have privacy, defeating the fairness we were trying to create.

One way the super rich can launder their money is to buy apartments, sit on them and then sell them making their money "clean". It's one reason why the apartment next door might be completely empty.[292]

The only truly fair world would be if everyone had access to the same tools, and if financial privacy would be available for all, not just the privileged few. Everyone could enjoy the security and peace of mind that privacy gives you, making it the preferable choice for me.

For better or worse, cryptocurrencies bring us closer to that world. Cryptocurrencies give everyone the ability to store their wealth privately, regardless of how rich you are. They make it possible for anyone to store their wealth "offshore" and off the grid; they act as a financial equalizer by giving everyone access to similar tools that the super rich already have.

Perfectly balanced, as all things should be.

While cryptocurrencies might make it easier to hide your money, it does not give you the ability to find the tax loopholes the super rich are exploiting.

Chapter 18
The cashless dystopia
The cashless society is a nightmare

If you want a picture of the future, imagine a boot stamping on a human face—for ever.

George Orwell, *1984*[Orw49]

In Sweden, and in the world in general, we're moving closer to the utopian cashless society. Businesses are safer from theft as they don't have to store large amounts of cash in stores, and payments are faster and more convenient. Tax fraud and illegal transactions are also harder.

But it's not all good. We've already touched on several problems in earlier chapters, for example how legitimate businesses might get banned in our attempts to ban illegal goods and services (p.55), or how the cashless society is a privacy nightmare (p.109) yet tax evasion is still a huge problem (p.133). In this chapter I'll try to tie together some of these issues and paint a picture of how the cashless society isn't a dream—it's a nightmare. But it's a nightmare cryptocurrencies might help us avoid.

A *utopia* is a dreamlike society that's perfect, or close to it. You might say that Heaven, the place some say you go to when you die, is an utopia.

Road to hell

In their ever-increasingly invasive attempts to counter money-laundering, governments all over the world have limited the amount of cash you can deposit or withdraw from banks, cash purchases and even how much cash you can carry. *Know-your-customer* laws for example require banks in the United States to report any cash deposits of $10,000, or multiple transactions adding up to that amount, to the IRS. The customers then have to be ready to provide extensive documentation to prove where the money is coming from.

The act of managing your deposits in a way to avoid triggering the report is called *structuring* and is—you guessed it—illegal[302]. Of course this might also affect innocent people or legitimate businesses who just happen to deposit using a suspicious pattern[303].

In the U.S., you also have to declare cash amounts over $10,000 you want to leave or enter the country with, otherwise you'll face a high risk of having it all confiscated[293]. Many countries have similar restrictions but North Macedonia takes it a step further: to prevent "money laundering and terrorism financing" cash payments above 30,000 MKD (around €500) are banned[294].

It sounds hypocritical to me when a major U.S. bank laundered **$378 billions** for Mexico's drug gangs[304], the kind of gangs that leaves behind enormous mass-graves[305].

Instead, we're encouraged to use digital payments (ignoring the unfortunate people without the ability to do so (p.73)), where banks are able to block large payments if they deem them suspicious—presumably to make it harder to do money laundering.

> I use WeChat to pay my rent. I use it to pay for my utilities. I use it to top up my phone credit. I use WeChat to pay for the metro system. I use it to scan QR codes on the back of shared-bike schemes throughout the city. I use it to call cabs.

Barclay Bram[295]

In many countries, we're already close to the cashless society. As we saw in the quote, WeChat is absolutely integral for many people in China and here in Sweden using cash is very rare, and many stores, restaurants and even banks have dropped cash completely.

A short story

Money should be **acceptable**, meaning that it must be usable by everyone (p.37). A move towards a society where you need permission to use its money is disastrous, which I'll try to exemplify using a short story:

Kevin was walking home after yet another failure. It had only been two weeks since he was declared a leech, but it felt like an eternity. Those bastards were so scared of being associated with a leech, they cut him off quicker than if he'd been a leper. Maybe he was as contagious as one.

He'd been trying to find some work, but nobody would take him in. He couldn't even get a cleaning job—what if he'd steal? And that condescending look on their faces. How his previous employer had told him he would get his salary when he was fired, knowing that the bank had frozen his account and he couldn't use it anyway. It would've felt so good to punch that ugly face in, but Kevin was glad he managed to hold back. As bad as the situation was, it surely would be worse in a prison cell.

Turning the corner, Kevin felt a stab of hunger. Hardly surprising, as he hadn't eaten anything today. But he still had some food at the apartment that Joe, bless his soul, had been so kind to help him buy. Everything would be better after eating some food.

When he reached his apartment door, he was met with an EVICTED sign. Horrified, Kevin tried to open the door, but they had already changed the lock. Anger washed over him again—the rent wasn't due for another week! Those bastards!

Trying to cool down, he tried to call the manager, but no answer. Maybe the bastard had blocked him. Instead he called Joe, who promised he could crash at his place, and that he'd call him back at 12 when he got off work.

That was still many hours away, and Kevin was still very hungry. So he decided to walk around downtown to search for something to eat. He asked around, but all he could find was a small coffee shop that would trade a gift card for a cup of coffee. He'd never realized how reliant he was on the plastic cards, and without them he was now risking to starve in the middle of downtown, with multiple restaurants at every corner.

A little happier, Kevin continued exploring downtown. He'd been here many times, but today it didn't quite look the same. He used to only see the fancy restaurants, the night clubs and the pretty girls. But now he noticed the people in the dark alleys, looking for cans or maybe even food in the trash. He saw homeless people trying to sleep, right next to the night clubs he used to visit. Maybe he would soon join them? Maybe they knew how to buy food?

Having to go pee, Kevin searched for a restroom. There was a small queue today, but Kevin was patient. The coffee had really raised his spirit— maybe everything would work out tomorrow?

It was Kevin's turn, so he walked to the door to the toilet and stopped. You had to pay with a plastic card to open the door.

The worst part of this story is that it's not even that far-fetched, and all examples are inspired by real life events:

1   "Leech" is literally a synonym for "deadbeat", the name for Chinese people on the wrong side of their social credit system. They also have trouble getting work and get shunned if their status is discovered.[296]

2   People have been thrown out of their homes for very minor things. For example a Michigan man underpaid his property taxes by **$8.41**, and the county seized his property, sold it and kept the profits[297].

This is related to *civil asset forfeiture*, which we'll look at in the next chapter (p.145).

3   I too was in trouble when I'd forgotten my credit cards, because many restaurants in Sweden don't accept cash. A girl in a coffee shop even helped me buy a warm chocolate drink, when I had trouble finding food. (I don't drink coffee.)

4   Here in Sweden I've seen public bathrooms you unlock with digital payments:

It says "5 SEK fee". Instead of inserting a 5 SEK coin, you use your card. Very convenient, when it works. I wonder if it unlocks when power disappears?

Perhaps the most unrealistic part of the story is how the potential employers knew about his status as a leech, and why he got marked in the first place. But a key problem with the cashless society, that's left implicit in the story, is the complete lack of financial privacy; everything you buy and do with your money is tracked.

For instance, Kevin's bank might have blocked him because they discovered he'd been buying weed or supporting its legalization (which Wells Fargo has done before[298]). Maybe Kevin's employer then saw that the bank account was blocked and started worrying that Kevin, now unable to pay for things, would resort to stealing things from the company for a living, and decided to fire him.

There are already companies that collect this kind of information, and sell it for profit. It's not unreasonable to think that employers would want this to help them decide who to hire, and who to fire.

When you think about it, we've already given up our financial privacy. All that's left is to wait for us to be abused, like in the story.

A dystopia

When you look closer at a *utopia*, you'll often find that it's not such a good place after all. You might even argue that a utopia cannot exist, since a society contains people with different desires that cannot be fulfilled simultaneously. (Is the Nazi Arian society a utopia? Maybe for the Nazis, but certainly not for the Jews.)

The cashless society isn't a utopia, but a *dystopia* that'll suppress the lowest class harder than we can imagine. If you cannot use the same money as others, you cannot have a home, pay your bills or buy food. You cannot get a normal job or even beg for money, since you cannot use the money they give you. You'll be completely closed off from the rest of society.

There are many examples of the utopia/dystopia theme, ranging from *Demolition Man (1993)* and *Hot Fuzz (2007)* to *The Hunger Games* and *Harry Potter*.

But you wouldn't be alone. 25 million Brits would struggle in a cashless society[299] and China has already banned millions from buying travel tickets[300] via their "social credit" system[301]. And don't forget about the 1.7 billion unbanked adults in the world, who don't fit into a cashless society (p.73).

What would happen to you then? My guess is you'd band together with others in the same situation, and you'll form a mini society where you'll use some other form of money. Maybe gift cards or "old" cash?

You might be able to interact with the normal society by bartering, but you'll probably turn to illegal activities like theft or prostitution.

A possible salvation

The lack of financial privacy and needing permission to use its money are the big problems with the cashless society. As we've seen in previous chapters, cryptocurrencies solve the permission problem very well, and some also give excellent privacy.

The cashless society does indeed have its benefits. It's more convenient to use digital money—just blip your card or your phone, instead of counting change—or how businesses don't have to store large amounts of cash in stores and risk break-ins. Cryptocurrencies also have these benefits.

It might hubris to claim that cryptocurrencies makes privacy better, as Bitcoin is more traceable than any other form of money in history. But there are other cryptocurrencies with much better privacy features; see the discussion about the privacy challenge for more information (p.193).

This is why cryptocurrencies are sometimes called "digital cash"; they combine the important permissionless and privacy properties of cash with the convenience of digital money, and it's the only way a cashless society would make sense.

Chapter 19

Protection against government confiscation

It's harder for governments to take cryptocurrencies from you

It came to me. My own. My love. My own. My precious.

Gollum, "The Lord of the Rings: The Fellowship of the Ring"

In this chapter, we'll see how governments around the world sometimes directly or indirectly take your money, and how cryptocurrencies might help you avoid it.

No, this chapter is **not** about tax evasion—do your taxes people.

It's about how laws meant to fight crime end up hurting innocent people and how they limit people's freedom. It's also about how difficult it can be for you to keep your money safe and your wealth intact; and of course, as this is about cryptocurrencies, how they might help.

Remember that legality doesn't imply morality, meaning just because it's legal doesn't make it right, which we explored in the chapter about *Darknet markets* (p.127).

Civil asset forfeiture

Perhaps, you've heard the phrase "innocent until proven guilty"? It's called *presumption of innocence* and it's a cornerstone in the modern justice system that says the default stance is that you're innocent of a crime and it's up to the prosecution to prove otherwise. It's an old legal principle that the United Nations has declared an universal human right[306].

If it was the other way around, "guilty until proven innocent", then it would open up abuse from inside the justice system and innocent people would end up in jail, either by being unlucky—despite being innocent you lack convincing evidence that you are—or you simply cannot afford competent defense to protect yourself. Therefore the presumption of innocence is a necessary requirement to keep the justice system fair.

However in the United States there's something called *civial asset forfeiture*. It's a legal tool that allows the police to seize your car, home, money or other assets without ever charging you with a crime. You read that right, they can seize your assets **without charging you with a crime**. There are tons of stories of innocent people[307][308][309] having their money or property confiscated, for example:

- NYPD officers stole $4,800 in a warrantless search.[310]

  When he went to retrieve his money he was told it was too late and it had already been deposited into the NYPD's pension fund.

- A couple had their house seized after their son sold heroin.[311]

  One day the police showed up and turned their power off, locked the doors with screws and forced them out on the street because their son had been arrested for selling $40 worth of heroin.

- A nurse got $41,377 confiscated before boarding a flight.[312]

  She was planning to start a medical clinic for women and children. She was never charged with a crime and was pressured to sign an unconstitutional agreement waiving important rights, including the right to interest on the cash and her right to sue back.

The limits placed on cash I referenced in the previous chapter are also examples of the presumption of innocence being turned on it's head. For example if you transfer €50,000 to a European bank it's up to you to prove where you got the money, not the bank or the government.

On a technical level it's not the owner that's charged with a crime, but the property itself. That's why it's legal for the police to seize a house because someone sold drugs in the house, even if the owners didn't know about it.

This really flips the "innocent until proven guilty" mantra on it's head. You're often—but not always!—able to contest the seizure to get back your assets. If you're lucky you'll get them back, but more likely you'll get locked down in a year long legal battle with expensive lawyer fees. Unfortunately it's often more expensive to contest the seizure so many are forced to accept the loss.

Maybe there were some good intentions when these laws mere made, but today they simply don't work as intended. I'll leave it to Columbia's former police chief to explain:

> It's usually based on a need—well, I take that back, there's some limitations on it. ... Actually, there's not really on the forfeiture stuff. We just usually base it on **something that would be nice to have** that we can't get in the budget, for instance. We try not to use it for things that we need to depend on because we need to have those purchased. It's kind of like pennies from heaven—**it gets you a toy** or something that you need is the way that we typically look at it to be perfectly honest.

(Emphasis mine)

Columbia's Police Chief Ken Burton, 2012[313]

He's saying that the police can take whatever they want, and that they're motivated by what would be "nice to have", not if there's a crime involved or not. Most of the money goes to funding the police, but the money has gone to extravagant Christmas parties, sirloin beef and a \$8,200 security system for the district attorney's private home[314]. And of course some managed to spend it on alcohol, prostitutes and marijuana[315]. Then there's the case where another district attorney spent \$27,000 to take his whole office to Hawaii, including the approving district judge[316].

In practice civil asset forfeiture is state-sanctioned theft where the police are acting like highway robbers[317].

"That's a nice car you have there, it would be a shame if anything happened to it."

So, how can cryptocurrencies protect you against the forfeiture laws? While they naturally can't prevent the police from seizing your house or your car, they allow you to easily store and travel with as much money as you can—without anyone noticing. Even if they know you have them there's nothing they can physically steal—they would need your password. (Of course they might be able to coerce you to unlock it for them.)

They say the laws are supposed to confiscate assets from criminals. For example from drug dealers who sells large amounts of drugs for cash. Because only criminals use large amounts of cash... well, that's the claim anyway.

If you're a cynic, like I tend to be, you have to love the incentives at play here. If the police seize money they directly help themselves yet there appears to be no negative consequences if they do.

An app on your phone can hold a practically unlimited amount of value in cryptocurrencies. Or if you want to be more secure you can encrypt your private key with a strong password and store it on your computer or online. Even the government cannot break strong encryption.

Safe deposit boxes aren't safe

So, we now know the dangers of walking around with a bunch of cash. Forget about moving it around, how about just finding a secure way to store them? What about storing them (or gold or jewelries) in a safe deposit box, surely they're called safe deposit boxes because they're *safe*?

Unfortunately, safe deposit boxes aren't safe:

> There are an estimated 25 million safe deposit boxes in America, and they operate in a legal gray zone within the highly regulated banking industry. There are no federal laws governing the boxes; no rules require banks to compensate customers if their property is stolen or destroyed.

> The New York Times, Safe deposit boxes aren't safe[318]

The contents of safety deposit boxes disappear all the time, and there's not a whole lot you can do if it happens to you. There are no hard laws to protect you, even if the bank's own records clearly show items vanishing. The banks instead cap their liability in the lease contract:

> If a loss results from our negligence or willful misconduct, our total liability will be the lesser of your actual uninsured loss or $500.

> The New York Times, Wells Fargo's safe-deposit-box-contract[319]

And they really are negligent. Did you know that the safe deposit box numbers aren't unique? So it may happen that a bank tries to evict another customer for not keeping up with payments, and they remove another box with the same number.[320]

Deposit boxes won't keep you safe from creditors, who may ask the bank for your deposit box[321], and of course they won't be safe from the government—or even the banks themselves—in bad economic times[322].

Confiscating money from your bank accounts

Alright, so if having physical goods isn't good enough how about storing money digitally in a bank account?

Similar to how safe deposit boxes aren't safe during a financial crisis, neither is your bank account. For example during the financial crisis in Cyprus in 2013 deposits over €100,000 had 47.5% of the value forcefully taken away[323]. The banks closed overnight and withdrawals were blocked. When banks were reopened capital control limits were in place to prevent a *bank run*.

I think this exemplifies our relationship with banks well. When we have our money at a bank, it's not really ours anymore. It's now the bank's money and we only have their promise to return our money when we ask for it. Which generally works well—until it doesn't.

Invalidating money

Fine. Let's say you know about all these ways someone can take your money and you've decided to hide your cash somewhere really safe, maybe buried in your yard or in a hidden safe somewhere in your house. Perhaps nobody even knows you have it so the risk of someone hitting you with a wrench until you give it up is minimized. That should do it, right?

Tough luck. In India they found an innovative way to "fight corruption" when they abolished the 500 and 1,000 rupee notes—that's 86% of all cash in circulation made invalid in one stroke[324][325].

Many turned to gold, jewelry and anything that could reasonably hold value to prevent their money and savings from disappearing in a puff of smoke. Cryptocurrencies could've also been used for protection because nobody can invalidate what you have, similar to having a physical gold bar.

Here are some tips if you want to install a safe:

1. Bolt it to the floor.
2. Hide it (not your master bedroom).
3. Make sure as few people as possible know about it and what you have inside, but do tell someone.
4. Consider another safe to act as a dummy.

Falling through the cracks when cash is renewed

I like cash. I like the feel of it and I like that I can store it at home and be reasonably sure that I can keep it. The government outright invalidating it, like in India, is exceptionally rare, and it's extremely unlikely that for example the Swedish government would do so without the ability to exchange the old cash into the new. For instance when Sweden upgraded to new bills the old ones were valid in stores for about a year, and you could exchange them at banks long after that too[326].

But the system isn't perfect. If you miss your window and have to go to a bank with your old, and now technically invalid bills, you have to prove where the cash came from. This can be quite hard if you've been saving some money here and there for many years, and if you don't your money is now lost.

Exactly this happened to a 91-year old Swedish woman couldn't deposit her old bills (worth around €10,000), because she couldn't prove where she got them[327]. There isn't anything outright evil going on here (maybe a little unintended evil?); there are rules which have to be followed and cash do have to get replaced from time to time. It's just unfortunate that some people may fall through the cracks.

Even though I like the idea of cash, I don't use it much. Simply because I'm *lazy*, and paying with cards is much easier.

It's not surprising that it was an old woman who got in trouble. When you're over 90 years old you probably didn't even know about the new bills and that the old ones were becoming invalid. She probably wasn't up-to-date with the ever-more strict KYC laws either. When she was younger she didn't have to track every single income-source, just to not lose her money.

Inflation

There is another way governments can take money from you: by inflating the money supply and using the excess money for themselves. We explored inflation in *A defective system* (p.97), and the extreme hyperinflation in *A global currency* (p.119), so I won't repeat myself too much here.

Just remember that inflation is a more indirect—and perhaps sinister—way to take money from you as you probably won't notice it. After all they aren't taking something physically from you—you still have your cash in your mattress and numbers in your bank account are unchanged—but they now get you less stuff.

With cryptocurrencies, nobody can "steal" money from you buy printing more of it.

What cryptocurrencies do

Here's a short summary on how cryptocurrencies can help protect our money and our wealth:

- It allows you to hold, and hide, any amount of money.
- If you use strong encryption, nobody can confiscate it (unless they use force).
- You can easily bring your money anywhere.
- The government cannot invalidate your money.
- Nobody can inflate the money supply and devalue your money.

Currently, cryptocurrencies are extremely volatile, and storing your wealth in them might be less preferable than letting it slowly wither away from inflation. With time, and increased adoption, I think this would change.

Here's a sad story I heard about what inflation can do to your savings:

This couple was quite frugal and saved a lot of their income. They were planning to give some of it to their son when he got older, so he could live a good life and not having to worry so much. After having saved a lot over many decades they gave a big gift to him as a lump sum.

After a few years they asked him what he did with the money and they were horrified by his answer—he had bought skiing equipment for all the money! But this money was supposed to buy a house or a car, how could he be this irresponsible?

Turns out the money wasn't worth that much anymore. They had just left the money alone letting inflation eat up most of the value.

Chapter 20
Separation of money and state
Countries that don't manage their own money

When I first started thinking about cryptocurrencies, I thought they were just useful for some people who couldn't use regular transactions, like buying weed or things on a darknet market. Or that it was simply a better payment system as there was no middleman to skim off large fees from all transactions. That's useful, but it didn't strike me as revolutionary.

But the idea of separating money from state made me go "Wow, that could actually have a huge impact." As we've seen earlier, the financial system relies heavily on manipulating the money supply (p.97) and on predicting and reacting to the market (p.91). This would, for better or worse, be largely impossible if states no longer controlled the money supply and if people used cryptocurrencies instead.

I do think avoiding up to 5% fees on practically all digital payments is an under-appreciated benefit of cryptocurrencies (p.49). It might be overshadowed by the volatility, but the potential benefit to the economy is absolutely huge.

Religion and state

I was chosen by heaven
Say my name when you pray
To the skies
See Carolus rise

Sabaton, "Carolus Rex"

I know it might be difficult to entertain the notion that a country shouldn't control their own money, and that the mere suggestion is outrageous. If this is the case for you, consider the historically similar relationship between religion and state:

For many centuries, millennia even, religion and the state were inseparable. I'm not even sure it was a conscious decision, rather the mere idea that it could be any other way was simply unthinkable. For many that's just how it was, like how the sun rose every morning or that you got hungry without food.

Countless rulers have based their legitimacy on religious grounds, that they should rule because God says so. This is useful since you have to question God to question them, and who are you to question God? For example both the Roman and Japanese emperors used this to legitimise themselves. Even today it's very common that the church should be the one to crown the kings and queens, as if to say "we give you the right to rule".

Charles XII of Sweden, also called "Carolus Rex", acknowledged the power of God but rejected the church when he placed the crown upon his own head, instead of letting someone from the church do it.

This is why it was a big deal when the Swedish king Gustav Vasa took steps towards the Protestant Reformation[328]. It wasn't motivated by religious reasons—he simply wanted control over the Catholic Church's property, which was the dominating religion at the time. In a sense the Diet at Västerås in 1527 was the first step in separating the church from the Swedish state, a process that was completed in 2000[329] when they were formally separated.

After the reformation Sweden largely became Protestantic and is now one of the least religious countries in the world.[332]

Separating church from the state was once unthinkable, yet it's now a given that religion shouldn't dictate what the state should do. In a similar way the notion that money could be separated from the state is today largely considered unthinkable, but this might change too.

Not that unusual

In practice some countries have already separated money from their state, as they use money someone else controls. For example the Euro is managed by the European Central Bank (ECB), and the countries that use the Euro have very little influence in the ECB's decision-making (well, most of them anyway). There are also countries that use the U.S. dollar as their official currency, while having no say in what the U.S. does with it[330].

Gold might also be an example of money outside of state control—there's nobody with exclusive access to gold after all. But in practice someone has to cast the gold to coins for it to be usable as money, including a "government approved" stamp on them, which gives some sort of control over the money. After all, it's difficult to determine what a coin is made of so we just trust the stamp on it.

Maybe a better example is shell money, or other money found in nature, where you just pick them up and start using them. Although they're lacking compared to coins or modern money, there's no one in charge of minting or stamping shells.

So the idea that a state doesn't require control over their own money isn't really that strange, as there are many examples of the contrary.

Because people don't actually verify the amount of gold in the coins, they could via *debasement*[333] slowly decrease the amount of gold in the coins. This would enable them to make more coins and effectively increase the money supply.

The difference with cryptocurrencies

With the various historical examples of how money can exist without state backing we might wonder what cryptocurrencies bring to the table. Why would they be different?

For starters all modern examples where a state doesn't control their own money simply mean they're using someone else's money. There's always someone in control of the money, in this case it's just some other country or institution. With cryptocurrencies there's no single entity in control, meaning it's money truly separate from state.

Cryptocurrencies are also different from the "natural" forms of money, such as shells or stones, because they have better monetary properties (p.31). For instance the supply in a cryptocurrency is provably limited, while you always run the risk of someone discovering a mountain of shells on some remote island somewhere. Cryptocurrencies being digital also means they're easier to transport and to send over larger distances, making global interaction much easier.

States can apply indirect control. For example if the U.S. passes anti-cryptocurrency laws, it would have a negative effect on the usefulness of cryptocurrencies. Similarly if they would pass beneficial laws, cryptocurrencies would become more useful, simply because the U.S. have such a large influence throughout the world.

While historical examples of states without direct control over their money exists, the excellent monetary properties (p.41) make cryptocurrencies well suited to separate money from state for real.

Assuming cryptocurrencies can solve their difficult challenges, such as scaling and privacy concerns (p.191).

What will the future hold?

It's impossible to predict the future. For example the iPhone was released in 2007 and today almost everyone carries a smartphone in their pocket. This is particularly crazy because each is *millions* of times more powerful than all of the combined computing power of NASA that put man on the moon 50 years ago[331].

Nobody could've predicted this explosive technological development, so how can we predict where cryptocurrencies will take us? I don't think they'll completely revolutionize the world in a decade, but it's impossible to say what will happen 50 or 100 years from now.

Will countries drop fiat and instead adopt cryptocurrencies? Would this force them to make more responsible decisions and to steer clear of moral hazard, which we saw during the last financial crisis (p.83)? Or would they fail spectacularly, issuing a new Great Depression?

It's possible cryptocurrencies will fail, but instead we adopt digital currencies issued and controlled by multinational corporations, truly fulfilling the cyberpunk dystopian nightmare that would make the cashless dystopia (p.139) seem like a dream?

Maybe cryptocurrencies will co-exist as an alternative to fiat, and as discussed in previous chapters provide payment options for the undesirable (p.55) and the unbanked (p.73)? Maybe they'll even slow down the money printing machines and limit the soaring debt (p.97)? But maybe they'll instead hamstring countries who need to act, but now cannot?

Of course cryptocurrencies might just be a fad that will be forgotten when people realize they don't provide any real value. (This would be quite unfortunate for me, since I've just written an entire book on how I think they do provide value.)

Which scenario is more likely? And what would the ideal scenario look like? That's something I'll leave up to you, the reader, to decide.

The Gold Standard was largely abandoned during the outbreak of World War I, so the countries could print money to pay for the war.

Part VI

Extensions

Non-currency usage of a blockchain

Blockchain is the tech. Bitcoin is merely the first mainstream manifestation of its potential.

Marc Kenigsberg

Money is perhaps the most obvious usage of cryptocurrencies but they support other use cases too. With embedded data and scripts cryptocurrencies can truly become "programmable money", where we use cryptocurrencies as a base and build new functionality on top.

There are many different ways this could be useful and I've selected some examples that I think have potential. I'll show how it's possible to tag a message with an unforgeable timestamp, create an uncensorable social media platform, and make gambles provably fair. We'll finish with the usefulness of tracking assets with tokens and how a cryptocurrency based voting system has some surprisingly attractive properties.

I generally try to avoid the word *blockchain* which sometimes refer to private blockchains or blockchains which use a consensus model with known and trusted actors. Facebook's Diem is such an example and IBM's blockchain is another.

Don't let the similar names fool you: consensus algorithms with known participants and those with unknown participants are **very** different. I only consider those using the latter to be cryptocurrencies.

Embedding data

The first thing we can observe is that it's possible to insert data into the ledgers of cryptocurrencies, essentially making the data immutable. It's not important exactly how, but if you're curious here are some ways:

Satoshi embedded his message in the "Coinbase data" entry of the block. Other miners usually include the name of their mining pool. Such as in block #595563 the coinbase data says "Mined by AntPool48".

Read Greg Walker's *Coinbase Transaction: A transaction used to claim a block reward* for more info about coinbase transactions.[336]

1   Miners can add data to blocks

    For example Satoshi left a message in the first ever Bitcoin block:

    ```
    The Times 03/Jan/2009 Chancellor on brink of second bailout for
    banks
    ```

2   Transactions can hold data

    See the OP_RETURN field in this Bitcoin Cash transaction[334] which says:

    ```
    Memo has reached 500,000 on-chain actions!
    ```

3   Addresses are user controlled

    Even if it's not intended you can always insert arbitrary data as long as you can control your address. For example you could chain transactions, by sending from address to address, and treat the second character of the receiving address as your message:

    ```
    ↳ 1HWXmyw…
    ↳ 1eLqUMf…
    ↳ 1lXGoQa…
    ↳ 1lvdhnx…
    ↳ 1oxCJio…
    ```

    To produce the message "Hello".

Scripts

Bitcoin does more than just transfer coins from one address to another. What it actually does is execute a small scripting language, which is responsible for unlocking funds and transferring them to new addresses. You can for example send funds from several addresses to many addresses or lock funds and require more than one key to spend them which is commonly called *multisig*).

This is the script of a standard Bitcoin transaction (amount, destination and other data is specified elsewhere):

```
OP_DUP OP_HASH160 <pubKeyHash>
OP_EQUALVERIFY OP_CHECKSIG
```

OP_RETURN is another type of opcode that marks the output as invalid. It's usually used to add data to transactions and is the preferred way to embed data because nodes concerned with storage can remove it and still be able to fully validate new transactions.

The scripting language in Bitcoin is fairly limited but the scripting language in Ethereum is much more powerful and can do more things. You can for example create games where you buy and sell cats on Ethereum[335].

Ethereum's powerful scripting language comes with all sorts of trade-offs. It makes it much more difficult to scale—which is already difficult with Bitcoin.

The scripting language in Ethereum is *Turing Complete*, meaning it's impossible to know if a script terminates. To avoid the problem of an infinite loop in the script every operation requires a fee (called *gas*), in contrast to a fee based on the script size as in Bitcoin.

Now it doesn't matter if you know what a script is or how it works, just remember this: cryptocurrencies can do more than just transfer coins from one address to another. We'll go into some of the examples in the following chapters.

Chapter 21

Timestamping service
Verifiable proof of knowledge at a certain time

Bitcoin is an extremely important innovation, but not in the way most people think. Bitcoin's real innovation is a globally verifiable proof publishing at a certain time. The whole system is built on that concept and many other systems can also be built on it. The blockchain nails down history, breaking Orwell's dictum of "He who controls the present controls the past and he who controls the past controls the future."

Julian Assange, Sep 16, 2014[337]

In *How do cryptocurrencies work?* (p.11) we saw that cryptocurrencies work by preventing double spending coins, and the system chooses one of two potentially valid transactions. While doing so it also creates an order between blocks and transactions, which can be used as the basis for a decentralized timestamping service.

What is a timestamping service?

A timestamping service offers proof that a message or document existed at a certain time with certain-contents. The idea of timestamping information is according to Wikipedia centuries old, dating back to *at least* the 17th century[338].

A modern example is the Wayback Machine, a service which allows you to see how a certain website looked at a certain time[339]. A bit like traveling back in time, but with your web-browser instead of a DeLorean.

Let's travel back in time and look at the site Hacker News, a tech oriented site where you can discuss news stores. I've lost a lot of time on the site reading insightful comments or getting upset at other less insightful comments.

The DeLorean is the time machine in the *Back To The Future* movies. They're amazing movies but unfortunately the time travel theory isn't really sound.[348]

I wanted to use a story of Bitcoin as an example, but they never got any traction that early on.

Interestingly enough Hacker News is full of people extremely skeptical of cryptocurrencies, who often comment that cryptocurrencies don't have a single legal use-case. This skepticism and misunderstanding, even from highly technical people, was one of the reasons I started writing this book.

Y **Hacker News** new | comments | ask | jobs | submit
1. ▲ Natalie Portman - Scientist (nytimes.com)   100 points by mhb 2 hours ago | 43 comments
2. ▲ Matt Blaze: How ACM and IEEE Shake Down Science (crypto.com)   50 points by alterego 2 hours ago | 9 comments
3. ▲ The Redis Manifesto (antirez.com)

The top three stories on Hacker News on Mars 1st, 2011 according to the Wayback Machine.[340]

As long as we can trust the Wayback Machine (and I do consider them generally trustworthy) we can be fairly sure this is correct. Letting a trusted party like the Wayback Machine handle timestamping, called *trusted timestamping*, is a solved problem with different kinds of standards but—as the name implies—there's always the caveat of requiring a trusted party to verify the timestamps.

Usage examples

What is a timestamping service useful for? Here are some examples:

- Proof of invention

  Surprisingly often in history a discovery happens independently and at around the same time[341]. What if you come up with an idea or an invention and you didn't want to reveal it yet but still wanted to claim priority?

  You would use timestamping. For example Robert Hook used it in 1660 when discovering Hooke's law by publishing the anagram *ceiiinosssttuv* and later published the translation *ut tensio sic vis* (latin for "as is the extension, so is the force")[342].

  Interestingly if you search for "ceiiinosssttuv" on Wikipedia you'll be redirected to Hooke's law, without an explanation why.

- Testaments

  If you're someone who likes to write testaments maybe you want to update the one you have. But after you die, how will people tell which is the newest? Sure you can write a date on the paper, but that can be altered by people who want the more beneficial one to be valid.

  The solution is to use a timestamping service. If you use one based on a cryptocurrency there's no possibility of altering the dates, not even by your lawyer.

  Of course the lawyer might try to forge your testament completely. If that's a worry you might want to sign your testament digitally, and make sure everyone has your key so they can themselves verify the validity of the document (p.204). (Strongly consider distributing a how-to document as well.)

- Proving discovery of software bugs

  What if you've discovered a major software bug and want to disclose it anonymously, but still want the ability to prove you were the one who found it? Later in the chapter (p.161) we'll go into details of how the discoverer of one of the most catastrophic bugs in Bitcoin ever accomplished this using timestamping.

Decentralized timestamping

With cryptocurrencies it's possible to do away with the trusted party requirement and offer a decentralized timestamping service. We know that there's no single trusted party that manages a cryptocurrency and instead many cooperate and reach consensus together. Therefore we only need to decide how to embed verifiable data and timestamps into a cryptocurrency:

1 Prepare data

Because we might want to reveal our message at a later date we don't want to store the message in the clear. We can use an anagram like Robert Hook used, some kind of encryption with a key or a hash function (p.202) to obfuscate the message.

After we have the obfuscated message we want to verify we can embed it into a cryptocurrency (p.155).

2 Retrieve timestamps

A blockchain creates a partial order between transactions where there's no order between transactions in the same block.

Transactions in an older block are older, transactions in a newer block are newer and transactions in the same block occur at the same time. You can observe, in a decentralized way, when a block with your transaction is created and use that as your message timestamp.

There is actually a timestamp in a block that the miner who creates the block can set themselves—with some constraints[349]. If we blindly trust that timestamp we put our trust in that miner.

The blocks themselves don't contain a trustworthy timestamp, but we can use the many different nodes observing the network to create an estimation. This could for example be the timestamps recorded by two nodes:

Using the time different nodes received the block is a more decentralized approach, but trusting the miner is probably good enough for most practical examples because the timestamp cannot diff too much. As more blocks are built on top by other miners we can be sure that the timestamp is reasonably correct.

Block number	Node #1	Node #2
#1001	2019-09-14 10:01	2019-09-14 10:01
#1002	2019-09-14 10:15	2019-09-14 10:27
...		
#1007	2019-09-14 11:07	2019-09-14 11:08

A couple of blocks and their observed timestamps by two different nodes. Blocks 1003–1006 are omitted.

In practice well connected nodes (with up to date clocks) will display a small time difference because blocks usually travel quickly through the network. A 12 minute time difference is extremely unlikely and unwanted, I only used it as an illustrative example.

Here we see that the timestamps differ, at most by 12 minutes. Although not visible in the table the nodes tell us that blocks 1003–1006 happened some time between 10:15 and 11:08. We cannot be sure down to seconds or minutes, but it gives a good estimate if we're only interested in an hourly or daily timestamp.

The network requires that blocks travel between miners quickly otherwise it increases the risk for forks (p.19) or hurts smaller miners disproportionally.

This way we have the basis for a decentralized timestamping service. Insert an obfuscated message in a transaction and afterwards you can reveal the message and use the creation time of the block the transaction is included in as your timestamp. Also comparing two messages to find which the oldest is very simple: just check which block came first—there's no need to look at a timestamp.

It's much easier to use (I'll go through an example step-by-step at the end of the chapter) compared to getting your message included in a publication like Hook did. You also don't have to trust a timestamping service—the solution is fully opaque and you can verify it yourself.

A real-life example

One of the most catastrophic bugs in recent years, CVE-2018-17144[343], which if left unpatched would allow an attacker to print an unlimited amount of Bitcoin. It was found and disclosed by someone who at least initially wanted to stay anonymous, but he wanted the ability to prove he was the one who found it.

Therefore he decided to create this message:

```
BitcoinABC does not check for duplicate inputs when processing
a block, only when inserting a transaction into the mempool.

This is dangerous as blocks can be generated with duplicate
transactions and then sent through e.g. compact block missing
transactions and avoid hitting the mempool, creating money out
of thin air.

/u/awemany
```

Which has the SHA-256 hash:

```
5c45a1ba957362a2ba97c9f8c48d4d59d4fa990945b7094a8d2a98c3a91ed9b6
```

And inserted it into the BTC blockchain using a timestamping service[344]. See "Advanced Verification" on the website to find the hash and see my explanation of hash functions for why the hash is enough (p.202).

This proves that reddit user awemany had knowledge of the inflation bug before it was disclosed and therefore that he was the one who found it.

Technically it doesn't conclusively prove he was the one who found it, only that he knew about the bug before everyone else.

Please read his writeup[345] of how he found the bug and the related discussion on reddit[346] for more info.

We can do it ourselves

The previous example used a timestamping service which did the conversions for us, but it's actually easy to do everything ourselves.

Let's say we want to obscure and timestamp the message Hook used:

    as is the extension, so is the force

Let's now encode and timestamp it using the Bitcoin Cash blockchain:

1   Encode the message using SHA-256

I'm sure you can find a tool for Windows if you search for it. Be sure to exclude the newline (which the -n flag is for). You can also find websites for it, but don't use them if the message is sensitive.

On Linux we can run the command:

```
echo -n "as is the extension, so is the force" | sha256sum
```

Giving us the SHA-256 hash:

    dab965bb19823669b8481846b9672c694a9af1b808314956b43154a0472942d8

2   Insert it in a transaction using OP_RETURN

For this step you need a wallet capable of creating a transaction with a custom OP_RETURN field, I used the desktop version of Electron Cash 4.0.14[347] and enabled the OP_RETURN field in settings. You need to have enough money to pay a small fee and use a small amount to transfer.

My transaction transferred around $0.05 with a $0.0008 fee. It might even be possible to transfer zero coins—as long as you pay the transaction fee—but the wallet I used had a minimum transaction limit.

Custom OP_RETURN using Electron Cash.

We can double-check the transaction on a blockexplorer, such as blockchair.com, to see that the OP_RETURN value matches our SHA-256 hash (look for the decoded OP_RETURN field).

Blockchair includes the prefix "j@" in the decoded OP_RETURN field while other blockexplorers I checked don't. It's the encoding (64) Electron Cash inserted into the transaction and isn't part of our hash.

With that our timestamp is prepared and nobody can see our original message, only the SHA-256 hash. When we're ready to reveal our message to the world, all we have to do is show everyone the message and how to verify the timestamp:

1   Locate the hash in the blockchain

    It's probably easiest if we point out which transaction we've included our hash in. This is the txid:

    `586783e17fadace136365490fd83ba59390ca55e7205ee74fbc7db2daa012ad3`

    You can try to look it up on a blockexplorer such as `blockchair.com`.

2   Verify the SHA-256 hash

    The message should encode to the the same hash that's included in the blockchain.

3   Lookup the timestamp

    According to Blockchair the transaction was included in a block mined 20:17 September 15, 2019 (UTC). Verifying the timestamp with other blockexplorers or full nodes is left as an exercise to the reader, just be cautious of timezone differences.

We now have a trusted timestamp for our message, backed by math instead of trust.

Chapter 22
Uncensorable Twitter
Permanent and uncensorable messages

*When you tear out a man's tongue, you are not proving him a liar,
you're only telling the world that you fear what he might say.*

Tyrion Lannister, "A Clash of Kings"

Another use for embeddable data in a cryptocurrency is a Twitter clone where messages are included into transactions, and are therefore uncensorable. One example is memo.cash which embeds data into the Bitcoin Cash blockchain. Like Twitter it only supports fairly short messages:

memo hitting over 1k regularly last days - https://memo.cash/charts

homopit[350]

https://youtu.be/5q3kDx1USPM

CashBack[351]

I can feel the anticipation rising...

Vidteks[352]

Images or videos aren't actually embedded but reference outside services. See their protocol[353] if you want more details.

Bitcoin Cash is a good option because it has low fees and a larger OP_RETURN limit, making it a cheap and easy base for a messaging platform.

Memo could potentially extend their message length from the current 217 character limit by chaining transactions as described before (p.155).

Not a purely good thing

For someone who is a big privacy supporter and who thinks the *Right to be forgotten* (the ability to remove yourself from the internet) is really important I'm quite conflicted. On the one hand, this tech can be used for good—as we'll get into later—but it might also be a bad idea for other reasons.

If this kind of social network becomes popular, you may end up in a position where you cannot delete your posts and really embarrass yourself. For example if you drunkenly post really negative opinions about your boss, there's no way to take that back.

People have gotten fired for things they post on social media—and they're not always drunk. Turns out employers, both current and potential future ones, do routinely check out social media and use it to decide if they will fire or hire you.

And what if someone posts something about you? I sometimes feel lucky I didn't grow up in the modern age, with the horrible cyber-bullying you hear about, but imagine if someone posts a degrading video of you? Today we might be able to get Facebook or someone to remove it, but if you base your social network on a cryptocurrency... No such luck.

An uncensorable forum

At the same time, there's something compelling about the idea of having a forum where your messages cannot be censored.

Another big issue, which I foresee as one of the biggest unsolved challenges of the internet age, is "intellectual DDOS". It basically tries to throw so much disinformation at you so cannot tell what's right and what's wrong. It's a denial-of-service attack which works by the fact that it's much easier to produce bullshit than to counter it.

In other words, "fake news". (Both actual fake news and the dismissal of real news is a form of DDOS on our minds.)

We've seen examples of censorship in *Uncensorable donations* (p.64), so let's not repeat ourselves too much. A quick example is that Twitter is completely censored in China, and you might get arrested if you bypass their internet-wide block of it.

A Twitter-like service based on a cryptocurrency does not have these problems. As we saw before, this kind of service is uncensorable, and there's no company or service China could put pressure on to get inconvenient content removed. Therefore we're free to discuss China's human rights abuses (like their forced organ harvesting[354]) and the information can never truly be removed.

Uncorrupted history

> Who controls the past controls the future. Who controls the present controls the past.
>
> George Orwell, *1984*[Orw49]

Have you heard about the barbarians? They're primitive and uncivilized humans who were more beast than man. Some say they're too stupid to farm and they live to fight. There's nobody more savage and if they catch you they will bathe in your blood...

Except those are exaggerated rumors, twisted by the passage of time. The Romans often liked to spread these kinds of rumors for propaganda purposes. If a Roman general came back from a successful campaign he might want to play up his opponent to make his feat bigger. As the saying goes: "history is written by the victors".

You can also actively rewrite the history, which is one of the main themes of the book *1984*[Orw49] (which I quote often, because I love it so much). The idea is that you can get away with anything, because you erase it in hindsight. Other times, you might deny events because they don't fit your world-view or your bias, which can happen subconsciously. There are many historic examples—some crazier than others[355]. Maybe you know about the holocaust denials or the moon landing skeptics? Even closer in time is how Bush declares victory in Iraq[356], despite there being no real victory there.

A nice example of the one-sided history is the Roman war against the Celts. We have a great recounting from the Roman general Julius Caesar—but nothing else.

Julius Caesar's "The Gallic Wars" is supposedly very good, but I'm content with Hardcore History's **fantastic** 6 hour episode *The Celtic Holocaust*[357].

I wonder what history would look like if we had an uncorrupted version of it? If we had access to several different unaltered versions of a story? What if we had access to an easily searchable Twitter-style feed—permanent and uncensorable—available to all?

With cryptocurrencies, we just might have that, for better or worse...

Chapter 23

Provably fair gambling
Gambling where you cannot cheat the odds

There's a sucker born every minute.

Attributed to Michael Cassius McDonald

I love the movie *Ocean's Eleven (2011)*. I've a fascination for heists and how they in the movie win against the house in various gambles—by cheating, of course. They hack the slot machines, they cheat in card games and they control the dice in craps like magicians. And they do it with style.

Cheating is possible in the real world, as well. For example you could do a coin toss, but with a coin with heads on both sides. Or a coin that's heavier on one side, making the odds 55% and 45%. Don't let the numbers fool you—this is a huge difference compared to a 50/50 gamble.

But it's hard to verify that a gamble is fair. With a coin, you *might* be able to feel it, and specialized anti-cheating machines might be able to measure dice, but you can never be sure. Gambling on the internet is a whole other can of worms, where you're often left trusting that the site isn't screwing you over.

With cryptocurrencies, we can devise a scheme where gambling is provably fair. We can create a gambling site where users are sure the bets are fair—with mathematical certainty—and without a trusted third-party facilitating the bets.

There was a big poker scandal several years ago where it was discovered that Ultimate Bet and Absolute Poker cheated in online poker. They were discovered by people who noticed certain users who had "abnormally high winning statistics". Turns out they were using a superuser account that could see all the cards.[358]

Seeds and pseudo-random generators

To understand how the gambling scheme I'll describe works, first it's important to understand *pseudo-random generators*. Take this random sequence for example:

```
1 2 2 9 0 3 3 8 5 9 …
```

The important thing about it is that you cannot predict what number comes next. That's why it's *random*.

But if we want to flip a coin, and verify how it was flipped without looking at it, how could we do that? It's simple—just flip it again in **exactly** the same way as you did before, and it should land exactly like it did before. (I didn't say it was easy!)

With a pseudo-random generator, that's what we can do. We give it a *seed*, which will produce a sequence that's unpredictable, except that when given the same seed it will always produce the same sequence. For example:

```
seed 7:   5 2 6 0 1 8 1 5 9 0 …
seed 13:  4 4 2 3 2 3 2 2 1 8 …
```

A pseudo-random generator can produce a sequence of numbers, a number of coin tosses or even generate the whole world in Minecraft.

They even call it a "seed" in Minecraft. There are many "Minecraft best seeds lists" out there, with seeds that generate some pretty impressive worlds. You do need to take care which version of Minecraft you're using, as the world generation can differ between versions.

This is also true for pseudo-random generators, where different generators will produce different results.

A simple provably fair gambling scheme

Here's a simple scheme that allows us to prove that a gamble has happened, what the results were and how to verify if it was fair.

Our gambling algorithm is simple. We'll concatenate the casino's seed with the player's seed and use it to initialize a pseudo-random generator, which will flip a coin to pick the winner. Here's a simple Python 3 script that does this for us:

```python
import random

casino_seed = input("Please enter the casino seed: ")
player_seed = input("Please enter the player seed: ")
our_seed = casino_seed + player_seed

print("Using seed:", our_seed)
random.seed(our_seed)

print("The winner is:", random.choice(["casino", "player"]))
```

Importantly, the casino should give out the seed encoded with a *cryptographic hash function* (p.202), otherwise the player can just pick the winning seed and there would be no gamble. When the player has sent their seed to the casino, the bet has been made, and the casino reveals their seed (which we can verify with the hashed value) and we know who won and who lost.

Concretely a game could play out like this:

1   The casino sends the player the seed, encoded with SHA-256:

    `4b227777d4dd1fc61c6f884f48641d02b4d121d3fd328cb08b5531fcacdabf8a`

2   The player sends their seed 1 to the casino

3   The casino says they won, and reveals that their seed was 4

To prove that the bet was made, the above interactions should be signed by both parties, complete with timestamps. It doesn't even have to be on a blockchain, just having a public key connected to their identity is enough. As long as either party has the signed messages, it's all good.

Now the player would like to verify that they did in fact lose:

1   First we verify that the casino indeed used the seed 4

    `echo -n "4" | sha256sum`

    Giving us the SHA-256 hash:

    `4b227777d4dd1fc61c6f884f48641d02b4d121d3fd328cb08b5531fcacdabf8a`

    Which matches the hash the casino gave out before the bet.

2   Then we can use the Python script to verify the gamble:

    ```
    Please enter the casino seed: 4
    Please enter the player seed: 1
    Using seed: 41
    The winner is: casino
    ```

It checks out; the casino won fair and square.

Let's see what we can prove, if either party aborts the bet.

If the player stops at 1, after having received the encoded seed, the bet simply never happens.

If the casino stops at 2, after the player has sent their seed to the casino, the bet should be considered played out. Here the casino knows the outcome, but hasn't told the player yet. The player can now prove they entered a bet with the casino, and on what terms.

If the casino doesn't reveal their seed at step 3, then the casino has most likely lost, and we should treat it like the casino is trying to cheat.

After step 3, there's proof that they entered the bet and what the outcome was. If the casino refuses to pay a winner, there's irrefutable proof that they in fact won the bet.

Limits to this scheme

There are limits to the simple toy example I've described:

- Seeds need to be longer

  A seed like 4 is far too simple. We'd need a much longer seed for the game to be secure. Maybe something like 65654687731080707945?

- Multiplayer games are more complex

  This scheme works fine for simple single player games, like flipping a coin. But if we wanted to create a provably fair poker game the implementation would be more complex, but it would still be possible.

- Only for digitally randomized gambles

  It's not possible to bet on real life events, like the outcome of an ice hockey game, without relying on a trusted third-party to announce the result of the game (often called an Oracle).

Here we'd have to encrypt your cards and hide them from other players, but they still need to be able to verify that they were dealt out correctly after the fact.

I leave the implementation details as an exercise for the reader.

How does this relate to cryptocurrencies?

Until now, nothing I've described requires a cryptocurrency (and if you don't need it, you shouldn't use it). So why bring it up in a book about cryptocurrencies?

By embedding the messages (p.155) between the casino and the player on the blockchain, we get a permanent record of all gambles that take place. It would be proof of dishonest behaviour and act as a reputation boost for honest casinos.

But we can go further. The biggest issue with our simple scheme is that the casinos can still decide not to pay. There's nothing forcing them to pay the players if they win big—they could just take the money and run.

With smart contracts, on a cryptocurrency with a powerful scripting language like Ethereum, we might enforce the payment as well. In our example when accepting the bet, both the casino and the player must lock up their funds in a smart contract that will play out the bet (like in the Python script) and send the funds to the winner. This removes the risk of the casino refusing to pay out if you manage to win, as it's enforced by the smart contract.

You can also include a timeout to return the funds and cancel the bet if the Oracle doesn't take any action. Or allow the player and casino to cancel the bet and return all funds, if they both agree.

You can also improve the state of sports betting. A smart contract can give an Oracle the power to transfer the money of a gamble to the winner—but it's only allowed to send it to either the player or the casino, so the Oracle cannot steal the money. This is good if you can trust the Oracle to call the result of a game, but you don't trust them to hold your money.

In this way cryptocurrencies can drastically reduce the risk of being cheated when we gamble.

Chapter 24

Tokens

Cryptocurrencies with centrally managed supply

The moment you think you got it figured, you're wrong.

Shooter (2007)

One of the most important properties that let cryptocurrencies function well as money is the limited supply. If someone was allowed to print coins from thin air, it would be very poor money and would essentially be worthless.

But would they really be completely useless? These cryptocurrency-like things are called *tokens*, and they aren't that useless. In this chapter, we'll look at how they can enable more accessible fund raising, improve gift cards or enable peer-to-peer derivative trading.

What are tokens?

Tokens are essentially cryptocurrencies, except there's a single entity with the power to create coins. Tokens retain the other useful properties of cryptocurrencies (p.5) such as counterfeit resistance, transaction irreversibility and double spend protection (p.13).

They achieve this by operating on top of an existing cryptocurrency. You might think of it as the issuer marking some coins with additional information, specifying what kind of token they are. (Technically tokens can be implemented in many different ways, but this is the core idea.)

Some properties are weakened when the value of tokens come from a central party.

Consider a gift card token for example. If the company backing the gift card goes bankrupt or if the company declares that the tokens cannot be redeemed, they're now useless.

The most popular class of tokens are probably the *ERC20 tokens*, implemented on top of Ethereum. For example USD Coin, Coinbase's stablecoin backed 1-to-1 by USD, is an ERC20 token. The Binance Coin, used for the bonus system on the cryptocurrency exchange Binance, is another.

Initial coin offering

The most famous—or infamous—use of tokens is for an *Initial Coin Offering (ICO)*. It's similar to an *Initial Public Offering (IPO)*, which aims to raise funds for companies or projects. In return for giving them money you'll receive a token as a sign of participation. ICOs are mostly unregulated and are easy for anyone to participate in.

One of the benefit of ICOs is that they're very easy to setup, and with the right tools it can be done in a few seconds. This is also a downside as there are countless of ICOs that function only as pyramid schemes with the only purpose of finding greater fools to dump on.

Although ICOs are mostly associated with scams (and rightfully so I'd say) there might be some usefulness here. What you're really doing is donating money to a cause you believe in, and hope you'll get a good outcome.

Does it sound insane? That's really no different from how *Kickstarter* works, where it's very popular to pledge money for an interesting board game project and you wait for months or years and hope you'll get something in return.

Why would you want a token for this? The benefit would be that anyone, anywhere, could participate and that participation could be done anonymously. And it all takes place on a platform where you have a guarantee that you can sell your token if you lose faith in the project (since properly implemented not even the issuer can prevent token transactions).

You could implement tokens on other cryptocurrencies as well. The Omni Layer is for example an extension network built on Bitcoin that supports tokens. The difference is that Ethereum's ERC20 tokens are miner validated, while Omni uses a different consensus mechanism.

ICOs are classified as securities and the Securities and Exchange Commission (SEC) has intervened on a number of occasions.

You might still say it sounds insane, but just realize Kickstarter is very popular and it mostly works out well. (At least for board games, which I'm most familiar with.)

Flipstarter is a platform that improves on Kickstarter by enforcing payments via smart contracts, cutting out the third-party from the picture. The money is automatically transferred when the funding goal has been reached, but otherwise it never leaves the pledger's wallet.[360]

It might be hard to claim anonymity if you want someone to send a board game to you, but it's relevant if you're expecting returns in cryptocurrencies or other digital goods.

Gift cards

People use gift cards all the time, but they're not always that great. How do you verify that they're valid, and haven't already been used? How do you do that in stores, when you're choosing which one to buy, and how do you verify digital gift cards?

For example, let's say you walk into a store and want to buy a gift card. How do you know it's not fake, or haven't been used? Luckily there's a code on the gift card, which you can enter into a website to verify if it's still valid. Okay! It's valid, so you buy it and walk out the store.

Unfortunately for you, the store clerk has already written down the gift card code, and shortly after you leave the store he decides to use it up, making your gift card useless. Physical gift cards, the one you hand in to a store when you use them up, don't really have this problem, but this is unsolved for digital gift cards.

This problem, of how to transfer ownership of a code, is really the same double spending problem that cryptocurrencies pioneered a solution for. And tokens inherit this property, allowing you to buy a token based gift card and be absolutely sure that it's unspent and that you're the only one who can spend it.

Physical gift cards can have problems with counterfeiting, which is also something cryptocurrencies completely solve.

Derivatives

It's quite difficult for us humans to truly understand very big numbers, because we don't have anything to relate them to. For example, what's the difference between $1 billion and $1 trillion? I know that the latter is 1000 times more, but that's just a number and I have difficulties to truly understand how large the difference is.

I think visualizations can help us compare large amounts like these, so here's one where the small box ▪ corresponds to $100 billion and the big box ■ corresponds to $1 trillion. (Although they may look small, the amounts are still *huge*.)

Jeff Bezos, the richest man in the world, is worth a staggering **$117.5 billion**[361]. (2019)

Around 190,040 tonnes of gold has been mined in the world[362]. At a spot price of $1,582.30/oz, or $50,872.09/kg, it would be worth around **$9.7 trillion**[363]. (2020-01-28)

All the money in the world, both physical and digital locked up with banks, is worth around **$90 trillion**[365]. (2017)

It's quite difficult to pinpoint the value of derivatives correctly. I've found a low end estimate at **$544 trillion** and a high end at **$1.2 quadrillion** (or $1,200 trillion).[366] (2017)

One quadrillion! As a non-native English speaker I hadn't even encountered "quadrillion" before, and to me it sounds like a made-up number found in Donald Duck.

There's been a lot of excitement around Bitcoin's meteoric rise in valuation. But compared to the really big markets Bitcoin's marketcap of **$164 billion**[364] isn't that impressive. (2020-01-28)

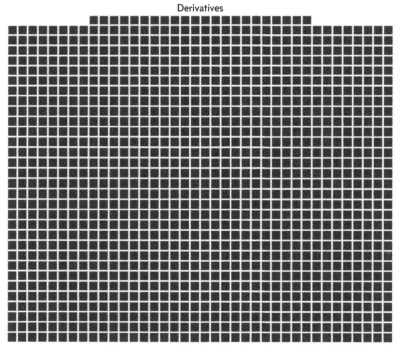

I bring this up just to say one thing: the value of derivatives is absolutely huge. Money, which makes the world go around, is dwarfed by the value of derivatives.

But what are derivatives?

In short, they're a bet on the value of something. A derivative is a contract that derives its price from fluctuations of the underlying asset. This commonly include bets on stocks, bonds, currencies and commodities. Have you heard about futures, forwards, swaps and options? They're all different types of derivatives.[359]

We've already seen how cryptocurrencies can improve currencies, but other types of derivatives might also find some benefit from being based on cryptocurrency tokens.

Take stock trading, for example. They're done through a stock exchange and intermediaries that manage the exchange. This is required because — like the problem with gift cards — there's no way to transfer ownership in a secure way. But now there is; with tokens you could create a decentralized derivative market and trade them directly between two people, without the need for an intermediary to manage the trade.

Similar to how cryptocurrencies can save fees by cutting out payment processors from digital purchases, there's financial gain here too.

If you wanted to, you could also create digital *bearer shares*, where the share of a security is given to whoever controls a specific token. (With typical bearer shares control is given to whoever holds a certain piece of paper.) They would protect the owners' anonymity, since their identity is never recorded or required, and could be used to for example create a company controlled by anonymous people.

I'm not suggesting that all derivatives should just use tokens, in many cases this wouldn't make sense and would only add inefficiencies to the system. But even if there's just a very small fraction of derivatives that could benefit, due to the sheer size of the derivative market, tokens could still bring a lot of value.

Chapter 25
Improved voting
A verifiable and resilient voting system

*Nobody is in favor of the power going down. Nobody is in favor of all
cell phones not working. But an election? There are sides. Half of the
country will want the result to stand and half the country will want the
result overturned; they'll decide on their course of action based on the
result, not based on what's right.*

Bruce Schneier, 80,000 Hours podcast[367]

In this chapter, we'll look at some of the problems with the way we vote
and how we might use cryptocurrencies (or "the blockchain") to make an
improved voting scheme.

I say they *might* help because it's not a use-case where I know they will
provide value; it's still unclear how much benefit it would bring and blockchain voting may even be a fundamentally bad idea. But as I'll argue, there
are some very good properties it can provide, so the idea isn't so bad it can
be thrown out directly.

If you're skeptical then don't worry—I'm not
entirely convinced of this use-case either.
I had written the chapter and was going to
throw it away, but in the end I decided to
keep it. If anything I hope the discussion is
interesting.

Bush v. Gore

But why do we talk about improving voting? What's the problem with the way we vote? Hasn't voting on paper and having people count them worked great for us so far?

Firstly, we shouldn't avoid looking for improvements just because the "old way" worked well. If so then we wouldn't have faster cars, bigger TV-screens or more effective medicine—the previous versions already worked well enough. There's always value in making something *better*.

But there are also serious problems with our voting system. A great example of some of them is the United States presidential election of 2000, where George W. Bush edged out Al Gore in a historically close election—at least according to Britannica[368], which I use as a source for the events.

I find it interesting that Gore got more total votes, but won fewer states, so he ended up losing the election.

To say that the election was close does it a disservice. After a day full of uncertainty, where Gore had called Bush to concede the election just to withdraw it later, it was clear Florida would be the decider. Bush appeared to have won in Florida with a margin of roughly 0.01%—a couple of hundred votes out of six million votes. This was so close that a machine recount was made, which showed that Bush had indeed won with only 327 votes!

Here we need to realize that the machines aren't computers that just count the votes digitally. They're machines that take the ballots, examines them and tries to figure out what vote is marked (or punched) on the ballot.

Then there's the infamous Butterfly Ballot disaster. Palm Beach County used a ballot design that was so bad that perhaps more than 20,000 voters voted for the wrong candidate or mistakenly voted for multiple candidates.[375]

The problem here is that some of the ballots weren't in good condition. Some ballots weren't punched through completely (so the machines couldn't detect the votes), others had voted for the same office multiple times or were incomplete in other ways. With the election being so close it's easy to see that these votes could very well change the outcome. Therefore the Florida Supreme Court ruled that these questionable ballots should be recounted by hand.

Because the stakes were fairly high (an understatement I know) there was a ton of legal action, and charges of conflict of interest were pushed by both parties. At the end the U.S. Supreme Court overturned the Florida decision and put a stop to the recounting, awarded Florida's votes to Bush and that no recount could be held in time.

So in the end the Supreme Court decided to end the election and might have changed the outcome in the process. That's a pretty big failure of the voting system right there.

The problems with paper voting

One of the issues with the U.S. election is that there are essentially only two parties and the winner of the election takes it all. Therefore such a small difference as a couple of hundred votes did have a huge impact. If Al Gore had won, our world might have looked completely different today.

But we also saw some problems that are caused by using paper votes:

- Inexact vote counting

  Humans counting votes will inevitably have a margin of error, but so will these voting machines that cannot see what we humans can.

- Counting votes is slow

  Counting, and recounting, can take weeks and at the end of the 2000 U.S. presidential election it would supposedly take too long so the human recount was skipped.

- Invalid ballots

  What if you accidentally leave a mark on an unintended place on your vote? Or if you don't leave a big enough mark? Now your vote might not count.

- Corruption

  Why was a human recount ordered and why was it thrown out? Who decides if a questionable ballot is invalid or not? These are all human decisions that are vulnerable to corruption (or incompetence).

I refer to voting with physical ballots as "paper voting", but the exact way we vote can differ. In the U.S. they use punchcards where you create a hole next to who you want to vote for, while in Sweden we select a piece of paper corresponding to the party we want to vote for. In other cases you might use a pen to leave a mark or write who you want to vote for.

The problems with electronic voting

In order to address some of the problems with paper voting, electronic voting is growing in popularity. The benefits are clear; you avoid the problem with questionable ballots and vote counting is precise and instant. But there are significant drawbacks that make them a "very bad idea"[369]:

- Lack of transparency

  How do you know that your vote has been counted correctly? That the machine didn't switch it out for some other vote? An electronic voting machine is largely a black box, one we're not sure how it works so we just hope it does the right thing.

- Hacking

  It's much easier to hack electronic voting machines—to change votes from Clinton to Trump for example[370]—than to hack paper voting. With paper voting you'd have to have people on site to exchange paper votes for new paper votes, but hacking a computer can be done from the other side of the world.

There's a lot of focus on "hackers" being a problem, but there are less nefarious problems too. For instance the app used to tabulate votes during the Iowa caucuses in 2020 was "inadequately tested"[376]. It simply didn't work properly, which is always a risk with software.

- Corruption

  In the same way hacking is a worry, so is corruption. If you want to influence votes all you'd have to do is switch out or reprogram the voting machine, and after that nobody would notice. With paper voting it's harder since there are many more constantly watching what happens to the votes, so you'd have to bribe more people to get away with it.

- Privacy concerns

  Paper voting preserves your privacy very well. You walk behind a screen, select a paper and put it a box with hundreds of other papers, making it basically impossible to trace that one vote back to you. Simple and very effective.

  Not so with electronic voting[371]. The voting machine needs to verify your identity some way and computers can—and therefore we must assume they will—record everything that happens on it. This is information that a hacker or election worker could gain access to, and would be able to see exactly who you voted for.

  Consider for example what would happen if the future government becomes corrupt. Like if a Nazi-like party comes to power and they decide to punish those who didn't vote for them in the election?

- Understandability

  It's easy to explain how paper voting works; you just count the pieces of paper and tally up which name occurs the most. It's much more difficult to explain how electronic voting works and what makes it trustworthy.

  How does it for example prevent someone from voting twice? With paper voting there are people who check that you're only placing a single vote in the box, but how does the computer do that? How do you know the computer counted your vote correctly? And how will the election worker know that connecting a USB memory stick into the voting machine opens it up for attacks?

  This is a general problem with technology, as people are often too trusting of them. We think they always do the right thing, but we underestimate the risk for faults or vulnerabilities in them. Just take self-driving cars as an example; they're still very much unsafe—both for passangers and pedestrians—but people don't seem to realize it.

  Understandability is important because people have to trust their election to be fair. If they don't trust their votes being counted correctly, then they can't trust the outcome of the election either.

For a convincing case against electronic voting, I recommend Jennifer Cohn's article *America's Electronic Voting System is Corrupted to the Core*[372]. On the other hand many of these problems can be mitigated, see the paper *Public Evidence from Secret Ballots*[373] for a good rundown.

In 2015 a database on the web had personal information on registered U.S. voters, 191 million in total. It contained your full name, home address, mailing address, phone number, date of birth and whether or not you voted in any election back to 2000.[377]

And it wasn't even a hack. The database was just lying there, open for anyone to read. It's like if someone had left a paper in the middle of the library, available to anyone who happened to walk by.[378]

With electronic voting this database might've also contained who you voted for.

A blockchain voting system

As an alternative I'll try to present a high level description of a blockchain voting scheme, which have some very good and beneficial properties:

+ Transparent

  The system is public so anyone can verify that it works like it's supposed to, which obstructs corruption and hacking. There's still trust here, trust that *someone* will audit the scheme, but it's a big step up from other black box voting systems where nobody can tell what's going on.

"Don't trust, verify." is a popular saying in the cryptocurrency sphere. A prerequisite is to have an open system that you can verify.

+ Verifiable

  Anyone can verify the integrity of the voting result. It can with certainty answer questions like:

  - Did my vote get counted?
  - Did it get counted correctly?
  - How many votes were given out in total?
  - How many votes were cast?
  - What was the outcome?

  If you happened to use a corrupt voting machine that changed your vote from Hillary to Trump, you could use another device and see that's what happened. You can also be sure that your vote was counted correctly, or if you didn't vote that it wasn't included and you can verify yourself that all votes were tallied correctly. In this scheme vote counting is alway verifiably correct.

+ No questionable votes

  The system will automatically reject invalid votes, so you cannot send a vote voting for multiple candidates for example. Either your vote is valid or it's not, which you can always verify when you vote. (Practically this would be done automatically by whatever voting program you use, radically reducing the risk for errors.)

+ Instant vote counting

  Because it's a form of electronic voting, votes can be counted instantly and you get real-time updates as the votes come in.

Even if possible, is it desirable to get a real-time update of voting? Couldn't that affect the election in a bad way?

+ Vote anywhere

  It's possible to set it up so you can vote with your mobile phone, from the other side of the world. This would allow for *direct democracy* where people can vote on policy directly, with very minor overhead.

+ Harder to disrupt

  Because the system only relies on a central party for the initial vote setup, and after that the voting is carried out by independent nodes in the network, it's more resilient against disruptions than a centralized scheme.

The scheme is similar to tokens that we discussed in the previous chapter (p.173). Here the issuer is the government, who still needs a way to identify voters and to give them a token (a single vote). The process would be similar to how it works today, where people have their identification verified by voting officials when they go to vote.

With the tokens distributed, you could cast a vote by sending them to predetermined addresses to cast your vote. For example if you want to vote for Trump, you send it to the Trump address. If you want to vote for Hillary, you send it to the Hillary address. And if you don't want to vote you don't do anything.

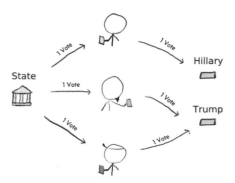

Each arrow corresponds to a token transaction and the "Hillary" and "Trump" boxes are addresses. The state is responsible for issuing the voting tokens to the voters and the voters in turn send them to the address they want to vote for. In this example Hillary got 1 vote and Trump got 2, and everyone voted.

These transactions work like cryptocurrency transactions, so you cannot counterfeit them or manufacture votes from thin air. Well, the state could issue new votes, but everyone can see exactly how many votes they give out, so if they give out more votes than eligible voters in the country... You know something is wrong.

It's easy to count the votes—just check how much each address holds. It's also easy for you to see that your vote has arrived to the correct voting address, and if it did you know your vote will count.

While I focus on government elections, voting is useful in other contexts too, for example shareholder voting or votes in a leaderless organization. (In my head I see a bunch of people sitting around a table, shrouded in shadows, voting on who to kill.)

It's easy to give multiple options. For example if you want to be able to differentiate between those who don't care, and those who want to vote but not any candidate, just have an additional "blank" address voters can send to.

Then how do you know that the votes are given out correctly and that the state distributes them fairly? The same way it works today—the voters are holding the state accountable.

Of course this this means that this voting scheme cannot fix voting in highly corrupt countries—only magic can do that.

Unsolved problems

The scheme I've presented is simple—too simple. There are many problems with it, some that are solvable but others that I don't have an answer to.

- Privacy

  The big flaw is the poor privacy. If you can connect token issuance with your identification—which the government will be able to do—then they can see who you voted for. It has the same privacy problem that Bitcoin has, except it's even worse as there's always a direct link between you and your address.

  The solution would be to obscure the coin history between issuance of the token and when you cast your vote. We could use the obfuscation techniques, described in the privacy and fungibility part of the appendix (p.193), to accomplish this.

  Imagine for example if all voters had to go through a mixing state, where people trade a vote for another vote. If done correctly the state can't connect the final votes to the identities, while still be sure the right people had the ability to vote.

  It's important to note that the privacy scheme has very high requirements. It's not enough that it seems to be good today, it has to hold up in 10, 20 or maybe even 100 years from now.

- Key delivery

  This whole scheme rests on the ability and the trust that the state can somehow distribute votes fairly and correctly. I don't think the trust issue is different from how it works today, but there many details on how votes are distributed that needs to be ironed out.

  I do think it's a problem that can be solved. For example in Sweden we have BankID, an electronic citizen identification solution, that we use to file our taxes, login to banks and many other things. It's really like an electronic identification card that could in theory be used to authenticate electronic votes as well.

  BankID is distributed by banks and not by the state, but in principle there's no reason why a similar system couldn't be.

- Stealing votes

  While the system itself could of course be hacked (anything could theoretically be broken), I see stealing individual votes as a bigger problem. For example if voting should be carried out on mobile phones, what if some malware has infected your phone and decides to change your vote? Or if a hacker can hack the voting app you use?

  One possible solution might be for people to change their votes before the voting is over, so they could verify their vote on another phone or computer, and do something about it if something has gone wrong. But this is problematic in other ways, like allowing you to change your vote if you see the vote isn't going your way.

– Vote buying

Another concern is that it might make buying and selling votes easier. With paper voting there's no easy way to prove you voted one way (other than bringing a camera with you and record your actions).

But with this scheme you can with 100% certainty prove who you voted for. If you wanted to you could also give your vote to someone else, or they might try to coerce you to do so.

– Understandability

If electronic voting was hard for people to understand and accept, this wouldn't be any easier. If anything "blockchain voting" is even harder to understand, especially as many technologically proficient people still regard the blockchain as a panacea that can solve any problem.

Why a blockchain?

The big question to ask is why would we want voting on a blockchain anyway? Why would we want to record our votes on a permanent database, when we might even want to allow people to change their votes before the voting is over? Why design a voting a scheme on an extremely inefficient system—that all cryptocurrencies and blockchain applications are?

As pointed out in the paper *Public Evidence from Secret Ballots*[374] it's possible to create an end-to-end verifiable electronic voting scheme even without the blockchain—which isn't surprising since the blockchain is just a database. They also say that because we already trust a central entity to give out the voting privileges, we can just trust them to publish a ledger of the events, making the blockchain obsolete.

They say a lot of other things too, and I recommend you read the paper as it goes through a lot of the difficulties and possible solutions with voting systems. It's not as simple as I may have led you to believe.

They're right that trust isn't an issue, since data will be independently verified for correctness anyway, but I don't agree that it makes a blockchain useless. A fault tolerant system—such as a blockchain—is inherently more difficult to disrupt. Because anyone can help collect, distribute and verify votes it doesn't matter if the government's servers gets overloaded in a *Denial of Service (DoS)* attack—as long as people have internet access the voting process will be uninterrupted.

While there are benefits to blockchain voting, there are many problems we need to solve first, with the privacy problem being the most important. And it's possible that when all things are considered, maybe paper voting is best after all.

Vote buying, or vote coercion, is really an unsolvable problem. Even if you have on-site voting with perfect secrecy, it's still vulnerable to people bringing a hidden camera that records the voting process.

The best we can do is reduce the target surface, and for an electronic voting scheme you'd want the ability to verify that your vote was counted correctly, but without you being able to prove how you voted.

Then again if we want a publicly verifiable voting system, where all data is publicly available, we must assume it will also exist forever. (On a related note this is the assumption we all should make when we interact with social media. The internet remembers.)

Part VII

Appendix
What didn't fit elsewhere

Chapter 26
The Bitcoin white paper
What started it all

A purely peer-to-peer version of electronic cash would allow online payments to be sent directly from one party to another without going through a financial institution. Digital signatures provide part of the solution, but the mainbenefits are lost if a trusted third party is still required to prevent double-spending.

Satoshi Nakamoto, "Bitcoin: A Peer-to-Peer Electronic Cash System"

The white paper is surprisingly easy to read and I highly recommend you read it[379]. If you prefer a simplified explanation with annotations I can recommend the beginner's guide on bitcoin.com[380] or if you would rather have it in podcast form I liked the one BitcoinNews.com made the 5th November 2018[381].

Note that the white paper was created in 2008 and some terminology and implementation details have changed. For example nodes in the paper refer to mining nodes, while today most people run nodes but don't mine. But the high level description is just as true today more than 10 years later.

Alterations

I'm sad I have to include this but there have been suggestions to alter the white paper hosted on bitcoin.org[382]. Rewriting an academic paper and rewriting Bitcoin's history for personal business interests is of course completely unacceptable, but here we are.

Therefore you might want to make sure you're reading the original unaltered white paper. There are those who try to keep track of the different versions found online[383] but it's always best to do it yourself. You can compare the PDF's SHA-256 hash with this:

```
b1674191a88ec5cdd733e4240a81803105dc412d6c6708d53ab94fc248f4f553
```

If you want to go even further the white paper is also embedded in the blockchain which guarantees nobody can change it. Instructions available on stackexchange[384].

Chapter 27
Challenges for cryptocurrencies
Large unsolved problems with cryptocurrencies

I have not failed. I've just found 10,000 ways that won't work.

Thomas A. Edison

While cryptocurrencies do some things very well, there are several hard unsolved problems with cryptocurrencies. For example:

- Adoption (p.192)
- Privacy and fungibility (p.193)
- Scalability (p.195)
- Energy usage (p.197)

Which I'll describe in more detail in this chapter.

Adoption

While this analogy might sound strange, money has an important similarity to social networks like Facebook, Twitter or Reddit: almost all their value come from them being used by others.

This is called the *network effect*, and Wikipedia has a succinct way to describe it[385]:

> When a network effect is present, the value of a product or service increases according to the number of others using it.

Wikipedia

You can have the best website in the world—beautiful, lightning fast and with all the features you could ever need—but if nobody's using it it's a worthless social network. Conversely you can have a shitty website, but it doesn't matter as long as many people use it. A beautiful example of such a site is Twitter, which has an absolutely atrocious user interface, but it's hugely valuable because so many people are invested in the platform.

I find Twitter's user experience so bad I can't stand to read, yet alone use it.

Another bad example is Reddit's new design, but luckily you still access the old design at old.reddit.com. I fear for the day when that option is removed.

The network effect is directly correlated to the functions of money: a medium of exchange, a unit of account and a store of value (p.36). If more people use a currency, the better it'll function as money, and the fewer that use it the worse it'll be.

Low adoption means it's difficult to both accept and pay with cryptocurrencies. It even compromises censorship-resistance, as you're forced through exchanges that can censor you instead of being able to spend cryptocurrencies directly. You might also partially attribute market immaturity to low adoption, as smaller markets are easier to manipulate and are more volatile.

As you might see, there's a circular reasoning here:

> I don't pay with cryptocurrencies because nobody accepts them.

and

> I don't accept cryptocurrencies because nobody pays with them.

This is a tough cycle to break, which explains why cryptocurrencies—despite their many strengths—aren't used more than they are.

It's fair to say that we shouldn't focus on adoption before we've solved the fundamental technical issues, as if we push too hard too soon the push back could be enormous, but it doesn't change the fact that adoption is the most important issue.

For these reasons I think the lack of adoption is the biggest problem cryptocurrencies face—both in difficulty and in importance—and it's much larger than the other issues we'll see later in this chapter.

Privacy and fungibility

Bitcoin, like most cryptocurrencies, uses a public ledger where all transactions and addresses are public. We might say that Bitcoin is *pseudo-anonymous*: while you can see all transactions and addresses, you don't know who owns an address. But if you know someone's address, for example if they sent money to you, you can then trace all past and future transactions moving through that address:

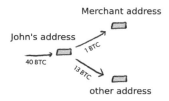

After the merchant receives a payment from John, the merchant can see that John has sent 13 BTC to another address, out of an initial 40 BTC.

John appears to be quite rich.

It's possible to trace coins further back in history. Here we see that John's coins come from a hacked exchange, whose address is known. It might mean John is the hacker or, more probably, that John has received *tainted* coins (coins associated with illegal behavior).

You can explore the Bitcoin blockchain, and see all transactions and addresses, on a blockchain explorer such as `blockchair.com`.

In an attempt to make Bitcoin more private "mixing" services such as CoinJoin can be used. They work by mixing together your coins with the coins of others, in an attempt to obscure where the coins are coming from:

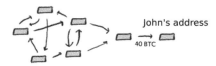

A mixing service makes several addresses send to each other, in order to obfuscate the history. Although not shown here, because it would be too messy, all addresses and amounts are still visible.

They're not perfect because you can still have a transaction graph, and you might be able to figure out where the coins originated from anyway.

For example, it's possible to build a list of the Bitcoin addresses with the most coins[395] and to monitor them to see when they send or receive coins.

There are also companies like Chainalysis that work to track your cryptocurrency assets and to analyze your financial activity.

Some who were tired of the moniker "privacy coins", given to coins that protect your privacy, have started referring to cryptocurrencies with a transparent blockchain as "surveillance coins".

I personally don't like either of them. They feel too tribal to me, like slurs used to belittle "the others".

Another approach is used by the shielded transactions of ZCash[386], where all information is hidden by *zero-knowledge-proofs:*

Shielded transactions hide both addresses and amount of transactions, but normal transactions still have their details visible.

Both mixing and the shielded transactions in ZCash has a major problem: people need to actively choose to use them. This is annoying for users but it's also bad for privacy[387] (you can always try to match inputs and outputs even with a perfect black box mixer). It also raises suspicion and people might ask why you're trying to hide your coins.

With this privacy scheme governments can still blacklist certain addresses[388], which might in the long run break *fungibility* as coins associated with those addresses become worth less than others.

As noted in the chapter *What is money?* fungibility is a core property of money (p.31). This is why it's wrong to label cryptocurrencies trying to address this problem as "privacy coins"—the issue goes beyond privacy.

Monero tries to solve this by hiding amounts and obscuring addresses for all transactions:

This is how the Monero blockchain appears to an observer. Each input is hidden among other transactions, but we cannot tell which one is real and which are fake. Receiving addresses are protected by *stealth addresses* and all amounts are also hidden.

Merchant address

1 XMR
"payment from John"

The merchant who receives the transaction can see which of the inputs is the correct one, the amount and a tag saying who the payment is from. (Alternatively the merchant could've given John a unique address and skip the transcation tagging.)

You can still verify the proof-of-work and even the coin supply on Monero, although verifying the coin supply isn't as simple as on a transparent blockchain. For more technical details on Monero I recommend *Mastering Monero*[Mas18] or *Zero to Monero* [Zer20].

There are other ideas of how to improve privacy and fungibility for cryptocurrencies, and cryptocurrencies of the future might work differently to what I've described here. There are weaknesses to the solutions we've seen so far, and they also come with disadvantages. For example, transactions in Monero are larger than transactions in Bitcoin, making Monero even more difficult to scale. But research is ongoing and I'm hopeful.

Scalability

Perhaps, the most famous technical issue cryptocurrencies face is how to scale them and to increase transaction throughput. This is the big drawback with a decentralized system compared to a centralized system; they're just so much less efficient.

Bitcoin can for example only process around 3-7 transactions per second (tx/s) at max capacity, while PayPal processes on average 400 tx/s[389] and VISA an average of 1 700 tx/s[390], with VISA's peak capacity being over 24 000 tx/s. If cryptocurrencies hope to live up to their potential then there's lots of work to do here.

But it's not quite as bad as the numbers seem to suggest. Bitcoin operates far from the technical limits because they didn't raise the *blocksize limit*, which controls how many transactions can fit in a block and essentially sets an artificial limit on transaction throughput. Bitcoin Cash, a fork of Bitcoin, has raised this limit and has more than 20 times the throughput of Bitcoin (around 150 tx/s). So, cryptocurrencies can at least be in the same playing field as PayPal.

But it's not as easy as "just increase the blocksize". Larger blocks have a centralizing effect, which compromises the core value proposition of a cryptocurrency, and if the network cannot handle them it may even break down.

There are a number of technical pain points that needs to be improved to scale a cryptocurrency. Here's a list of some that I think are important:

- Block propagation

  When a miner finds a block it's important that it propagates around the world to all other miners, so they can continue building on it. This should be done quickly, otherwise it'll increase *orphan rates* (the risk that a block will get discarded as another one was found at the same time), which will have a centralizing effect as it harms smaller miners more than larger miners.

See Daniel Morgan's *The Great Bitcoin Scaling Debate—A Timeline*[396] for the history of the blocksize debate (it only goes up to Dec 2017, but as of May 2019 no significant development has happened). Because Bitcoin didn't raise the blocksize, Bitcoin Cash was created in 2017, keeping fees low and transaction capacity high.

There are **no valid** reasons against a moderate blocksize increase[397], yet there are Bitcoin developers who to this day think we should decrease it to 300 kB[398].

As of 2020-03-04, the total blockchain size of Bitcoin is 265 GB[399]. That's not small, but a 1 TB SSD harddisk costs around $120 and can at the current rate store the entire BTC blockchain for almost 15 more years (it grows around 50 GB/year).

- Blockchain size

  Because full nodes must store transactions *forever*, it's important that the blockchain size (containing all transactions) doesn't outgrow the storage capacity of nodes.

- Bandwith usage

  It's important that nodes have internet connections with enough bandwidth to share transactions with each other.

- Initial sync

  When you first start up a node from scratch you need to download and validate the whole blockchain. This must be fast enough so that nodes are able to catch up in a reasonable amount of time.

- Validation speed

  Whenever a node sees blocks and transactions they must also validate them.

Miners can delay transaction validation and only validate the POW of a block and start mining it directly. This is a fair assumption as it's very expensive to produce a valid POW for a block.

When we increase transaction throughput we also increase the burden of full nodes (those who validate and store the blockchain), it might mean that fewer people can run nodes, harming the node decentralization of the network. It's not a problem as long as enough people can and want to run a node; exchanges, researchers, developers, payment processors, mining pools, and enthusiasts will want to as long as it's not extremely expensive.

Most people won't run a full node anyway as they will use light wallets or SPV wallets on the mobile phone, which will ask other full nodes for the data they need.

Besides optimizing the standard basic structure defined by Bitcoin, there are other scaling proposals out there. Some say we should offload transactions to "layer two" networks, which will only occasionally settle back to a cryptocurrency thereby increasing transaction throughput.

While I'm not against layer two solutions, I'm deeply skeptical of them being a solution to the scaling problem. Simply because if you transact on another network, you're not actually using a cryptocurrency, but something else with different properties.

Others suggest we should use a completely different system, maybe giving up *proof-of-work* for *delegated proof-of-stake* or base it on the *Avalanche protocol*[391].

It may ultimately be impossible to scale a cryptocurrency so that *everyone* in the world uses it for their daily transactions, but I'm confident it's possible to scale it to be useful on a global scale.

Energy usage

Do you know that it's common to have two conflicting beliefs at the same time? You might know that eating too much candy is very bad for your health—and you really would like to lose weight—but you still eat it. Another example is how you think that cheating for an exam is wrong, but you still do it because "you had to".

This is called *cognitive dissonance* and it can cause great discomfort when we have to face it. It's also something I, as a cryptocurrency supporter and an environmentalist, struggle with.

The issue is that cryptocurrencies with proof-of-work use a lot of energy. Bitcoin uses more energy than entire countries!

When we experience cognitive dissonance we try to reduce it in some way, which often happens unconsciously. We might downplay the importance on one side of the conflict ("it's just one chocolate bar"), we might rationalize it in some way ("I'll exercise harder later") or we might suppress the issue entirely (stop talking to anyone who reminds you that you're on a diet).

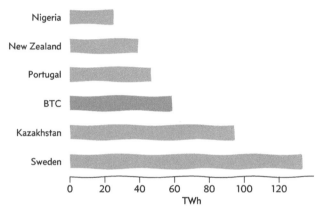

Energy usage for Bitcoin and different countries. The consumption for all entries are still quite small if you compare to USA's 3902 TWh or China's 5564 TWh.

I used Blockchainanalytics to estimate Bitcoin's energy consumption to 58.2 TWh[392], and worlddata.info to estimate energy consumption for the countries[393]. (2020-03-11)

This is absolutely a big problem, but there are some important points we need to keep in mind:

- **The energy isn't wasted**

  The energy is used to secure the chain, because to attack it you need to expend at least that amount of energy. If the energy usage was low, it would be easy to attack.

- **Unrelated to transaction throughput**

  Critics like to look at how much energy is spent to process a single transaction—which makes Bitcoin look extremely bad—but it's a bit misleading since transaction throughput is an unrelated problem.

- **Mostly cheap and renewable energy**

  According to CoinShare's research 73% of Bitcoin mining uses renewable energy, mostly in the form of cheap hydropower in China.[394]

- **Energy consumption follow mining profitability**

  Bitcoin mining is purely profit driven; when the price of Bitcoin goes up, it becomes more profitable to mine and when the price goes down, it's less profitable to mine. Similarly if the energy price would go up, then it's less profitable to mine and Bitcoin would use less energy.

  In fact, it's already difficult to run a profitable mining operation, which is why most mining is based in countries with cheap energy.

There's no other way to drastically reduce the energy usage than to replace proof-of-work with another consensus mechanism. I think this is one reason why proof-of-stake appeals to so many people, despite unsolved problems and large drawbacks.

If we're stuck with proof-of-work, then we just have to accept that it uses a lot of energy, and we have to decide if it's worth it. Are the use-cases valuable enough to warrant spending this much energy? Or are the skeptics right, and Bitcoin mining is just a terrible waste of energy?

Although hydropower is good from a CO_2 perspective, building large dams is very disruptive for the enviroment.

More problems

An exhaustive list and description of all problems would require much more than one book. Still, I'd like to at least mention a couple of other problems:

1. User experience

   The user experience of cryptocurrencies isn't that good. Wallets are hard to understand and if you mess up you might lose your funds forever.

2. Scams everywhere

   For every legitimate cryptocurrency, there are thousands of scams, and it can be very difficult for outsiders to identify them.

3. Regulation

   Having to calculate and declare taxes for *every* cryptocurrency purchase you make is a clear hindrance to adoption. Not to mention cryptocurrencies are illegal in some countries.

4. Development organization

   A cryptocurrency is supposed to remove third parties, but that raises the question how should you upgrade a cryptocurrency? In practice, the development has been dictated by a single development team, which gives them a great deal of power and is a source of centralization.

5. Confirmation time

   Even though I did write that cryptocurrencies are faster than alternatives (p.52), the system isn't fool-proof. While 0-conf is often good enough, if you need more security then due to variance you sometimes need to wait up to an hour or two before your first confirmation.

I don't trust my parents to be able to manage a cryptocurrency wallet themselves, and I certainly don't trust them to choose which cryptocurrency or cryptocurrency project to invest in.

What's the easiest way to disrupt a cryptocurrency? Executing a 51% attack can be extremely expensive and so far cryptocurrencies have largely been impossible to hack.

But how about bribing or infiltrating a developer team? That's much easier and it could allow you to block important changes or even sneak in vulnerabilities.

Chapter 28
A hitchhiker's guide to cryptography
An introduction to cryptography

Don't Panic.

Douglas Adams, "The Hitchhiker's Guide to the Galaxy"

This chapter serves as an introduction to the cryptographic terms and constructs mentioned in the book. The aim is to give you an idea of what they are and how they might be used in a cryptocurrency context. I won't go into low-level details of how they work, so you don't need to know any mathematics or programming to follow along. If this interests you, I hope this introduction will be helpful as a starting point when researching the topic on your own.

If the history of cryptography interests you, I can also recommend the book *The Codebreakers* by David Kahn[Cod96]. You can enjoy it even without much math knowledge.

Hash functions

Hash functions, or to be more precise *cryptographic hash functions*, are commonly used in the cryptocurrency space. They're used as the basis of proof-of-work, to verify the integrity of downloaded files and we used them when we created a timestamped message (p.157).

Hashes are *one-way functions*. As the name implies we can give data to a function to get a result, but we cannot go the other way to get back the original data if we only have the hashed result.

It's similar to how we can break an egg, but there's no easy way to "unbreak" it.

The difference between a cryptographic hash function and a normal hash function is that a cryptographic hash function is created to make finding the reverse of it difficult, and it should be infeasible to find two values with the same hash (called a *collision*).

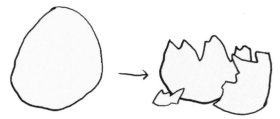

It's easy to break an egg.

But it's very hard to piece it together again.

In the digital world we can use the popular SHA-256 hash function as an example:

```
hello →
5891b5b522d5df086d0ff0b110fbd9d21bb4fc7163af34d08286a2e846f6be03
```

But there's no function to reverse a hash directly:

```
084c799cd551dd1d8d5c5f9a5d593b2e931f5e36122ee5c793c1d08a19839cc0
→ ???
```

To find out what's hidden behind the hash we have to try all possibilities:

```
1  →  4355a46b19d348dc2f57c...
2  →  53c234e5e8472b6ac51c1...
...
42 →  084c799cd551dd1d8d5c5f9a5d593b2e
       931f5e36122ee5c793c1d08a19839cc0
```

Found it! The answer is "42". But we were lucky that we only had to test 42 possibilities, we could have continued a **very** long time depending on the input.

Don't believe me? Then try to guess what message this SHA-256 output comes from, and I can even give you a hint that it's only spaces, upper- and lower-case letters:*

```
b409d7f485033ac9f52a61750fb0c54331bfdd966338015db25efae50984f88f
```

To get a sense for how hard it can be to figure out the matching data for a hash, let's look at Bitcoin mining. Because that's really what miners do — they calculate SHA-256 hashes with different kinds of input again and again until they find a match. And they don't require an exact match either, they only want to find a hash with a certain number of leading zeroes.

The current hashrate for Bitcoin is around 113 exahashes per second[400] (2020-02-18). That's a staggering 113 x 10^{18}, or 133 000 000 000 000 000 000, hashes per second, yet they're still only expected to find a single solution every 10 minutes.

Even all of Bitcoin's hashrate, working for millions of years, are not expected to find the reverse of a single hash. Even though there's theoretically an infinite number of inputs that produce the same hash, it's computationally infeasible to ever find one, therefore we can consider it practically impossible to reverse a hash.

I've simplified the explanation here a little. There's not a one-to-one correspondence between an input and a hash, as several inputs can result in the same hash.

For security it's important that the data you want to protect is sufficiently large and has enough variation to make it difficult to guess what it is.

It's the same way you should choose a password; a short one made of only numbers is easy to guess, but a 30 character password is much harder.

We can say it's impossible to reverse a hash if we have to brute force the solution like this, but there could be weaknesses in the hash function that could allow us to find it much faster. The SHA-1 hash function is for example not secure anymore, as weaknesses have been found that can be used to generate collisions[403].

---

*   The hash was encoded from: *Iron Man is my favorite superhero*

Public-key cryptography

If you jump into the mathematical definitions of *public-key cryptography* it might look very complicated. While some details are complicated, the cryptography is conceptually simple; it's a digital version of a locked mailbox.

A locked mailbox.

Cryptographic schemes commonly use a single large number as their secret key, but public-key cryptography uses two keys: the *public key*, which is like the mailbox, and the *private key*, which is like the key to the mailbox. Anyone can give you mail—just slide it into the mailbox at the top—but you're the only one who can read them, because you're the only with the key to the mailbox.

You *encrypt* a message by placing it in the mailbox, this way nobody but the owner of the mailbox can *decrypt* and read it. The owner of the mailbox can also prove they own the mailbox by placing their name on it, an action that requires you to open the mailbox with the key. In digital terms this is how you *sign* a message.

This is where our mailbox metaphor breaks down a bit. It may seem that it's more inconvenient to sign a message than to encrypt one, but digitally they're both straightforward.

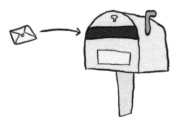

Placing a message inside the mailbox ensures that only the one with the key can read it.

The mailbox contains the label "Jonas", which you have to open the mailbox to change. By putting my name on the mailbox I prove that I own it.

Large parts of the internet depends on public-key cryptography. For example when you connect to your bank over the internet, this scheme helps ensure that nobody can see how much money you have, who you pay and that you're the only one that can transfer your money.

The lock icon or the "https" label means you're using public-key cryptography (among other things) to secure your connection to the website.

I won't go into details on the mathematics behind public-key cryptography, as I'm not able to without making the explanation needlessly complicated, but if this interests you I encourage you to look it up—I personally find it fascinating.

We'll look at public-key cryptography in practice when we look at how Bitcoin addresses work.

RSA is one of the first public-key cryptography schemes and it was also the first one I studied. It's fairly simple, so I think it's a good starting point to understand public-key cryptography.

Bitcoin uses another, more secure, scheme called ECDSA, which uses *elliptic-curve cryptography*.

Bitcoin addresses

The addresses in Bitcoin (and other cryptocurrencies) use public-key cryptography to protect your funds. The address is a public key that everyone can send coins to, but to send coins from an address you need the private key.

This is for example a standard **Bitcoin address**:

```
19WoNYNXnfNPmLteC8YmZFsTQoN9gBSbCG
```

Which corresponds to the **public key**:

```
049f6aad24669d180cfe4c974a677407cbf26f03242a
09126ebf88621d31f01a218d40fcbcb769b44b014d50
2a1c9ce8c2ca629bc339fe14b4db56e27e80ac30a7
```

The address could be displayed in various different ways, Bitcoin just happened to do it this way. Using an address is more convenient as it's shorter and includes error checking codes.

The **private key** to this address looks like this:

```
5298e83a0c0884cdcf34294f663220bc73e3c6689e95b53158a9a89e95fd78bb
```

The private key is just a large number and can be be displayed in different ways. Here's the same key in the *Wallet Import Format*[401], which is shorter and includes error checking codes:

```
5JSfRE8qNQZTtdwuRx6pxVohC3C3VeAHvzKvLsZWHEGPdW2zF3o
```

It's important to note that you should *never* reveal your private key like this. Don't take a screenshot of it, email it or post it on social media. Because if someone sees your key, they can steal all the coins from your address. The private key really is the key to the castle, and if you lose it you'll lose all your funds forever. So please back up your private key somewhere safe (or the more user-friendly *seed*, but we'll get to that shortly).

There are other types of addresses and other formats for the private and public keys, and other cryptocurrencies may handle them differently, but the concepts are the same.

Bitcoin Cash is a fork of Bitcoin and it has an additional address format. The same Bitcoin address, with the same public key, could also be displayed as this Bitoin Cash address:

```
qpwk83ew0xwpe87mmm9v4
3nvzj2y4d783cmv7ayctd
```

The reason Bitcoin uses public-key cryptography for the addresses is because you can **sign** messages with it. For example if I sign the message:

```
Jonas sent the money
```

With the private key to the address:

```
19WoNYNXnfNPmLteC8YmZFsTQoN9gBSbCG
```

I'll get this signature:

```
HCZl2+vEZboqXgaVYi1nLNgwoa/INLiEsA2yXe+87j5iFoo/
G96m4AoA5dL5T+rTiFKpXHuS5w3rP1IWSPZZv0Q=
```

Which lets you **verify** that I know the private key to the address, even if I never showed it to you. This can be useful if we've sent money to someone and we want to prove who did it.

This is also what happens in the background when you authorize a transaction; you sign it with your private key and your signature is verified before the transaction is accepted. If the signature doesn't verify then the transaction is invalid and gets discarded, ensuring that coins can only be spent by the owner of the address.

Encrypting messages using your bitcoin keys isn't that common to my knowledge—people typically use protocols such as PGP—but it's possible. I'll include a short example for completeness sake.

For example if you want to send me the message:

```
I secretly love your book!
```

But only want me to be able to read it, you can encrypt it with my public key:

```
049f6aad24669d180cfe4c974a677407cbf26f03242a
09126ebf88621d31f01a218d40fcbcb769b44b014d50
2a1c9ce8c2ca629bc339fe14b4db56e27e80ac30a7
```

And you'll get the encrypted message:

```
QklFMQJ+CTugTvsEmuB7owU3DvC5taXqC5DhsJ3Wq8EmUM
HwgsE54GlY1PI9d1R/oGfq1mG9dcThW5T9fpUtQTY+ogLL
vKsrN6ngeulLMrfoyCxFtLTjH78PGSd8eROQ1yPq1k=
```

Which only I can **decrypt** to the original message. (Since I've given out the private key, you can decrypt it as well.)

Payment systems are usually smarter, so it's normally not needed to sign a message to prove you sent them a payment.

How hard is it to fake a signature? Very hard, as there's no known attack that can do it. The biggest threat is quantum computers, which *if* they live up to the hype could break public-key cryptography.

Quantum computers wouldn't actually be able to steal all Bitcoins directly, since they can only discover the private key if there's a signature. And if you have coins in your address, but you've never sent any coins from it before, no signature exists.

If quantum computers can break public-key cryptography we as a society would have much bigger problems than the security of Bitcoin, as it would break the security of the internet itself. (There is quantum secure cryptography we could potentially move to, so everything isn't lost yet.)

Seeds

Variations among cryptocurrencies exist. A Monero seed is for example 25 words long.

Because private keys aren't very user-friendly, Bitcoin wallets use seeds. The seed is made up of a sequence of 12, or sometimes 24, words selected from a pre-determined set of 2048 possible words[402].

This is for example a 12-word seed:

```
reward tip because lock general culture
below strike frog fox chunk index
```

Which corresponds to the private key:

```
KyRoQMYWAtfj5cGLThb1fznm5Utjq7Etmn9DLtdxYCiE3Vntcz3E
```

Much more user friendly right? Even though memorizing the public key directly is very difficult, you can see that it would not be too difficult to memorize the seed!

In addition to being easy to use, seeds act as a starting point in deterministic wallets to generate multiple private and public key pairs (giving you multiple addresses).

See the discussion about *pseudo-random generators* (p.170) for some theory of how it might be possible to generate a set of random-looking outputs from a seed.

Giving out a new address each time you receive money is useful for privacy purposes, as it makes it harder to connect your transactions with your identity. This is why all modern wallets generates a new address each time you press receive.

Here are for example the first 10 addresses and their private keys of our seed:

Adress	Private Key
19oN2GWEH1uiPz11WyChkUp2che9Z11Q5A	KyRoQMYWAtfj5cGLThb1fznm5Utjq7Etmn9DLtdxYCiE3Vntcz3E
1LverDkyaWMEyyFHiEWQaJt6UGxRjeBfQR	L1NH4wpuKzafbq2PtVXaGCE8hjc7KGzRfyfYik73APu7kZvdJxUp
1QHQ8uFrEL29WAkMLQgkoDzHimEQNqubM1	Kx3c9ZeS2pzYPuLa2NoA14SavnsWpkf1BJDLDu1N52oGoNWgv9KM
1HiohATeEm6BBeRCgWZ5vY3ZKFrCDsJnt9	KyCWZEpJ3AYUmB7MGEVvZfr6eiwgag89jmZtHC1tEVv9XynSqmot
1KJ5oMUEJTyd3igAYjJGvpdVjGDvF1Brc6	L4exrFikcfgSYm1ZZBkJrbwouLjzrrJB6VPyaH4vyK8cAkK2V2nt
1DzZJ6R1xXiQ3HJ3BsBAcviVdtUEeiu2UG	Kx37aUKrHRVdinxzHWTK8ebXWeMtRSbtshzonTMTQBrssQ2ms1JV
134TjnZ8xiu4wxfyy4xQQtiMiKhhe6AVur	KwPqA3XUaWCX2dhRRm4WXArm5DJKXko1ydgwwApJ3BC3dgnQ3Ydg
12XiJHvYT6TyaWcUhzdcBgqFZc3bNWpYdd	L2WakaNFfBehyL17c13iQwJKR8H1hQtsVvR5jsdugFfj9si8DZm2
12MuxMtJb9jbrzMQrr7zDiLYcn6xwaXMkq	L2ScmsyKJYzW2koEPjHmLKzjFMYNfR8UZMifP2yvggrRrJEBU4UJ
1MqBeJiVW6FqxKbrMq8mVUcukjXWMzuYew	KypFcqzaJRHPwxQfGDiYyJMtAdyKNSQuR78yZPTU57baS42dp4tr

I reiterate the importance of backing up and protecting your seed. Here are just some ways you could lose your money:

- You have a wallet on your phone but you lose it or it breaks down.
- You've written down your seed on paper, but it burns up.
- You forgot where you wrote down your seed.
- Someone finds your seed, and steals your money.

Therefore it's of utmost importance for you to backup and protect your seed. Ideally you should have multiple encrypted copies in different locations, protected from fire and theft.

Does this sound too difficult? It's true, there are many pitfalls and it's easy to do a bad job. But in practice, for reasonably small amounts, it's enough just to write down your seed somewhere.

Chapter 29

Cryptocurrencies are antifragile

They grow stronger from resistance

Antifragility is beyond resilience or robustness. The resilient resists shocks and stays the same; the antifragile gets better.

Nassim Nicholas Taleb, "Antifragile"

It's common to separate things into two categories: those that are fragile and those that are robust. Regular glass is for example fragile as it breaks easily, often by accident, and bullet-proof glass is robust as it can withstand a significant amount of force before it breaks.

But there's a third category that we often don't think about. It's called *antifragile* and it goes beyond robustness as it grows even stronger when stressed. I think the phrase "what doesn't kill you makes you stronger" explains antifragility quite well.

The concept of antifragility was minted by Nassim Taleb in his book series *Incerto*. It includes the famous book *The Black Swan*[Bla08], but I think *Antifragile*[Ant12] is the most important in the series.

At first it might sound impossible; how could something grow stronger from pressure? It would be like if we had armor that was self-healing but after getting shot it also learned from the bullet and adapted to resist the next shot better. Clearly that's only possible in science-fiction.

But that's exactly how our immune system works. After defeating a virus that might make us very sick, our body learns to recognize the virus so it can attack and kill it much earlier. This is how we might develop immunity against COVID-19 and it's the basic principle that make vaccines work.

If you're a comic reader you might recognize this ability from the X-men villains *The Sentinels* that in some variants learn to be immune against any kind of attack.

Fragile	Robust	Antifragile
Glass	Bullet-proof glass	The immune system

Taleb describes a myriad of things that are antifragile; for instance financial long options, street fights, love and religion.[Ant12] As I'll argue in this chapter cryptocurrencies also belong to this group.

The longer it lives the longer it's expected to live

Time is one of the things that break down the fragile and make the antifragile stronger. This is exemplified by the *Lindy Effect*:

> The old is expected to stay longer than the young in proportion to their age.

Nassim Nicholas Taleb, "Antifragile"

In other words the longer something lives, the longer it can be expected to live. The Lindy Effect is only relevant to non-perishable goods; it applies to things like inventions or money, but doesn't apply to humans or food.

Week-old food isn't better than newly cooked food. I know, I've tried.

It's a heuristic, not a natural law, but the implications generally make sense. For instance that Bitcoin will survive another decade, that a newly created cryptocurrency promising to solve all of Bitcoin's problems will fail and that gold will outlive them all by a few millennia.

The largest bug bounty in the world

In the software development world a *bug bounty* is a reward for someone who finds a vulnerability and reports it in a responsible manner. This is vastly preferable to them exploiting it or selling it on the black market, in particular if it's a serious one. For example it's easy to imagine the problem caused by a bug that allowed an attacker to view all private messages in Facebook, so Facebook might we willing to pay a hacker a lot of money if they help them patch this security issue[404].

Note that not all companies have generous bounties and it's likely you can make more money on the black market by reselling the exploit. Some companies might even thank you by taking legal action against you!

While a decentralized project like Bitcoin doesn't have an official bug bounty, Bitcoin itself functions like a very large bug bounty. Because if you find a way to break Bitcoin, and transfer coins to yourself, you could steal billions of dollars worth of Bitcoin and nobody would know who did it.

This is why I think the Lindy Effect applies to cryptocurrencies; with each day that pass without a fatal bug being found in a cryptocurrency, the probability that it will survive another day increases. With such a large sum of money to incentivize people to search for bugs, the fact that no fatal bugs have been found yet inspire confidence.

Antifragility loves small errors

What kills me makes others stronger

Nassim Nicholas Taleb, "Antifragile"

Another property of the antifragile is that they like small errors, because after recovering after an error they grow stronger. Therefore they want many small errors, but not errors so big the recovery time becomes too long.[Ant12]

This is how our muscles grow stronger. When we do strength training we break down our muscles by causing micro tears, and with rest they heal and make the muscles stronger. But we must be careful to not overdo it otherwise we'll break down, only becoming weaker.

And it also holds true for the immune system. Some types of vaccines even give you a very small dose of the virus—just enough to activate your immune system and teach it how to kill the virus—but not so large to make you so sick you couldn't function as normal. And of course you don't want to die in the process.

Cryptocurrencies work the same way. When a weakness is discovered developers will introduce a fix, eliminating the weakness. As long as the cryptocurrency doesn't completely die, tweaknesses will only strengthen it, making it harder to disrupt.

Splitting ensures antifragility

While you can argue that an individual cryptocurrency is antifragile, antifragility also applies to the cryptocurrency concept itself. People like to point at the thousands of cryptocurrencies as some sort of drawback, but it's actually the opposite. Cryptocurrencies being created and then dying off en mass is good as each time one fails we might learn something new and use that to improve the survivors.

People have found very serious bugs. In the chapter about the timestamping service (p.161) we mentioned that awemany found a bug in Bitcoin that would allow an attacker to print an unlimited amount of Bitcoin. While serious, even if exploited it wouldn't have been fatal.

As thanks for reporting it awemany received some substantial donations from the community.

As I'm proof-reading this chapter late December 2020, Monero is currently being attacked, preventing some nodes from syncing.[409]

It's a variation of the *sybil attack* we saw earlier in the chapter *How do cryptocurrencies work?* (p.16) that exploits weaknesses in the p2p network implementation.

While this is disruptive, workarounds exists[410] and these attacks will ultimately make Monero more resistant to similar attacks in the future.

Cryptocurrencies are like a Hydra.

Cut off one head, two more shall take its place.

Forking a cryptocurrency is a fundamental antifragility force. This means forking the ledger, where a cryptocurrency splits into several but all the addresses and coins are still there, or forking the code but restarting from an empty ledger.

Another way is to reimplement everything from scratch. This is also antifragility in action as it reuses the idea of how cryptocurrencies work (p.11).

This process allows a community with different ideals to explore their own path, it allows us to explore different ways to solve a problem and it even allows a cryptocurrency to recover from a catastrophic bug. Forking is the ultimate fail-safe.

Concrete examples

Let's look at some concrete examples of how antifragility might come into play for a cryptocurrency:

1   **Developers disagree on the best way forward**

The coin splits in two and both paths are explored.

For example in Bitcoin there was a big argument of how best to scale. Some wanted to explore on-chain scaling to find the limits and others wanted to move away from the blockchain to "second layer solutions" and depend on them to scale.

On-chain scaling and second layer solutions aren't mutually exclusive as you can explore both at the same time on the same chain.

This lead to the BTC/BCH split where a part of the community left Bitcoin (BTC) to create Bitcoin Cash (BCH) that aims to prioritize on-chain scaling.

You may wonder, which approach is the correct one? That's the best part: it doesn't matter as the cryptocurrency idea will live on regardless. The big issue is if both approaches are a dead-end.

2   Reference client abandons core values

What would happen if the developers of a cryptocurrency decided to print coins from thin air and make themselves rich? Or make some other change that would destroy the cryptocurrency?

Then they would be replaced.

For example Monero replaced—or kicked out—the old developer team early on in it's history when the developers pushed changes that the community disagreed with.[405]

A more recent example is the BCH/ABC split. Since Bitcoin Cash split from Bitcoin in 2017, Bitcoin ABC (Bitcoin Adjustable Blocksize Cap) has been the reference client that has dictated every change that went into the protocol. This ended in 2020 when ABC wanted to reroute 8% of the block reward to an address under their control.[406] The change had serious centralization concerns[407], and in the end the miners and the BCH community rejected them and they split away to their own minority fork.

Not only did Bitcoin Cash replace the reference client, they replaced it with a handful of cooperating developer teams, reducing the damage a rogue developer could cause.

As of now it's not yet clear how viable the ABC chain will be. Some exchanges use the ticker BCHA, but most don't support it at all at this time.

I think the developers is the weak-link in a cryptocurrency. While proof-of-work ensures that even state level actors will find it difficult to disrupt the network, influencing a few developers is much easier.

This is why I think these examples of replacing developer teams are so significant. It shows that the community can, and will, reject malicious developers.

3   Marketplaces freeze your assets

Decentralized marketplaces that allow for non-custodial trades are created. This means the marketplaces never control your funds and all trades are made directly with the other person, making it impossible for anyone to freeze your funds.

4   Governments declare cryptocurrencies illegal

Governments have declared drugs and prostitution illegal for centuries, but they still manage to thrive. Making them legal would paradoxically make them easier to control, and I think it's the same with cryptocurrencies.

If governments banned cryptocurrencies people would still trade them in person and move to decentralized marketplaces, which are inherently harder to disrupt. We would move away from centralized payment services and move towards a peer-to-peer economy, like how Satoshi envisioned.

For example Monero supporters worry that governments will declare cryptocurrencies with good privacy features illegal (a reasonable thing to worry about). This will soon be a smaller issue as work on a Bitcoin-Monero atomic swap project is underway[408], which would allow people to trade Bitcoin and Monero without any third-party.

Remember that cryptocurrencies are completely global. Even if they're illegal in your country, you can always find an exchange, service or marketplace online that operates in another country where they're legal. The tricky part is to buy or sell cryptocurrencies for fiat.

5   A 51% attack

One of the worst things that can happen to a cryptocurrency is a *51% attack* (p.22), but even such an event can strengthen it.

For example an attacked chain could change the mining algorithm, making all existing mining rigs worthless. This would make it impervious to the same type of attack and if an attacker wants to make another attempt brand new mining rigs would have to be purchased or created.

As another example during the BCH/BSV split the BSV (Bitcoin Satoshi's Vision) miners threatened to attack the BCH chain, and to not allow any transactions to be confirmed. This would essentially kill the chain, but this attack was never carried out and protection was added to the BCH software that made it more difficult to carry out such an attack.

The *block finalization* of Bitcoin Cash is highly controversial. It ensures that whenever a block has 10 confirmations it will never be invalidated, even if a longer chain is found.

While it might make it harder to *reorg*, it's unsound in the sense that newly connected nodes may be unable to decide which chain is the correct, but without it the nodes would simply follow the longest chain.

Antifragility brings confidence

There's a worry that governments will kill cryptocurrencies by making them illegal; that PayPal will co-opt Bitcoin and turn it into a corporate coin; that Facebook or governments will create a centralized digital currency that out-competes real cryptocurrencies; that developers will go rogue; or that a fatal bug will bring it all down.

I've gotta be honest, they don't worry me too much. I see them as temporary setbacks that are harmful in the short-term, but will in the end make cryptocurrencies even stronger.

Therefore I'm convinced that as long as internet exists, so will cryptocurrencies.

About me, the author
Hello, I'm Jonas

I have no special talents. I am only passionately curious.

Albert Einstein

I wonder what you might think of someone who is writing a book about cryptocurrencies? Maybe you'll think of a teenage multi-millionaire or an old neckbeard raving about free software? Or perhaps an anarchist saying things like "governments are evil" and "taxation is theft"?

I am none of those. I'm just a normal person, perhaps a bit introverted. I only have a short beard, and I pay my taxes and enjoy the benefits we get here in Sweden. Unfortunately I'm neither a teenager nor a multi-millionaire.

It's easy to see why cryptocurrencies might attract people like this. Cryptocurrencies are all about freedom, and the free software movement (saying that all software should be free) and anarchism seek freedom to the extreme.

I first heard about Bitcoin in 2010, about one year after its creation. I installed a Bitcoin wallet and played around with it a little. It was just another internet thing for me and like many others, it failed to hold my attention. After about 10 or 15 minutes, I removed it and promptly forgot about it.

I did have a couple of Bitcoins at that time. It hurts to admit this as today a single Bitcoin is worth around $50,000, but sadly I've lost them. After all, back then they weren't worth anything.t

It wasn't until four or maybe five years that later I looked at Bitcoin again. I studied computer science and we had a course in cryptography—a very fun course I might add—with a part about cryptocurrencies. We went through the technical details, and it made me curious about Bitcoin on a deeper level. I read the white paper and began following the news and development in the space.

Before writing this book, I wasn't actively involved in cryptocurrencies. While I love programming, ever since I started programming full-time it's been difficult to find energy for side-projects, like I had during my University years.

The free time I've had has been taken up by my two boys, my girlfriend and other hobbies. Saying no to something is saying yes to something else.

After my parental leave we decided that I should work part time to avoid long days at pre-school. Working less has also opened up time and energy for me to work on a side project, and writing a book has been on my bucket-list so I thought "why not do it now"? My girlfriend, wonderful as she is, has always been super supportive of my silly ideas.

As the book project has been finishing up, I've started working on another cryptocurrency project: a self-hosted payment processor[411]r, that allows you to accept payments online without any third-party.

Am I qualified to write about cryptocurrencies? Am I a cryptocurrency expert? I don't know. I just see myself as an enthusiast who is trying to write down and share my thoughts. Please keep that in mind when you consider any claims I make—I may very well miss something important.

My current hobbies include Brazilian Jiu-Jitsu, boardgames, and standard low-effort ones such as reading books or watching videos.

I have a very on-and-off relationship with my hobbies, which I pick up and do intensely for a short period of time. For instance, I've been into lockpicking, Go, and learning Korean, which I would like to start again some day.

I have a blog at jonashietala.se where I write about random stuff, mostly for myself. It's also, as you might imagine, not updated regularly.

References

[Ant12]   Nassim Nicholas Taleb (2012) *Antifragile : Things That Gain from Disorder*

[Big10]   Michael Lewis (2010) *The Big Short: Inside the Doomsday Machine*

[Bla08]   Nassim Nicholas Taleb (2008) *The Black Swan: The Impact of the Highly Improbable*

[Box16]   Marc Levinson (2016) *The Box: How the Shipping Container Made the World Smaller and the World Economy Bigger* 2nd ed.

[Cod96]   David Kahn (1996) *The Codebreakers : The Comprehensive History of Secret Communication from Ancient Times to the Internet* Revised Edition

[Fed94]   Murray N. Rothbard (1994) *The Case Against the Fed*

[Mas18]   SerHack (2018) *Mastering Monero*

[Mus13]   Alan S. Blinder (2013) *After the Music Stopped: The Financial Crisis, the Response, and the Work Ahead*

[Old06]   David Edgerton (2006) *The Shock of the Old: Technology and Global History Since 1900*

[Orw45]   George Orwell (1945) *Animal Farm*

[Orw49]   George Orwell (1949) *1984*

[Pea16]   K. Anders Ericsson, Robert Pool (2016) *Peak: Secrets from the New Science of Expertise*

[Per19]   Edward Snowden (2019) *Permanent Record*

[Thi11]   Daniel Kahneman (1949) *Thinking, Fast and Slow*

[Wat18]   Scott Harrison (2018) *Thirst: A Story of Redemption, Compassion, and a Mission to Bring Clean Water to the World*

[Zer20]   koe, Kurt M. Alonso, Sarang Noether (2020) *Zero to Monero: Second Edition*

[1]   Daniel Shane (2017) *The bitcoin rally is back on: It just zoomed above $13,000*
        https://money.cnn.com/2017/12/06/investing/bitcoin-rally-hits-12000
        (Accessed: 2020-02-18)

[2]   Independent (2018) *Cryptocurrencies are about to become worthless–and this is what will happen when they crash*
        https://www.independent.co.uk/voices/bitcoin-cryptocurrency-price-crash-bank-of-england-agustin-
        carstens-a8645356.html
        (Accessed: 2020-02-18)

[3]   CNN Business (2017) *Bitcoin boom may be a disaster for the environment*
        https://money.cnn.com/2017/12/07/technology/bitcoin-energy-environment
        (Accessed: 2020-02-18)

[4]   Independent (2018) *Bitcoin price is so high because criminals are using it for illegal trades, research suggests*
        https://www.independent.co.uk/life-style/gadgets-and-tech/news/bitcoin-price-fall-criminals-
        blockchain-anonymous-cryptocurrency-zcash-monero-dash-a8174716.html
        (Accessed: 2020-02-18)

[5]   Bruce Schneier (2019) *Blockchain and trust*
        https://www.schneier.com/blog/archives/2019/02/blockchain_and_.html
        (Accessed: 2020-02-18)

[6]   New York Post (2015) *How the Beanie Baby craze was concocted—then crashed*
        https://nypost.com/2015/02/22/how-the-beanie-baby-craze-was-concocted-then-crashed/
        (Accessed: 2020-02-18)

[7]   CNBC (2017) *Meet CryptoKitties, the $100,000 digital beanie babies epitomizing the cryptocurrency mania*
        https://www.cnbc.com/2017/12/06/meet-cryptokitties-the-new-digital-beanie-babies-selling-for-100k.
        html
        (Accessed: 2020-02-18)

[8]   Britannica (no date) *Tulip Mania*
        https://www.britannica.com/event/Tulip-Mania
        (Accessed: 2020-02-18)

[9]   Inflation matters (no date) *Keynesian Inflation Theory*
        http://inflationmatters.com/keynesian-inflation-theory/
        (Accessed: 2019-04-24)

[10]   Austrian Economics Wiki (no date) *Inflation*
        https://austrianeconomics.fandom.com/wiki/Inflation
        (Accessed: 2019-04-24)

[11]   The Bitcoin.com Podcast Network (2019) *Austrian Economics for Bitcoiners with Jeffrey Tucker (part 1)*
        https://podcast.bitcoin.com/e799-Austrian-Economics-for-Bitcoiners-with-Jeffrey-Tucker-part-1
        (Accessed: 2019-04-24)

[12]   fullstacks.org (no date) *Ethereum Fork History*
        https://fullstacks.org/materials/ethereumbook/16_appdx-forks-history.html
        (Accessed: 2019-04-24)

[13]   Leslie Lamport Robert Shostak Marshall Pease (1982) *The Byzantine Generals Problem* ACM Transactions on Pro-
        gramming Languages and Systems | July 1982, pp. 382-401

[14]   Ken Shirriff (2014) *Mining Bitcoin with pencil and paper: 0.67 hashes per day*
         http://www.righto.com/2014/09/mining-bitcoin-with-pencil-and-paper.html
         (Accessed: 2019-05-03)

[15]   Blockchair (no date) *Transaction*
         https://blockchair.com/bitcoin/
         transaction/0c4c723ea0b78722a79c3e34fb714b92e5aac355041f490cd56937c14458d44f
         (Accessed: 2019-05-03)

[16]   xmrchain.net (no date) *Monero explorer*
         https://xmrchain.net/
         (Accessed: 2019-05-03)

[17]   blockchain.com (no date) *Total Hash Rate (TH/s)*
         https://www.blockchain.com/charts/hash-rate
         (Accessed: 2021-01-31)

[18]   Bitmain (no date) *Antminer S9i*
         https://shop.bitmain.com/promote/antminer_s9i_asic_bitcoin_miner/specification
         (Accessed: 2021-01-31)

[19]   CryptoCompare (no date) *Antminer S9I*
         https://www.cryptocompare.com/mining/blokforge/antminer-s9i-14-ths/
         (Accessed: 2020-04-20)

[20]   coindesk (2017) *The Bitcoin Mining Arms Race: GHash.io and the 51% Issue*
         https://www.coindesk.com/bitcoin-mining-detente-ghash-io-51-issue
         (Accessed: 2019-05-03)

[21]   Fullstacks (2018) *Ethereum Fork History*
         https://fullstacks.org/materials/ethereumbook/16_appdx-forks-history.html
         (Accessed: 2019-04-24)

[22]   Stackexchange (2016) *What exactly is the Nothing-At-Stake problem?*
         https://ethereum.stackexchange.com/questions/2402/what-exactly-is-the-nothing-at-stake-problem
         (Accessed: 2019-05-03)

[23]   Practical Cryptography (no date) *Caesar Cipher*
         http://practicalcryptography.com/ciphers/caesar-cipher/
         (Accessed: 2019-05-03)

[24]   Jonald Fyookball (2017) *Why Every Bitcoin User Should Understand "SPV Security"*
         https://medium.com/@jonaldfyookball/why-every-bitcoin-user-should-understand-spv-security-
         520d1d45e0b9
         (Accessed: 2019-05-03)

[25]   awemany (2018) *Solving the 0-conf problem using forfeits*
         https://gist.github.com/awemany/619a5722d129dec25abf5de211d971bd
         (Accessed: 2019-05-03)

[26]   Bitcoin Gold forum (2018) *Double Spend Attacks on Exchanges*
         https://forum.bitcoingold.org/t/double-spend-attacks-on-exchanges/1362
         (Accessed: 2019-05-03)

[27]   YouTube (2017) *Baltic Honeybadger 2017 Bitcoin Conference*
https://www.youtube.com/watch?v=DHc81OL_hk4&t=21235
(Accessed: 2019-05-06)

[28]   Chris Dolmetsch (2019) *OneCoin Leaders Charged in Multibillion-Dollar Pyramid Scam*
https://www.bloomberg.com/news/articles/2019-03-08/onecoin-leaders-charged-in-u-s-with-operating-pyramid-scheme
(Accessed: 2019-05-06)

[29]   BBC Sounds (no date) *The Missing Cryptoqueen*
https://www.bbc.co.uk/programmes/p07nkd84/episodes/downloads
(Accessed: 2020-09-21)

[30]   FBI (2019) *Seeking Victims in Bitconnect Investigation*
https://www.fbi.gov/resources/victim-services/seeking-victim-information/seeking-victims-in-bitconnect-investigation
(Accessed: 2019-05-06)

[31]   Olga Kharif (2019) *Tether Says Stablecoin Is Only Backed 74% by Cash, Securities*
https://www.bloomberg.com/news/articles/2019-04-30/tether-says-stablecoin-is-only-backed-74-by-cash-securities
(Accessed: 2019-05-06)

[32]   SEC (2021)
https://www.sec.gov/news/press-release/2020-338
Accessed: 2021-01-04

[33]   bitcointalk.org (2015) *Why the darkcoin/dash/dashpay instamine matters*
https://bitcointalk.org/index.php?topic=999886.0
(Accessed: 2019-05-06)

[34]   John Blocke (2016) *A (brief and incomplete) history of censorship in /r/Bitcoin*
https://medium.com/@johnblocke/a-brief-and-incomplete-history-of-censorship-in-r-bitcoin-c85a290fe43
(Accessed: 2019-05-06)

[35]   Trustnodes (2019) *The Cryptocurrency Sub Tests Censorship After Bitcoin Core Supporter Suddenly Becomes Top Mod*
https://www.trustnodes.com/2019/05/01/the-cryptocurrency-sub-tests-censorship-after-bitcoin-core-supporter-suddenly-becomes-top-mod
(Accessed: 2019-05-06)

[36]   Wezz (2017) *September 2017 Stats Post*
https://www.reddit.com/r/noncensored_bitcoin/comments/7414nf/september_2017_stats_post/
(Accessed: 2019-05-06)

[37]   thepaip (2018) *A collection of evidence regarding Bitcoin's takeover and problems*
https://www.reddit.com/r/btc/comments/83vgdm/a_collection_of_evidence_regarding_bitcoins/
(Accessed: 2019-05-06)

[38]   Ingrid Van Damme (2007) *Cowry Shells, a trade currency*
https://www.nbbmuseum.be/en/2007/01/cowry-shells.htm
(Accessed: 2019-05-16)

[39]   Mia Sogoba (2018) *The Cowrie Shell: Monetary and Symbolic Value*
         https://www.culturesofwestafrica.com/cowrie-shell-monetary-symbolic-value/
         (Accessed: 2019-05-16)

[40]   Mark Cartwright (2016) *Ancient Greek Coinage*
         https://www.ancient.eu/Greek_Coinage/
         (Accessed: 2019-05-16)

[41]   Robert Michael Poole (2018) *The tiny island with human-sized money*
         http://www.bbc.com/travel/story/20180502-the-tiny-island-with-human-sized-money
         (Accessed: 2019-05-16)

[42]   Boban Docevski (2017) *The Rai Stones are huge stone wheels used as currency on the island of Yap*
         https://www.thevintagenews.com/2017/12/28/rai-stones/
         (Accessed: 2019-05-16)

[43]   Sveriges Riksbank (no date) *1644 - The world's largest coin*
         https://www.riksbank.se/en-gb/about-the-riksbank/history/1600-1699/the-worlds-largest-coin/
         (Accessed: 2019-05-16)

[44]   Alex Q. Arbuckle (2016) *Hyperinflation in Germany*
         https://mashable.com/2016/07/27/german-hyperinflation/
         (Accessed: 2019-05-16)

[45]   Wikipedia (no date) *Weimar Republic (1920–24)*
         https://en.wikipedia.org/wiki/German_Papiermark#Weimar_Republic_(1920%E2%80%9324)
         (Accessed: 2019-05-16)

[46]   Alex Q. Arbuckle (2016) *Hyperinflation in Germany*
         https://mashable.com/2016/07/27/german-hyperinflation/
         (Accessed: 2019-05-16)

[47]   Steven Tomlinson (no date) *Case Study: Cigarettes as Money*
         https://www.cengage.com/economics/tomlinson/transcripts/8520.pdf
         (Accessed: 2019-05-16)

[48]   Matt Davis (2014) *Five Suprising Things Prisoners Use As Currency*
         https://www.therichest.com/business/economy/five-surprising-things-prisoners-use-as-currency/
         (Accessed: 2019-05-16)

[49]   Maria Godoy (2016) *Ramen Noodles Are Now The Prison Currency Of Choice*
         https://www.npr.org/sections/thesalt/2016/08/26/491236253/ramen-noodles-are-now-the-prison-currency-of-choice?t=1557205041822
         (Accessed: 2019-05-16)

[50]   Kimberley Amadeo (no date) *History of the Gold Standard*
         https://www.thebalance.com/what-is-the-gold-standard-3306137
         (Accessed: 2019-05-16)

[51]   Owen Ferguson (2019) *Hoarding Nickels: Why Your Pocket Change Might Be Worth More Than You Think*
         https://www.thepennyhoarder.com/smart-money/hoarding-nickels-pocket-change-might-worth-think/
         (Accessed: 2019-05-16)

[52]   Georg Friedrich Knapp (1924) *The State Theory of Money* 4th ed.
London: Macmillan & Company Limited, St. Martin's Street, 1924

[53]   Mises Wiki (no date) *Subjective theory of value*
https://wiki.mises.org/wiki/Subjective_theory_of_value
(Accessed: 2019-05-16)

[54]   Khan Academy (no date) *definition, measurement, and functions of money*
https://www.khanacademy.org/economics-finance-domain/ap-macroeconomics/ap-financial-sector/
definition-measurement-and-functions-of-money-ap/a/definition-measurement-and-functions-of-money
(Accessed: 2019-05-16)

[55]   Dan Sanchez (2012) *Mises on the Basics of Money*
https://mises.org/library/mises-basics-money
(Accessed: 2019-05-16)

[56]   Principles of Economics (no date) *Defining Money by Its Functions*
https://opentextbc.ca/principlesofeconomics/chapter/27-1-defining-money-by-its-functions/
(Accessed: 2019-05-16)

[57]   Macrotrends (no date) *Gold Prices - 100 Year Historical Chart*
https://www.macrotrends.net/1333/historical-gold-prices-100-year-chart
(Accessed: 2019-05-16)

[58]   The Money Project (no date) *Properties of money*
http://money.visualcapitalist.com/tag/properties-of-money/
(Accessed: 2019-05-16)

[59]   Sound Money Defense League (no date) *What is Sound Money? Sound Money Explained*
https://www.soundmoneydefense.org/sound-money-explained
(Accessed: 2019-05-16)

[60]   Gary North (1969) *The Fallacy of "Intrinsic Value"*
https://fee.org/articles/the-fallacy-of-intrinsic-value/
(Accessed: 2019-05-16)

[61]   Federal Reserve Bank of Atlanda (no date) *Fractional Reserve Banking - An Economist's Perspective (Transcript)*
https://www.frbatlanta.org/education/classroom-economist/fractional-reserve-banking/economists-
perspective-transcript
(Accessed: 2019-05-16)

[62]   Thorsten Polleit (2010) *The Faults of Fractional-Reserve Banking*
https://mises.org/library/faults-fractional-reserve-banking
(Accessed: 2019-05-16)

[63]   U.S. Department of the Treasury (2018) *Treasury Designates Iran-Based Financial Facilitators of Malicious Cyber Activity and for the First Time Identifies Associated Digital Currency Addresses*
https://home.treasury.gov/news/press-releases/sm556
(Accessed: 2019-05-23)

[64]   Investing.com (no date) *Bitcoin historical price data*
https://www.investing.com/crypto/bitcoin/historical-data
(Accessed: 2020-09-29)

[65]   Skatteverket (2018) *HFD, mål nr 2674-18. Avyttring av bitcoin*
        https://www4.skatteverket.se/rattsligvagledning/373946.html?date=2018-12-17
        (Accessed: 2018-12-17)

[66]   CURIA (2015) *Judgement of the court (Fifth Chamber): Case C-264/14*
        http://curia.europa.eu/juris/document/document.
        jsf?text=&docid=170305&pageIndex=0&doclang=en&mode=req&dir=&occ=first&part=1&cid=604646
        (Accessed: 2019-05-23)

[67]   luigi1111, Riccardo Spagni (2017) *Disclosure of a Major Bug in CryptoNote Based Currencies*
        https://www.getmonero.org/2017/05/17/disclosure-of-a-major-bug-in-cryptonote-based-currencies.html
        (Accessed: 2019-05-23)

[68]   Bitcoin Core (2018) *CVE-2018-17144 Full Disclosure*
        https://bitcoincore.org/en/2018/09/20/notice/
        (Accessed: 2019-05-23)

[69]   Kevin Simler (2019) *Going Critical*
        https://www.meltingasphalt.com/interactive/going-critical/
        (Accessed: 2019-05-23)

[70]   Electronic Frontier Foundation (2013) *Deep Dive: Software Patents and the Rise of Patent Trolls*
        https://www.eff.org/deeplinks/2013/02/deep-dive-software-patents-and-rise-patent-trolls
        (Accessed: 2019-05-23)

[71]   US5960411A United States (1999) *Method and system for placing a purchase order via a communications network*
        https://patents.google.com/patent/US5960411
        (Accessed: 2019-05-23)

[72]   BitInfoCharts (no date) *Bitcoin, Litecoin, Bitcoin Cash, Monero, Dogecoin Median Transaction Fee historical chart*
        https://bitinfocharts.com/comparison/median_transaction_fee-btc-ltc-bch-xmr-doge.html
        (Accessed: 2019-05-25)

[73]   Monero.how (no date) *How much are Monero transaction fees?*
        https://www.monero.how/monero-transaction-fees
        (Accessed: 2019-05-25)

[74]   Kroger (2019) *Kroger Announces Second Division to Stop Accepting Visa Credit Cards Due to Excessive Transaction Fees*
        http://ir.kroger.com/file/Index?KeyFile=396935873
        (Accessed: 2019-06-03)

[75]   Spencer Tierney (2019) *Wire Transfers: What Banks Charge*
        https://www.nerdwallet.com/blog/banking/wire-transfers-what-banks-charge/
        (Accessed: 2019-06-03)

[76]   Ben Dwyer (no date) *Average Credit Card Processing Fees*
        https://www.cardfellow.com/blog/average-fees-for-credit-card-processing/
        (Accessed: 2019-06-03)

[77]   PayPal (no date) *Credit Card Fees, Send Money Fees & Other Charges - PayPal US*
        https://www.paypal.com/us/webapps/mpp/paypal-fees
        (Accessed: 2019-06-03)

[78]   Swish (no date) *Get started with Swish*
         https://www.getswish.se/foretag/vara-erbjudanden/
         (Accessed: 2019-06-03)

[79]   Sydney Vaccaro (2018) *Growing Cost of Fraud For Digital Goods*
         https://chargeback.com/growing-cost-of-fraud-for-digital-goods/
         (Accessed: 2019-06-03)

[80]   Chargebacks 911 (no date) *Chargeback Fees*
         https://chargebacks911.com/knowledge-base/chargeback-fees/
         (Accessed: 2019-06-03)

[81]   Emily Vuitton (2016) *MasterCard Chargeback Time Limits*
         https://chargeback.com/mastercard-chargeback-time-limits/
         (Accessed: 2019-06-03)

[82]   Gregory Maxwell (2017) *Total fees have almost crossed the block reward*
         https://lists.linuxfoundation.org/pipermail/bitcoin-dev/2017-December/015455.html
         (Accessed: 2019-06-03)

[83]   John Blocke (2016) *The Fee Market Myth*
         https://medium.com/@johnblocke/the-fee-market-myth-b9d189e45096
         (Accessed: 2019-06-03)

[84]   Kim P, personal finance expert at CreditDonkey (no date) *Credit Card Processing Fees: What You Need to Know*
         https://www.creditdonkey.com/credit-card-processing-fees.html
         (Accessed: 2019-06-03)

[85]   UniBul (no date) *How Visa's Payment System Works*
         http://blog.unibulmerchantservices.com/how-visas-payment-system-works/
         (Accessed: 2019-06-03)

[86]   Dakota Skye (2014) *@DirectorJoshua something has to be done. #chase has fucked with people before with other issues. Should not get away with shit like this*
         https://mobile.twitter.com/dakota_skyexxx/status/458517153323712513
         (Accessed: 2019-06-12)

[87]   Chris Morris (2013) *Porn and Banks: Drawing a Line on Loans*
         https://www.cnbc.com/id/100746445
         (Accessed: 2019-06-12)

[88]   Wikipedia (no date) *Legality of cannabis by U.S. jurisdiction*
         https://en.wikipedia.org/wiki/Legality_of_cannabis_by_U.S._jurisdiction
         (Accessed: 2019-06-12)

[89]   Robb Mandelbaum (2016) *Where Pot Entrepreneurs Go When the Banks Just Say No*
         https://www.nytimes.com/2018/01/04/magazine/where-pot-entrepreneurs-go-when-the-banks-just-say-no.html
         (Accessed: 2019-06-12)

[90]   Oscar (2018) *The State of Payment Processing for Cannabis E-Commerce*
         http://stayregular.net/blog/the-state-of-payment-processing-for-cannabis-e-commerce
         (Accessed: 2019-06-12)

[91]   Stripe (no date) *Restricted Businesses—Sweden*
         https://stripe.com/restricted-businesses
         (Accessed: 2019-06-12)

[92]   Wikipedia (no date) *First they came …*
         https://en.wikipedia.org/wiki/First_they_came%E2%80%A6
         (Accessed: 2019-06-12)

[93]   Tyler (2019) *32 Incredible Cannabis Industry Statistics 2020*
         https://www.marijuanaseo.com/cannabis-industry-statistics/
         (Accessed: 2019-06-12)

[94]   New York Post (2014) *Chase closes hundreds of porn stars' accounts*
         https://nypost.com/2014/04/28/chase-closes-the-accounts-of-hundreds-of-porn-stars/
         (Accessed: 2019-06-12)

[95]   Emily Flitter (2018) *A candidate backed medical marijuana. Wells Fargo closed her bank account.*
         https://www.cnbc.com/2018/08/22/wells-fargo-closes-bank-account-of-candidate-who-supports-marijuana.html
         (Accessed: 2019-06-12)

[96]   Lester Coleman (2015) *Australian Commission Investigates Banks Closing Bitcoin Companies' Accounts*
         https://www.ccn.com/banks-still-closing-accounts-bitcoin-activity
         (Accessed: 2019-06-12)

[97]   Kyle Caldwell (2015) *Barclays closed down my bank account after Bitcoin trade*
         https://www.telegraph.co.uk/finance/personalfinance/investing/11537972/Barclays-closed-down-my-bank-account-after-Bitcoin-trade.html
         (Accessed: 2019-06-12)

[98]   Jeremy Woertink (2018) *Programming in the Adult Entertainment Industry is Broken*
         https://dev.to/jwoertink/programming-in-the-adult-entertainment-industry-is-broken-hgn
         (Accessed: 2019-06-12)

[99]   Hacker News (2018) *Programming in the Adult Entertainment Industry Is Broken*
         https://news.ycombinator.com/item?id=17756219
         (Accessed: 2019-06-12)

[100]   Alexa (no date) *pornhub.com ranking*
         https://www.alexa.com/siteinfo/pornhub.com
         (Accessed: 2020-12-30)

[101]   Samantha Cole (2019) *PayPal Pulls Out of Pornhub, Hurting 'Hundreds of Thousands' of Performers*
         https://www.vice.com/en/article/d3abgv/paypal-pulls-out-of-pornhub-payments
         (Accessed: 2020-12-30)

[102]   Noor Zainab Hussain, Munsif Vengattil (2020) *Mastercard, Visa halt payments on Pornhub over allegations of child sex-abuse content*
         https://www.reuters.com/article/us-pornhub-mastercard/mastercard-to-stop-processing-payments-on-pornhub-cites-unlawful-content-idUSKBN28K30C
         (Accessed: 2020-1-30)

[103] Werner Almesberger (2015) *PayPal trouble delays project*
https://neo900.org/news/paypal-trouble-delays-project
(Accessed: 2019-06-14)

[104] Emmie Martin (2018) *Only 39% of Americans have enough savings to cover a $1,000 emergency*
https://www.cnbc.com/2018/01/18/few-americans-have-enough-savings-to-cover-a-1000-emergency.html
(Accessed: 2019-06-14)

[105] Notch (2010) *Working on a Friday update, crying over paypal*
https://notch.tumblr.com/post/1096322756/working-on-a-friday-update-crying-over-paypal
(Accessed: 2019-06-14)

[106] Jake Morrison (2018) *PayPal Know Your Customer failure*
https://www.cogini.com/blog/paypal-know-your-customer-failure/
(Accessed: 2019-06-14)

[107] Dejan Murko (2019) *We got banned from PayPal after 12 years of business*
https://blog.niteo.co/paypal-ban-after-12-years/
(Accessed: 2019-06-14)

[108] schockergd (2013) *PayPal just froze over $70,000 in my account - Say they won't return it for 180 days*
https://www.reddit.com/r/Entrepreneur/comments/1rkkd7/paypal_just_froze_over_70000_in_my_account_say/
(Accessed: 2019-06-14)

[109] PayPal - Horror Stories, Lawsuits, Reviews PayPal Problems (2012) *PayPal destroyed my business of 8 years in a day*
http://www.aboutpaypal.org/paypal-destroyed-business-8-years-day/
(Accessed: 2019-06-14)

[110] Mark Gavalda (2019) *Should Startups Avoid Stripe? How We Got Our Account Back*
https://kinsta.com/blog/startups-avoid-stripe/
(Accessed: 2019-06-14)

[111] Olav Småriset (2019) *Why Stripe is the worst choice for your new startup business*
https://medium.com/@OlavOlsm/why-stripe-is-the-worst-choice-for-your-new-startup-business-e4d9f515e116
(Accessed: 2019-06-14)

[112] WikiLeaks (no date) *Drafts:About*
https://wikileaks.org/wiki/Draft:About
(Accessed: 2019-08-28)

[113] Mark Oliver (2017) *33 Haunting Photos From The Killing Fields Of The Cambodian Genocide*
https://allthatsinteresting.com/cambodian-genocide
(Accessed: 2019-08-28)

[114] John Sudworth (2019) *Tiananmen 30 years on - China's great act of 'forgettance'*
https://www.bbc.com/news/blogs-china-blog-48455582
(Accessed: 2019-08-28)

[115] PEN America (2019) *Arrest of Chinese Filmmaker Deng Chuanbin Represents the Extreme Lengths of Chinese Authorities to Silence Artistic Voices*
https://pen.org/press-release/deng-chuanbin-arrest/
(Accessed: 2019-08-28)

[116]   Committee to Protect Journalists (2015) *10 Most Censored Countries*
          https://cpj.org/2015/04/10-most-censored-countries.php
          (Accessed: 2019-08-28)

[117]   Allum Bokhari (2016) *Reddit Mods Delete Orlando Shooting Posts Because Attacker Was Muslim*
          https://www.breitbart.com/tech/2016/06/12/reddit-topics-censored-users-banned-linking-orlando-
          shootings-islam/
          (Accessed: 2019-08-28)

[118]   BBC (2019) *Julian Assange: A timeline of Wikileaks founder's case*
          https://www.bbc.com/news/world-europe-11949341
          (Accessed: 2019-08-28)

[119]   Emma Grey Ellis (2016) *WikiLeaks Has Officially Lost the Moral High Ground*
          https://www.wired.com/2016/07/wikileaks-officially-lost-moral-high-ground/
          (Accessed: 2019-08-28)

[120]   WikiLeaks (2012) *Collateral Murder*
          https://collateralmurder.wikileaks.org/
          (Accessed: 2019-08-28)

[121]   WikiLeaks (no date) *Collateral Murder Transcript*
          https://collateralmurder.wikileaks.org/en/transcript.html
          (Accessed: 2019-08-28)

[122]   YouTube (2010) *Collateral Murder (39 min)*
          https://www.youtube.com/watch?v=is9sxRfU-ik
          (Accessed: 2019-08-28)

[123]   Matthew Schofield (2011) *Iraqi children in U.S. raid shot in head, U.N. says*
          https://www.mcclatchydc.com/news/special-reports/article24696685.html
          (Accessed: 2019-08-28)

[124]   Russell Goldman, Luis Martinez (2010) *WikiLeaks Documents Reveal Death Count, Torture*
          https://abcnews.go.com/Politics/wikileaks-iraqi-civilian-deaths-higher-reported/story?id=11953723
          (Accessed: 2019-08-28)

[125]   BBC (2010) *Wikileaks founder Julian Assange accused of rape*
          https://www.bbc.com/news/world-11047025
          (Accessed: 2019-08-28)

[126]   BBC (2010) *Wikileaks' Assange faces international arrest warrant*
          https://www.bbc.com/news/world-europe-11803703
          (Accessed: 2019-08-28)

[127]   WikiLeaks (2010) *PayPal freezes WikiLeaks donations*
          https://wikileaks.org/PayPal-freezes-WikiLeaks-donations.html
          (Accessed: 2019-08-28)

[128]   WkiLeaks (2011) *Banking Blockade*
          https://wikileaks.org/Banking-Blockade.html
          (Accessed: 2019-08-28)

[129]   WikiLeaks (2014) *Protesters against WikiLeaks banking blockade, the "PayPal 14", largely victorious*
          `https://wikileaks.org/Protesters-against-WikiLeaks.html`
          (Accessed: 2019-08-28)

[130]   bitcointalk.org (2010) *Satoshi Re: Wikileaks contact info?*
          `http://archive.fo/Gvonb#msg26999`
          (Accessed: 2019-08-28)

[131]   Julian Assange (2014) *AMA with Julian Assange on Reddit*
          `https://www.reddit.com/r/technology/comments/2ghp54/i_am_julian_assange_ama_about_my_new_book_`
          `when/ckjcmyw/`
          (Accessed: 2019-08-28)

[132]   BBC (2012) *Julian Assange loses extradition appeal at Supreme Court*
          `https://www.bbc.com/news/uk-18260914`
          (Accessed: 2019-08-28)

[133]   BBC (2012) *Julian Assange: Ecuador grants Wikileaks founder asylum*
          `https://www.bbc.com/news/uk-19281492`
          (Accessed: 2019-08-28)

[134]   Charlie Savage (2017) *Chelsea Manning to Be Released Early as Obama Commutes Sentence*
          `https://www.nytimes.com/2017/01/17/us/politics/obama-commutes-bulk-of-chelsea-mannings-sentence.`
          `html`
          (Accessed: 2019-08-28)

[135]   Erin Durkin (2019) *Chelsea Manning jailed for refusing to testify to grand jury in WikiLeaks case*
          `https://www.theguardian.com/us-news/2019/mar/08/chelsea-manning-judge-jails-wikileaks-case`
          (Accessed: 2019-08-28)

[136]   Charlie Savage (2019) *Assange Indicted Under Espionage Act, Raising First Amendment Issues*
          `https://www.nytimes.com/2019/05/23/us/politics/assange-indictment.html`
          (Accessed: 2019-08-28)

[137]   BBC (2019) *Julian Assange: Sweden reopens rape investigation*
          `https://www.bbc.com/news/world-europe-48253343`
          (Accessed: 2020-09-22)

[138]   BBC (2019) *Julian Assange: Sweden drops rape investigation*
          `https://www.bbc.com/news/world-europe-50473792`
          (Accessed: 2020-09-22)

[139]   Stefan Simanowitz, Amnesty International (2020) *Why are Amnesty International monitors not able to observe the Assange hearing?*
          `https://www.amnesty.org/en/latest/news/2020/09/why-are-amnesty-international-monitors-not-able-to-`
          `observe-the-assange-hearing/`
          (Accessed: 2020-09-22)

[140]   Craig Murray - Historian, Former Ambassador, Human Rights Activist (no date)
          `https://www.craigmurray.org.uk/`
          (Accessed: 2020-09-30)

[141]   Craig Murray (2020) *Your Man in the Public Gallery: Assange Hearing Day 14*
https://www.craigmurray.org.uk/archives/2020/09/your-man-in-the-public-gallery-assange-hearing-day-14/
(Accessed: 2020-09-30)

[142]   Craig Murray (2020) *Your Man in the Public Gallery: Assange Hearing Day 17*
https://www.craigmurray.org.uk/archives/2020/09/your-man-in-the-public-gallery-assange-hearing-day-17/
(Accessed: 2020-09-30)

[143]   Judiciary of England and Wales (2021) *USA vs. Julian Assange Judgemenet*
https://www.judiciary.uk/wp-content/uploads/2021/01/USA-v-Assange-judgment-040121.pdf
(Accessed: 2021-03-10)

[144]   Associated Press, Wire Service Content (2019) *Trump Considers Pardons for Soldiers Accused of War Crimes*
https://www.usnews.com/news/politics/articles/2019-05-24/trump-considers-pardons-for-soldiers-accused-of-war-crimes
(Accessed: 2019-08-28)

[145]   Wikipedia (no date) *Eddie Gallagher (Navy SEAL)*
https://en.wikipedia.org/wiki/Eddie_Gallagher_(soldier)
(Accessed: 2019-08-28)

[146]   Support Hong Kong Free Press (no date)
https://www.hongkongfp.com/support-hkfp/
(Accessed: 2019-08-28)

[147]   Chris Hoffman (2017) *How the "Great Firewall of China" Works to Censor China's Internet*
https://www.howtogeek.com/162092/htg-explains-how-the-great-firewall-of-china-works/
(Accessed: 2019-08-28)

[148]   Amnesty (2018) *Up to one million detained in China's mass "re-education" drive*
https://www.amnesty.org/en/latest/news/2018/09/china-up-to-one-million-detained/
(Accessed: 2019-08-28)

[149]   David Leigh, James Ball, Ian Cobain and Jason Burke (2011) *Guantánamo leaks lift lid on world's most controversial prison*
https://www.theguardian.com/world/2011/apr/25/guantanamo-files-lift-lid-prison
(Accessed: 2019-08-28)

[150]   Rob Evans and David Leigh (2010) *WikiLeaks cables: Secret deal let Americans sidestep cluster bomb ban*
https://www.theguardian.com/world/2010/dec/01/wikileaks-cables-cluster-bombs-britain
(Accessed: 2019-08-28)

[151]   Von John Goetz, Matthias Gebauer (2010) *US Pressured Italy to Influence Judiciary*
https://www.spiegel.de/international/europe/cia-rendition-case-us-pressured-italy-to-influence-judiciary-a-735268.html
(Accessed: 2019-08-28)

[152]   Wikipedia (no date) *Tunisian Revolution*
https://en.wikipedia.org/wiki/Wikileaks_Revolution
(Accessed: 2019-08-28)

[153]   Arshad Mohammed, Ross Colvin (2010) *Saudi king urged U.S. to attack Iran: WikiLeaks*
https://www.reuters.com/article/us-wikileaks-usa-idUSTRE6AP06Z20101129
(Accessed: 2019-08-28)

[154]   Chris Floyd (2006) *Children of Abraham: Death in the Desert (Wayback Machine)*
https://web.archive.org/web/20150416062019/http://www.chris-floyd.com/march/
(Accessed: 2019-08-28)

[155]   Halimah Abdullah (2016) *Guantanamo Bay: Obama Announces Plan to Close Controversial Detention Facility*
https://www.nbcnews.com/news/us-news/president-obama-expected-make-statement-guantanamo-n524131
(Accessed: 2019-08-28)

[156]   Wikipedia (no date) *Repatriation of Ahmed Agiza and Muhammad al-Zery*
https://en.wikipedia.org/wiki/Repatriation_of_Ahmed_Agiza_and_Muhammad_al-Zery
(Accessed: 2019-08-28)

[157]   BBC (2019) *Julian Assange: Wikileaks co-founder arrested in London*
https://www.bbc.com/news/uk-47891737
(Accessed: 2019-08-28)

[158]   Caroline Davies, Simon Murphy and Damien Gayle (2019) *Julian Assange faces US extradition after arrest at Ecuadorian embassy*
https://www.theguardian.com/uk-news/2019/apr/11/julian-assange-arrested-at-ecuadorian-embassy-wikileaks
(Accessed: 2019-08-28)

[159]   YouTube (2012) *Dschinghis Khan - Moskau 1979*
https://www.youtube.com/watch?v=NvS351QKFV4
(Accessed: 2019-08-28)

[160]   City News Service (2019) *Navy dismisses case against SEAL accused of covering up war crimes*
https://fox5sandiego.com/news/navy-dismisses-case-against-seal-accused-of-covering-up-war-crimes/
(Accessed: 2020-09-22)

[161]   Ian Vásquez (2001) *Ending Mass Poverty*
https://www.cato.org/publications/commentary/ending-mass-poverty
(Accessed: 2019-09-05)

[162]   The Balance (no date) *The Impact of Globalization on Economic Growth*
https://www.thebalance.com/globalization-and-its-impact-on-economic-growth-1978843
(Accessed: 2019-09-05)

[163]   BBC (2019) *Trade wars, Trump tariffs and protectionism explained*
https://www.bbc.com/news/world-43512098
(Accessed: 2019-09-05)

[164]   The Global Findex Database (2017) *Measuring Financial Inclusion and the Fintech Revolution*
https://globalfindex.worldbank.org/sites/globalfindex/files/2018-04/2017%20Findex%20full%20report_0.pdf
(Accessed: 2019-09-05)

[165]   Agence France-Presse (2019) *Venezuela opposition clings to social media lifeline*
https://news.abs-cbn.com/overseas/02/01/19/venezuela-opposition-clings-to-social-media-lifeline
(Accessed: 2019-09-05)

[166]   Kevin Helms (2019) *Venezuelan Explains How Bitcoin Saves His Family*
          https://news.bitcoin.com/venezuelan-bitcoin-saves-family/
          (Accessed: 2019-09-05)

[167]   Wikipedia (no date) *Haijin*
          https://en.wikipedia.org/wiki/Haijin
          (Accessed: 2019-09-05)

[168]   YouTube (2011) *The Crisis of Credit Visualized - HD (11 min)*
          https://www.youtube.com/watch?v=bx_LWm6_6tA
          (Accessed: 2019-10-25)

[169]   Trading Economics (no date) *United States GDP Growth Rate*
          https://tradingeconomics.com/united-states/gdp-growth
          (Accessed: 2019-10-25)

[170]   Trading Economics (node date) *Germany GDP Growth Rate*
          https://tradingeconomics.com/germany/gdp-growth
          (Accessed: 2019-10-25)

[171]   Trading Economics (no date) *Japan GDP Growth Rate*
          https://tradingeconomics.com/japan/gdp-growth
          (Accessed: 2019-10-25)

[172]   Trading Economics (no date) *Euro Area GDP Growth Rate*
          https://tradingeconomics.com/euro-area/gdp-growth
          (Accessed: 2019-10-25)

[173]   Brady Dennis (2011) *TARP moves into the black as some loans are repaid*
          https://www.washingtonpost.com/business/economy/tarp-moves-into-the-black-as-some-loans-are-re-
          paid/2011/03/30/AFDrEc6B_story.html
          (Accessed: 2019-10-25)

[174]   Ciarán Hancock (2019) *Was it worth paying €41.7bn to bail out Irish banks?*
          https://www.irishtimes.com/business/financial-services/was-it-worth-paying-41-7bn-to-bail-out-
          irish-banks-1.4036792
          (Accessed: 2019-10-25)

[175]   Blockchair (no date) *Bitcoin block 0*
          https://blockchair.com/bitcoin/block/0
          (Accessed: 2019-10-25)

[176]   Imgur (2014) *The Times | 1/3/2009 | Chancellor on Brink of Second Bailout for Banks | Satoshi Nakamoto*
          https://imgur.com/pGYXHJh
          (Accessed: 2019-10-25)

[177]   Jesse Eisinger (2014) *Why Only One Top Banker Went to Jail for the Financial Crisis*
          https://www.nytimes.com/2014/05/04/magazine/only-one-top-banker-jail-financial-crisis.html
          (Accessed: 2019-10-25)

[178]   Andrew Ross Sorkin, Mary Williams Walsh (2009) *A.I.G. Reports Loss of $61.7 Billion as U.S. Gives More Aid*
          https://www.nytimes.com/2009/03/03/business/03aig.html
          (Accessed: 2019-10-25)

[179]   CNN (2009) *Obama tries to stop AIG bonuses: 'How do they justify this outrage?'*
http://edition.cnn.com/2009/POLITICS/03/16/AIG.bonuses/
(Accessed: 2019-10-25)

[180]   Wikipedia (no date) H*owie Hubler*
https://en.wikipedia.org/wiki/Howie_Hubler
(Accessed: 2019-10-25)

[181]   YouTube (2013) *The Psychology of Human Misjudgement - Charlie Munger Full Speech (1 hour 16 min)*
https://www.youtube.com/watch?v=pqzcCfUglws
(Accessed: 2019-10-25)

[182]   Lisa Abramowicz (2015) *Goldman Sachs Hawks CDOs Tainted by Credit Crisis Under New Name*
https://www.bloomberg.com/news/articles/2015-02-04/goldman-sachs-hawks-cdos-tainted-by-credit-crisis-under-new-name
(Accessed: 2019-10-25)

[183]   Ben Eisen, Telis Demos (2019) *Banks Warm to Mortgage Bonds That Burned Them in 2008*
https://www.wsj.com/articles/banks-warm-to-mortgage-bonds-that-burned-them-in-2008-11568626202
(Accessed: 2019-10-25)

[184]   Francis Elliott, Gary Duncan (2009) *Chancellor Alistair Darling on brink of second bailout for banks*
https://www.thetimes.co.uk/article/chancellor-alistair-darling-on-brink-of-second-bailout-for-banks-n9l382mn62h
(Accessed: 2019-10-25)

[185]   Edward Robinson, Omar Valdimarsson (2016) *This Is Where Bad Bankers Go to Prison*
https://www.bloomberg.com/news/features/2016-03-31/welcome-to-iceland-where-bad-bankers-go-to-prison
(Accessed: 2019-10-25)

[186]   Richard Best (2019) *Why Bank Bail-Ins Will Be the New Bailouts*
https://www.investopedia.com/articles/markets-economy/090716/why-bank-bailins-will-be-new-bailouts.asp
(Accessed: 2019-10-25)

[187]   Trent Gillies (2017) *Warren Buffett says index funds make the best retirement sense 'practically all the time'*
https://www.cnbc.com/2017/05/12/warren-buffett-says-index-funds-make-the-best-retirement-sense-practically-all-the-time.html
(Accessed: 2019-11-11)

[188]   John Hackett (no date) *Economic planning*
https://www.britannica.com/topic/economic-planning
(Accessed: 2019-11-11)

[189]   Jim Chappelow (no date) *Command Economy*
https://www.investopedia.com/terms/c/command-economy.asp
(Accessed: 2019-11-11)

[190]   Matthew Johnston (no date) *Why the USSR Collapsed Economically*
https://www.investopedia.com/articles/investing/021716/why-ussr-collapsed-economically.asp
(Accessed: 2019-11-11)

[191]   Mark Felsenthal (2017) *Fed says inflation main worry, but cites risks*
          https://www.reuters.com/article/us-usa-fed-rates-idUSN0722343620070808
          (Accessed: 2019-11-11)

[192]   The Federal Reserve Board (2002) *Remarks by Governor Ben S. Bernanke*
          https://www.federalreserve.gov/boarddocs/speeches/2002/20021108/default.htm
          (Accessed: 2019-11-11)

[193]   Jose Viñals, Simon Gray, Kelly Eckhold (2016) *The Broader View The Positive Effects of Negative Nominal Interest Rates*
          https://blogs.imf.org/2016/04/10/the-broader-view-the-positive-effects-of-negative-nominal-interest-rates/
          (Accessed: 2019-11-11)

[194]   David Dayen (2014) *This Is the Fed's Most Brazen and Least Known Handout to Private Banks*
          https://newrepublic.com/article/116913/federal-reserve-dividends-most-outrageous-handout-banks
          (Accessed: 2019-11-11)

[195]   omega tau (2015) *181–Why Megaprojects Fail (and what to do about it)*
          http://omegataupodcast.net/181-why-megaprojects-fail-and-what-to-do-about-it/
          (Accessed: 2019-11-11)

[196]   The World Bank (no date) *Inflation, consumer prices (annual %) - Sweden*
          https://data.worldbank.org/indicator/FP.CPI.TOTL.ZG?locations=SE
          (Accessed: 2019-11-13)

[197]   Kimberly Amadeo (no date) *Inflation Targeting and How It Works*
          https://www.thebalance.com/inflation-targeting-definition-how-it-works-3305854
          (Accessed: 2019-11-13)

[198]   ProPublica (2014) *Inside the New York Fed: Secret Recordings and a Culture Clash*
          https://www.propublica.org/article/carmen-segarras-secret-recordings-from-inside-new-york-fed
          (Accessed: 2020-12-08)

[199]   Kimberly Amadeo, Michael J Boyle (no date) *New Deal Summary, Programs, Policies, and Its Success*
          https://www.thebalance.com/fdr-and-the-new-deal-programs-timeline-did-it-work-3305598
          (Accessed: 2019-11-13)

[200]   Matt Phillips (2012) *The Long Story of U.S. Debt, From 1790 to 2011, in 1 Little Chart*
          https://www.theatlantic.com/business/archive/2012/11/the-long-story-of-us-debt-from-1790-to-2011-in-1-little-chart/265185/
          (Accessed: 2019-11-13)

[201]   Kimberly Amadeo, Thomas J. Brock (no date) *Keynesian Economics Theory*
          https://www.thebalance.com/keynesian-economics-theory-definition-4159776
          (Accessed: 2019-11-13)

[202]   James Chen (no date) *Velocity of Money*
          https://www.investopedia.com/terms/v/velocity.asp
          (Accessed: 2019-11-13)

[203]   Federal Reserve Bank of St. Louis (no date) *Federal Debt: Total Public Debt*
          https://fred.stlouisfed.org/graph/?id=GFDEBTN,
          (Accessed: 2021-01-31)

[204]   Kimberly Amadeo (no date) *Interest on the National Debt and How It Affects You*
          https://www.thebalance.com/interest-on-the-national-debt-4119024
          (Accessed: 2019-11-13)

[205]   countryeconomy.com (no date) *General government gross debt*
          https://countryeconomy.com/national-debt
          (Accessed: 2019-11-13)

[206]   World Inequality Report 2018
          https://wir2018.wid.world/
          (Accessed: 2019-11-13)

[207]   Federal Reserve of New York (2019) Statement Regarding Repurchase Operations
          https://www.newyorkfed.org/markets/opolicy/operating_policy_190920
          (Accessed: 2019-11-13)

[208]   Federal Reserve Bank of St. Louis (no date) *M2 Money Stock*
          https://fred.stlouisfed.org/series/M2
          (Accessed: 2020-10-01)

[209]   Nathan Lewis (2019) *The Problem With "Modern Monetary Theory" Is That It's True*
          https://www.forbes.com/sites/nathanlewis/2019/02/21/the-problem-with-modern-monetary-theory-is-
          that-its-true/
          (Accessed: 2019-11-13)

[210]   Steven J. Murdoch (2004) *Software Detection of Currency*
          https://murdoch.is/projects/currency/
          (Accessed: 2019-11-13)

[211]   The Money Project (no date) *The Buying Power of the U.S. Dollar Over the Last Century*
          http://money.visualcapitalist.com/buying-power-us-dollar-century/
          (Accessed: 2019-11-13)

[212]   Finansinspektionen (2019) *Capital requirements for the Swedish banks, second quarter 2019*
          https://www.fi.se/contentassets/67c0bdcc4ddf4d1dbea616cb48fb1f01/kapitalkrav-sv-banker-2019-kv2_
          eng.pdf
          (Accessed: 2019-11-13)

[213]   European Central Bank (2016) *What are minimum reserve requirements?*
          https://www.ecb.europa.eu/explainers/tell-me/html/minimum_reserve_req.en.html
          (Accessed: 2019-11-13)

[214]   Money Metals Exchange (no date) *The Gold Confiscation Of April 5, 1933*
          https://www.moneymetals.com/resources/executive-order-6102
          (Accessed: 2019-11-13)

[215]   Tyler Cowen (2008) *The New Deal Didn't Always Work, Either*
          https://www.nytimes.com/2008/11/23/business/23view.html?_r=0
          (Accessed: 2019-11-13)

[216]   Matt Phillips (2012) *The Long Story of U.S. Debt, From 1790 to 2011, in 1 Little Chart*
          https://www.theatlantic.com/business/archive/2012/11/the-long-story-of-us-debt-from-1790-to-2011-
          in-1-little-chart/265185/
          (Accessed: 2019-11-13)

[217] Will Kenton (no date) *Nixon Shock*
https://www.investopedia.com/terms/n/nixon-shock.asp
(Accessed: 2019-11-13)

[218] Bob Woodward, Robert Costa (2016) *In a revealing interview, Trump predicts a 'massive recession' but intends to eliminate the national debt in 8 year*
https://www.washingtonpost.com/politics/in-turmoil-or-triumph-donald-trump-stands-alone/2016/04/02/8c0619b6-f8d6-11e5-a3ce-f06b5ba21f33_story.html?utm_term=.d6b42cbf9b8c
(Accessed: 2019-11-13)

[219] World Inequality Database
https://wid.world/data/
(Accessed: 2019-11-13)

[220] Sveriges Riksbank (2015) *Negative repo rate is introduced*
https://www.riksbank.se/en-gb/about-the-riksbank/history/2000-2018/negative-repo-rate-is-introduced/
(Accessed: 2019-11-13)

[221] Reuters (2019) *1-Denmark's Jyske Bank lowers its negative rates on deposits*
https://www.reuters.com/article/denmark-rates-jyske-bank/update-1-denmarks-jyske-bank-lowers-its-negative-rates-on-deposits-idUSL5N26B1AA
(Accessed: 2019-11-13)

[222] Kevin Kallmes (2019) *Hyperinflation and trust in Ancient Rome*
https://notesonliberty.com/2019/09/16/hyperinflation-and-trust-in-ancient-rome/
(Accessed: 2019-11-13)

[223] Clay Halton: *Debasement*
https://www.investopedia.com/terms/d/debasement.asp
(Accessed: 2020-02-05)

[224] Edward Snowden (2015) *Ask Me Anything on Reddit*
https://www.reddit.com/r/IAmA/comments/36ru89/just_days_left_to_kill_mass_surveillance_under/crglgh2/
(Accessed: 2019-12-09)

[225] Bobbie Johnson (2010) *Privacy no longer a social norm, says Facebook founder*
https://www.theguardian.com/technology/2010/jan/11/facebook-privacy
(Accessed: 2019-12-09)

[226] Dusten Carlson (2013) *Facebook's Zuckerberg Buys His Neighborhood Because, Get This, He Wants Privacy*
https://www.inquisitr.com/989057/facebooks-zuckerberg-buys-his-neighborhood-because-get-this-he-wants-privacy/
(Accessed: 2019-12-09)

[227] Laura Shin (2014) *'Someone Had Taken Over My Life': An Identity Theft Victim's Story*
https://www.forbes.com/sites/laurashin/2014/11/18/someone-had-taken-over-my-life-an-identity-theft-victims-story/
(Accessed: 2019-12-09)

[228] Reddit (no date) *What's the happiest 5-word sentence you could hear?*
https://www.reddit.com/r/AskReddit/comments/24vo34/whats_the_happiest_5word_sentence_you_could_
hear/chb4v05/?context=1
(Accessed: 2019-12-09)

[229] Charles Duhigg (2012) *How Companies Learn Your Secrets*
https://www.nytimes.com/2012/02/19/magazine/shopping-habits.html?pagewanted=all&_r=0
(Accessed: 2019-12-09)

[230] Hillary Mayell (2002) *Thousands of Women Killed for Family "Honor"*
https://www.nationalgeographic.com/culture/2002/02/thousands-of-women-killed-for-family-honor/
(Accessed: 2019-12-09)

[231] Wikipedia (no date) *Dowry murder*
https://en.wikipedia.org/wiki/Dowry_system_in_India#Dowry_murder
(Accessed: 2019-12-09)

[232] Sarah Dai (2019) *'Worse than doing time': life on the wrong side of China's social credit system*
https://www.inkstonenews.com/china/chinas-13-million-discredited-individuals-face-discrimination-
thanks-social-credit-system/article/3003319
(Accessed: 2019-12-09)

[233] Madeline Chambers (2009) *No remorse from Stasi as Berlin marks fall of Wall*
https://www.reuters.com/article/us-germany-wall-stasi/no-remorse-from-stasi-as-berlin-marks-fall-
of-wall-idUSL118487020091104
(Accessed: 2019-12-09)

[234] Amy Davidson Sorkin (2013) *The N.S.A.-Verizon Scandal*
https://www.newyorker.com/news/amy-davidson/the-n-s-a-verizon-scandal
(Accessed: 2019-12-09)

[235] Von SPIEGEL (2013) *The NSA's Secret Spy Hub in Berlin*
https://www.spiegel.de/international/germany/cover-story-how-nsa-spied-on-merkel-cell-phone-from-
berlin-embassy-a-930205.html
(Accessed: 2019-12-09)

[236] Simon Sharwood (2015) *GCHQ's SMURF ARMY can hack smartphones, says Snowden. Again.*
https://www.theregister.co.uk/2015/10/06/gchqs_smurf_army_can_hack_smartphones_says_ed_snowden/
(Accessed: 2019-12-09)

[237] Barton Gellman, Laura Poitras (2013) *U.S., British intelligence mining data from nine U.S. Internet companies in broad
secret program*
https://www.washingtonpost.com/investigations/us-intelligence-mining-data-from-nine-us-internet-
companies-in-broad-secret-program/2013/06/06/3a0c0da8-cebf-11e2-8845-d970ccb04497_story.html
(Accessed: 2019-12-09)

[238] Barton Gellman, Ashkan Soltani (2013) *NSA infiltrates links to Yahoo, Google data centers worldwide, Snowden documents say*
https://www.washingtonpost.com/world/national-security/nsa-infiltrates-links-to-yahoo-google-data-
centers-worldwide-snowden-documents-say/2013/10/30/e51d661e-4166-11e3-8b74-d89d714ca4dd_story.html
(Accessed: 2019-12-09)

[239]   Micah Lee (2019) *The Metadata Trap: The Trump Administration Is Using the Full Power of the U.S. Surveillance State Against Whistleblowers*
https://theintercept.com/2019/08/04/whistleblowers-surveillance-fbi-trump/
(Accessed: 2019-12-09)

[240]   Raphael Satter (2020) *U.S. court: Mass surveillance program exposed by Snowden was illegal*
https://www.reuters.com/article/us-usa-nsa-spying-idUSKBN25T3CK
(Accessed: 2020-09-22)

[241]   UK Legislation (no date) *Metropolitan Police Act 1839* Section 54
https://www.legislation.gov.uk/ukpga/Vict/2-3/47/section/54
(Accessed: 2019-12-09)

[242]   Jamie Redman (2019) *Snowden: US Seizing My Book Revenue is 'Good for Bitcoin'*
https://news.bitcoin.com/snowden-us-seizing-my-book-revenue-is-good-for-bitcoin/
(Accessed: 2019-12-09)

[243]   Geoffrey A. Fowler (2019) *You watch TV. Your TV watches back.*
https://www.washingtonpost.com/technology/2019/09/18/you-watch-tv-your-tv-watches-back/
(Accessed: 2019-12-09)

[244]   Karl Bode (2019) *Vizio Admits Modern TV Sets Are Cheaper Because They're Spying On You*
https://www.techdirt.com/articles/20190114/08084341384/vizio-admits-modern-tv-sets-are-cheaper-because-theyre-spying-you.shtml
(Accessed: 2019-12-09)

[245]   Mark Bergen, Jennifer Surane (2018) *Google and Mastercard Cut a Secret Ad Deal to Track Retail Sales*
https://www.bloomberg.com/news/articles/2018-08-30/google-and-mastercard-cut-a-secret-ad-deal-to-track-retail-sales
(Accessed: 2019-12-09)

[246]   Rosa Marchitelli (2019) *'Is that even legal?': Companies may be sharing new credit or debit card information without you knowing*
https://www.cbc.ca/news/business/banking-information-shared-with-third-parties-1.5102931
(Accessed: 2019-12-09)

[247]   Wikipedia (no date) *Great man theory*
https://en.wikipedia.org/wiki/Great_man_theory
(Accessed: 2019-12-09)

[248]   YouTube (2013) *James Clapper (DNI) Lies to the Senate About the NSA (30 sec)*
https://www.youtube.com/watch?v=AGYn7ER5U_0
(Accessed: 2019-12-09)

[249]   Edward Snowden (2019) *in conclusion this is good for bitcoin*
https://twitter.com/snowden/status/1174090027648868353?s=21
(Accessed: 2019-12-09)

[250]   ACLU Foundation (2017) *BAD TRIP Debunking the TSA's 'Behavior Detection' Program (PDF)*
https://www.aclu.org/sites/default/files/field_document/dem17-tsa_detection_report-v02.pdf
(Accessed: 2019-12-09)

[251]   Western Union (no date) *Send Money Online*
          https://www.westernunion.com/us/en/web/send-money/start
          (Accessed: 2019-12-10)

[252]   Kathryn Reid Venezuela crisis (no date) *Facts, FAQs, and how to help*
          https://www.worldvision.org/disaster-relief-news-stories/venezuela-crisis-facts
          (Accessed: 2019-12-10)

[253]   Steven Russolillo, Joanne Chiu, Eli Binder (2019) *Worried Hong Kong Residents Are Moving Money Out as Protests Escalate*
          https://www.wsj.com/articles/worried-hong-kong-residents-are-moving-money-out-as-protests-escalate-11566120603
          (Accessed: 2019-12-10)

[254]   John Greenwood, Steve H. Hanke (2018) *How China Copes With Capital Flight*
          https://www.wsj.com/articles/how-china-copes-with-capital-flight-1542672901
          (Accessed: 2019-12-10)

[255]   Hanke-Krus hyperinflation table (2013)
          https://www.cato.org/sites/cato.org/files/pubs/pdf/hanke-krus-hyperinflation-table-may-2013.pdf
          (Accessed: 2019-12-10)

[256]   Kaushik Patoway (2018) *Hungary's Hyperinflation: The Worst Case of Inflation in History*
          https://www.amusingplanet.com/2018/08/hungarys-hyperinflation-worst-case-of.html
          (Accessed: 2019-12-10)

[257]   New York Post (2019) *Zimbabwe struggles with hyperinflation: 'It's a nightmare'*
          https://nypost.com/2019/10/10/zimbabwe-struggles-with-hyperinflation-its-a-nightmare/
          (Accessed: 2019-12-10)

[258]   International Monetary Fund (no date) *Inflation rate, average consumer prices*
          https://www.imf.org/external/datamapper/PCPIPCH@WEO/WEOWORLD/VEN/ARG/SDN/ZWE
          (Accessed: 2019-12-10)

[259]   Trading Economics (no date) *Lebanon Inflation Rate*
          https://tradingeconomics.com/lebanon/inflation-cpi
          (Accessed: 2020-09-21)

[260]   The Daily Star (2019) *Top banking official: operations to fully resume when Lebanon crisis ends*
          http://www.dailystar.com.lb/News/Lebanon-News/2019/Oct-24/494282-top-banking-official-operations-to-fully-resume-when-lebanon-crisis-ends.ashx
          (Accessed: 2019-12-10)

[261]   Kimberly Amadeo (no date) *Why the US Dollar Is the Global Currency*
          https://www.thebalance.com/world-currency-3305931
          (Accessed: 2019-12-10)

[262]   Chris Troutner (2019) *I wanted to help someone in #Venezuela, so I'm tutoring a novice #JavaScript developer as he writes #opensource software.*
          https://twitter.com/christroutner/status/1142080363981709313
          (Accessed: 2019-12-10)

[263]   Blockchair (no date) *Bitcoin tx 4410c8d14ff9f87ceeed1d65cb58e7c7b2422b2d7529afc675208ce2ce09ed7d*
https://blockchair.com/bitcoin/
transaction/4410c8d14ff9f87ceeed1d65cb58e7c7b2422b2d7529afc675208ce2ce09ed7d
(Accessed: 2019-12-10)

[264]   Carlos Hernández (2019) *Bitcoin Has Saved My Family: "Borderless money" is more than a buzzword when you live in a collapsing economy and a collapsing dictatorship.*
https://www.nytimes.com/2019/02/23/opinion/sunday/venezuela-bitcoin-inflation-cryptocurrencies.html
(Accessed: 2019-12-10)

[265]   bitcoinuptime (no date) *Bitcoin uptime tracker*
https://www.buybitcoinworldwide.com/bitcoin-uptime/
(Accessed: 2019-12-10)

[266]   Craig Cohen (2019) *Is the dollar's "exorbitant privilege" coming to an end?*
https://privatebank.jpmorgan.com/gl/en/insights/investing/is-the-dollar-s-exorbitant-privilege-
coming-to-an-end
(Accessed: 2019-12-10)

[267]   Wikipedia (no date) *Cryptolocker*
https://en.wikipedia.org/wiki/CryptoLocker
(Accessed: 2019-12-15)

[268]   Dan Carlin (2017) *The Destroyer of Worlds*
https://www.dancarlin.com/hardcore-history-59-the-destroyer-of-worlds/
(Accessed: 2019-12-15)

[269]   Lee Banfield (2018) *Darknet Markets and the Shadow Economy*
https://weeklyglobalresearch.wordpress.com/2018/05/12/darknet-markets-and-the-shadow-economy/
(Accessed: 2019-12-15)

[270]   Liz Alderman (2017) *Greeks Turn to the Black Market as Another Bailout Showdown Looms*
https://www.nytimes.com/2017/02/18/world/europe/greece-bailout-black-market.html
(Accessed: 2019-12-15)

[271]   Gian Volpicelli (2018) *The unbelievable tale of a fake hitman, a kill list, a darknet vigilante… and a murder*
https://www.wired.co.uk/article/kill-list-dark-web-hitmen
(Accessed: 2019-12-15)

[272]   Free Ross Ulbricht
https://freeross.org/
(Accessed: 2019-12-15)

[273]   Mark Townsend (2018) *Dark web dealers voluntarily ban deadly fentanyl*
https://www.theguardian.com/society/2018/dec/01/dark-web-dealers-voluntary-ban-deadly-fentanyl
(Accessed: 2019-12-15)

[274]   Jen Christensen (2018) *The 5 most expensive drugs in the United States*
https://edition.cnn.com/2018/05/11/health/most-expensive-prescription-drugs
(Accessed: 2019-12-15)

[275]   Raphael Satter (2020) *U.S. court: Mass surveillance program exposed by Snowden was illegal*
https://www.reuters.com/article/us-usa-nsa-spying-idUSKBN25T3CK
(Accessed: 2020-09-22)

[276]   Seth D. Ginsberg (2017) *5 Ways Insurance Companies Meddle in Your Health Care*
https://health.usnews.com/health-care/for-better/articles/2017-07-13/5-ways-insurance-companies-meddle-in-your-health-care
(Accessed: 2019-12-15)

[277]   Armando Mombelli (2019) *Switzerland in the age of automatic exchange of banking information*
https://www.swissinfo.ch/eng/financial-transparency_switzerland-in-the-age-of-automatic-exchange-of-banking-information/45234706
(Accessed: 2020-01-02)

[278]   SWI swissinfo.ch (2019) *Switzerland grants 18 more countries access to bank details*
https://www.swissinfo.ch/eng/automatic-exchange-_switzerland-grants-18-more-countries-access-to-bank-details/45424544
(Accessed: 2020-01-02)

[279]   The Panama Papers (no date) *Exposing the Rogue Offshore Finance Industry*
https://www.icij.org/investigations/panama-papers/
(Accessed: 2020-01-02)

[280]   Secrecy for Sale (no date) *Inside the Global Offshore Money Maze*
https://www.icij.org/investigations/offshore/
(Accessed: 2020-01-02)

[281]   ICIJ (2016) *Former EU Official Among Politicians Named in New Leak of Offshore Files from The Bahamas*
https://www.icij.org/investigations/offshore/former-eu-official-among-politicians-named-new-leak-offshore-files-bahamas/
(Accessed: 2020-01-02)

[282]   Paradise Papers (no date) *Secrets of the Global Elite*
https://www.icij.org/investigations/paradise-papers/
(Accessed: 2020-01-02)

[283]   Tom Morgan (2016) *Panama Papers: Emma Watson named in latest offshore data release*
https://www.telegraph.co.uk/news/2016/05/10/panama-papers-emma-watson-named-in-latest-data-release/
(Accessed: 2020-01-02)

[284]   YouTube (2016) *Trump Brags About Not Paying Taxes: "That Makes Me Smart" (30 sec)*
https://www.youtube.com/watch?v=uBZR1-onmAo
(Accessed: 2020-01-02)

[285]   Annette Alstadsæter, Niels Johannesen, Gabriel Zucman (2019) *Tax Evasion and Inequality*
http://gabriel-zucman.eu/files/AJZ2019.pdf
(Accessed: 2020-01-02)

[286]   Paul Kiel, Jesse Eisinger (2018) *How the IRS Was Gutted*
https://www.propublica.org/article/how-the-irs-was-gutted
(Accessed: 2020-01-02)

[287]   Institute for Policy Studies (2017) *Offshore Leaks Database*
          `https://ips-dc.org/report-billionaire-bonanza-2017/`
          (Accessed: 2020-10-27)

[288]   Inequality.org (no date) *Income Inequality*
          `https://inequality.org/facts/income-inequality/`
          (Accessed: 2020-01-02)

[289]   Chuck Collins (2018) *Trump, Kavanaugh and the myth of self-made success*
          https://edition.cnn.com/2018/10/04/opinions/trump-nyt-kavanaugh-yale-self-made-man-myth-collins
          (Accessed: 2020-01-02)

[290]   The Panama Papers (2016) *All Putin's Men: Secret Records Reveal Money Network Tied to Russian Leader*
          `https://www.icij.org/investigations/panama-papers/20160403-putin-russia-offshore-network/`
          (Accessed: 2020-01-02)

[291]   Megan Cerullo (2019) *60 of America's biggest companies paid no federal income tax in 2018*
          https://www.cbsnews.com/news/2018-taxes-some-of-americas-biggest-companies-paid-little-to-no-federal-in-
          come-tax-last-year/
          (Accessed: 2020-01-02)

[292]   Emily Badger (2017) *When the (Empty) Apartment Next Door Is Owned by an Oligarch*
          `https://www.nytimes.com/2017/07/21/upshot/when-the-empty-apartment-next-door-is-owned-by-an-`
          `oligarch.html`
          (Accessed: 2020-01-02)

[293]   Institute for Justice (no date) *Ordinary Americans Are Victims of Policing for Profit in Our Nation's Airports*
          https://ij.org/case/kentucky-civil-forfeiture/
          (Accessed: 2020-01-05)

[294]   Xinhua (2019) *North Macedonia limits payment in cash up to 500 euros*
          `http://www.china.org.cn/world/Off_the_Wire/2019-06/01/content_74845553.htm`
          (Accessed: 2020-01-05)

[295]   Barclay Barm (2019) *WeChat Is Watching: Living in China with the app that knows everything about me.*
          `http://nautil.us/issue/73/play/wechat-is-watching`
          (Accessed: 2020-01-05)

[296]   Sarah Dai (2019) *'Worse than doing time': life on the wrong side of China's social credit system*
          `https://www.inkstonenews.com/china/chinas-13-million-discredited-individuals-face-discrimination-`
          `thanks-social-credit-system/article/3003319`
          (Accessed: 2019-12-09)

[297]   Eric Boehm (2019) *A Michigan Man Underpaid His Property Taxes By $8.41. The County Seized His Property, Sold It—and Kept the Profits.*
          `https://reason.com/2019/11/06/a-michigan-man-underpaid-his-property-taxes-by-8-41-the-county-`
          `seized-his-property-sold-it-and-kept-the-profits/`
          (Accessed: 2020-01-05)

[298]   Emily Flitter (2018) *A candidate backed medical marijuana. Wells Fargo closed her bank account.*
          https://www.cnbc.com/2018/08/22/wells-fargo-closes-bank-account-of-candidate-who-supports-marijuana.html
          (Accessed: 2020-01-05)

[299]   Reena Sewraz (2018) *25 million Brits would struggle in a cashless society*
          https://www.which.co.uk/news/2018/12/25m-brits-would-struggle-in-a-cashless-society/
          (Accessed: 2020-01-05)

[300]   Lily Kuo (2019) *China bans 23m from buying travel tickets as part of 'social credit' system*
          https://www.theguardian.com/world/2019/mar/01/china-bans-23m-discredited-citizens-from-buying-
          travel-tickets-social-credit-system
          (Accessed: 2020-01-05)

[301]   Planet Money (2018) *Episode 871, Blacklisted In China*
          https://www.npr.org/sections/money/2018/10/26/661163105/episode-871-blacklisted-in-
          china?t=1577261607993
          (Accessed: 2020-01-05)

[302]   Cornell Law School (no date) *31 U.S. Code § 5324. Structuring transactions to evade reporting requirement prohibited*
          https://www.law.cornell.edu/uscode/text/31/5324
          (Accessed: 2020-01-05)

[303]   Institute for Justice (no date) *Connecticut Forfeiture - IRS Seizes First, Questions Later—Much Later*
          https://ij.org/case/connecticut-forfeiture/
          (Accessed: 2020-01-05)

[304]   Ed Vulliamy (2011) *How a big US bank laundered billions from Mexico's murderous drug gangs*
          https://www.theguardian.com/world/2011/apr/03/us-bank-mexico-drug-gangs
          (Accessed: 2020-01-05)

[305]   Associated Press in Mexico City (2017) *More than 250 skulls found in 'enormous mass grave' in Mexico*
          https://www.theguardian.com/world/2017/mar/14/mexico-skulls-mass-grave-drug-cartel-veracruz
          (Accessed: 2020-01-05)

[306]   United Nations (no date) *Universal Declaration of Human Rights*
          https://www.un.org/en/universal-declaration-human-rights/
          (Accessed: 2020-01-09)

[307]   J. Francis Wolfe (2015) *10 Egregious Abuses Of Civil Asset Forfeiture*
          https://listverse.com/2015/06/29/10-egregious-abuses-of-civil-asset-forfeiture/
          (Accessed: 2020-01-09)

[308]   Casey Harper (2015) *The 7 Most Egregious Examples Of Civil Asset Forfeiture*
          https://dailycaller.com/2015/01/30/the-7-most-egregious-examples-of-civil-asset-forfeiture/
          (Accessed: 2020-01-09)

[309]   End Civil Forfeiture (no date) *Cases*
          http://endforfeiture.com/#cases
          (Accessed: 2020-01-09)

[310]   Max Rivlin-Nadler (2014) *How The NYPD's Use Of Civil Forfeiture Robs Innocent New Yorkers*
          https://gothamist.com/news/how-the-nypds-use-of-civil-forfeiture-robs-innocent-new-yorkers
          (Accessed: 2020-01-09)

[311]   Pamela Brown (2014) *Parents' house seized after son's drug bust*
          https://edition.cnn.com/2014/09/03/us/philadelphia-drug-bust-house-seizure/
          (Accessed: 2020-01-09)

[312]   Institute of Justice: Houston Forfeiture (no date) *Nurse Files Class Action Challenging CBP's Abusive Civil Forfeiture Practices*
          `https://ij.org/case/houston-forfeiture`
          (Accessed: 2020-01-09)

[313]   Laurien Rose (2012) *Police Chief Ken Burton calls forfeiture funds 'pennies from heaven'*
          https://www.themaneater.com/stories/outlook/police-chief-ken-burton-calls-forfeiture-funds-pen
          (Accessed: 2020-01-09)

[314]   J.F. (2013) *Fighting crime through superior steak*
          `https://www.economist.com/democracy-in-america/2013/10/15/fighting-crime-through-superior-steak`
          (Accessed: 2020-01-09)

[315]   POLICE Magazine (2011) *Prosecutor: Mich. Cops Spent Forfeiture Funds on Alcohol, Prostitutes*
          `https://www.policemag.com/348174/prosecutor-mich-cops-spent-forfeiture-funds-on-alcohol-prostitutes`
          (Accessed: 2020-01-09)

[316]   John Burnett (2009) *Texas Case May Spur Drug Money Rule Change*
          `https://www.npr.org/templates/story/story.php?storyId=104065589&t=1567527486222`
          (Accessed: 2020-01-09)

[317]   ACLU (2012) *ACLU Announces Settlement in "Highway Robbery" Cases in Texas*
          https://www.aclu.org/press-releases/aclu-announces-settlement-highway-robbery-cases-texas
          (Accessed: 2020-01-09)

[318]   Stacy Cowley (2019) *Safe Deposit Boxes Aren't Safe*
          `https://www.nytimes.com/2019/07/19/business/safe-deposit-box-theft.html`
          (Accessed: 2020-01-09)

[319]   New York Times (2019) *Wells Fargo's safe-deposit-box-contract*
          `https://int.nyt.com/data/documenthelper/1425-wells-fargo-safe-deposit-box-l/a4a2ec35134500f23c01/`
          `optimized/full.pdf#page=1`
          (Accessed: 2020-01-09)

[320]   Stacy Cowley (2019) *Safe Deposit Boxes Aren't Safe*
          `https://www.nytimes.com/2019/07/19/business/safe-deposit-box-theft.html`
          (Accessed: 2020-01-09)

[321]   Caleb Jones (2017) *Bank Safety Deposit Boxes Are No Longer Safe*
          `https://calebjonesblog.com/bank-safety-deposit-boxes-no-longer-safe/`
          (Accessed: 2020-01-09)

[322]   Jeff Thomas (2017) *Say Goodbye to Your Safe Deposit Box*
          `https://internationalman.com/articles/say-goodbye-to-your-safe-deposit-box/`
          (Accessed: 2020-01-09)

[323]   Menelaos Hadjicostis (2013) *Bank of Cyprus depositors lose 47.5% of savings*
          https://eu.usatoday.com/story/money/business/2013/07/29/bank-of-cyprus-depositors-lose-savings/2595837/
          (Accessed: 2020-01-09)

[324]   Rajesh Kumar Singh, Iain Marlow (2016) *India Abolishes 500 and 1,000 Rupee Notes to Fight Corruption*
          https://www.bloomberg.com/news/articles/2016-11-08/india-abolishes-inr500-1-000-rupee-notes-to-fight-corruption
          (Accessed: 2020-01-09)

[325]   Justin Rowlatt (2016) *Why India wiped out 86% of its cash overnight*
https://www.bbc.com/news/world-asia-india-37974423
(Accessed: 2020-01-09)

[326]   Nya Sedlar (no date) *New Swdish bills and coins for 2015 and 2016*
http://nyasedlar.nu/
(Accessed: 2020-01-09)

[327]   Per Carlsson (2016) *91-årig kvinna vägras lösa in sedlar*
https://www.svt.se/nyheter/lokalt/skane/91-arig-kvinna-vagras-losa-in-sina-sedlar
(Accessed: 2020-01-09)

[328]   Britannica (no date) *Reformation*
https://www.britannica.com/event/Reformation
(Accessed: 2020-02-05)

[329]   Thorsten Sandberg (2002) *Kyrkan och staten–en historisk separation*
https://popularhistoria.se/sveriges-historia/kyrkan-och-staten-en-historisk-separation
(Accessed: 2020-02-05)

[330]   Troy Adkins (no date) *Countries That Use The U.S. Dollar*
https://www.investopedia.com/articles/forex/040915/countries-use-us-dollar.asp
(Accessed: 2020-02-05)

[331]   Tibi Puiu (2020) *Your smartphone is millions of times more powerful than the Apollo 11 guidance computers*
https://www.zmescience.com/research/technology/smartphone-power-compared-to-apollo-432/
(Accessed: 2020-02-05)

[332]   Oishimaya Sen Nag (2018) *The Least Religious Countries In The World*
https://www.worldatlas.com/articles/least-religious-countries-in-the-world.html
(Accessed: 2020-02-05)

[333]   Clay Halton: *Debasement*
https://www.investopedia.com/terms/d/debasement.asp
(Accessed: 2020-02-05)

[334]   Blockchair (no date) *Bitcoin tx 786816d4f92e9b8e78bf281e2b498daa526c93dc69a5e6b493c901928ee3f51d*
https://blockchair.com/bitcoin-cash/
transaction/786816d4f92e9b8e78bf281e2b498daa526c93dc69a5e6b493c901928ee3f51d
(Accessed: 2019-09-21)

[335]   CryptoKitties (no date) *Collect and breed furrever friends!*
https://www.cryptokitties.co/
(Accessed: 2019-09-21)

[336]   Greg Walker (2017) *Coinbase Transaction: A transaction used to claim a block reward.*
https://learnmeabitcoin.com/glossary/coinbase-transaction
(Accessed: 2019-09-21)

[337]   Julian Assange (2014) *I am Julian Assange. AMA about my new book, "When Google Met WikiLeaks."*
https://www.reddit.com/r/technology/comments/2ghp54/i_am_julian_assange_ama_about_my_new_book_
when/ckjasj0/
(Accessed: 2019-09-21)

[338]   Wikipedia (no date) *Trusted timestamping*
         https://en.wikipedia.org/wiki/Trusted_timestamping
         (Accessed: 2019-09-21)

[339]   Internet Archive (no date) *Wayback Machine*
         https://archive.org/
         (Accessed: 2019-06-12)

[340]   Hacker News (Wayback Machine, Mars 1st, 2011)
         https://web.archive.org/web/20110301181127/http://news.ycombinator.com/
         (Accessed: 2019-09-21)

[341]   Wikipedia (no date) *List of multiple discoveries*
         https://en.wikipedia.org/wiki/List_of_multiple_discoveries
         (Accessed: 2019-09-21)

[342]   Catalyst (2009) *Hooke's law of springs (PDF)*
         https://www.stem.org.uk/system/files/elibrary-resources/legacy_files_migrated/8469-
         catalyst_20_2_438.pdf
         (Accessed: 2019-09-21)

[343]   National Vulnerability Database (2018) *CVE-2018-17144 Detail*
         https://nvd.nist.gov/vuln/detail/CVE-2018-17144
         (Accessed: 2019-09-21)

[344]   originstamp (no date) *Timestamp Information: 5c45a1ba957362a2ba97c9f8c48d4d59d4fa990945b7094a8d2a-
         98c3a91ed9b6*
         https://originstamp.org/s/5c45a1ba957362a2ba97c9f8c48d4d59d4fa990945b7094a8d2a98c3a91ed9b6
         (Accessed: 2019-09-21)

[345]   awemany (2018) *600 Microseconds: A perspective from the Bitcoin Cash and Bitcoin Unlimited developer who discovered
         CVE-2018-17144*
         https://medium.com/@awemany/600-microseconds-b70f87b0b2a6
         (Accessed: 2019-09-21)

[346]   awemany (2018) *600 Microseconds - How CVE-2018-17144 was discovered*
         https://www.reddit.com/r/btc/comments/9huu11/600_microseconds_how_cve201817144_was_discovered/
         (Accessed: 2019-09-21)

[347]   Electron Cash (no date) *A Bitcoin Cash SPV Wallet*
         https://electroncash.org/
         (Accessed: 2020-04-08)

[348]   Overthinking it (2009) *How Time Travel Works (and doesn't) in Back To The Future [BTTF Week]*
         https://www.overthinkingit.com/2009/01/16/how-time-travel-works-in-back-to-the-future/
         (Accessed: 2019-09-21)

[349]   bitcoin.it wiki (no date) *Block timestamp*
         https://en.bitcoin.it/wiki/Block_timestamp
         (Accessed: 2019-09-21)

[350]   homopit (2019) *memo hitting over 1k regularly last days - https://memo.cash/charts*
https://memo.cash/post/9649592301c43b168db94b66a110f8b5aa4a8fad2ff5752aec9d963a8c4a2849
(Accessed: 2019-09-25)

[351]   CashBack (2019) *https://youtu.be/5q3kDx1USPM*
https://memo.cash/post/c2503a1aecb55e2584b41ea183c3c355c527790a1ef9cb0dc3f90d8d7ae654bd
(Accessed: 2019-09-25)

[352]   Vidteks (2019) *I can feel the anticipation rising...*
https://memo.cash/post/5e614e32e679df162cc04582769b09fd88e7f0ea32f537dcc72cae38efcb7fe9
(Accessed: 2019-09-25)

[353]   memo.cash Protocol
https://memo.cash/protocol
(Accessed: 2019-09-25)

[354]   China Tribunal (2019) *Independent Tribunal into Forced Organ Harvesting from Prisoners of Conscience in China, Final Judgement Report*
https://chinatribunal.com/final-judgement-report/
(Accessed: 2019-08-28)

[355]   Debra Kelly (2016) *10 Insane Attempts At Rewriting History*
https://listverse.com/2016/01/05/10-insane-attempts-at-rewriting-history/
(Accessed: 2019-08-28)

[356]   BBC News (2003) *Bush declares victory in Iraq*
http://news.bbc.co.uk/2/hi/middle_east/2989459.stm
(Accessed: 2019-08-28)

[357]   Dan Carlin (2017) *The Celtic Holocaust*
https://www.dancarlin.com/hardcore-history-60-the-celtic-holocaust/
(Accessed: 2019-08-28)

[358]   Natalie Faulk (2018) *Ultimate Bet and Absolute Poker: What Happened?*
https://upswingpoker.com/ultimate-bet-absolute-poker-scandal/
(Accessed: 2019-12-17)

[359]   James Chen (no date) *Derivative*
https://www.investopedia.com/terms/d/derivative.asp
(Accessed: 2020-02-07)

[360]   Flipstarter (no date)
https://flipstarter.cash/
(Accessed: 2020-05-07)

[361]   Dan Western (2020) *The 25 Richest People in the World 2020*
https://wealthygorilla.com/top-20-richest-people-world/
(Accessed: 2020-02-07)

[362]   World Gold Council (no date) *How much gold has been mined?*
https://www.gold.org/about-gold/gold-supply/gold-mining/how-much-gold
(Accessed: 2020-02-07)

[363]   APMEX (no date) *Live USD Gold Price Charts & Historical Data*
          https://www.apmex.com/gold-price
          (Accessed: 2020-02-07)

[364]   Coinlib - Crypto Prices, Charts, Lists & Crypto Market News
          https://coinlib.io/
          (Accessed: 2020-02-07)

[365]   Jeff Desjardins (no date) *Comparing the World's Money & Markets*
          https://www.visualcapitalist.com/all-of-the-worlds-money-and-markets-in-one-visualization-2020/
          (Accessed: 2020-02-07)

[366]   Jeff Desjardins (no date) *Comparing the World's Money & Markets*
          https://www.visualcapitalist.com/all-of-the-worlds-money-and-markets-in-one-visualization-2020/
          (Accessed: 2020-02-07)

[367]   80,000 hours (2019) *Bruce Schneier on how insecure electronic voting could break the United States—and surveillance
          without tyranny*
          https://80000hours.org/podcast/episodes/bruce-schneier-security-secrets-and-surveillance/
          (Accessed: 2020-01-31)

[368]   Britannica (no date) *Bush v. Gore, law case*
          https://www.britannica.com/event/Bush-v-Gore
          (Accessed: 2020-01-31)

[369]   Ellen Nakashima (2018) *In Georgia, a legal battle over electronic vs. paper voting*
          https://www.washingtonpost.com/world/national-security/in-georgia-a-legal-battle-over-electronic-
          vs-paper-voting/2018/09/16/d655c070-b76f-11e8-94eb-3bd52dfe917b_story.html
          (Accessed: 2020-01-31)

[370]   Jessica McBride (2016) *Vote Flipping: Were Clinton Votes Changed to Trump in Georgia?*
          https://heavy.com/news/2016/10/vote-flipping-georgia-texas-north-carolina-nevada-hillary-clinton-
          machines-donald-trump-rigged-fraud/
          (Accessed: 2020-01-31)

[371]   UpGuard Team (2017) *The Chicago Way: An Electronic Voting Firm Exposes 1.8M Chicagoans*
          https://www.upguard.com/breaches/cloud-leak-chicago-voters
          (Accessed: 2020-01-31)

[372]   Jennifer Cohn (2019) *America's Electronic Voting System is Corrupted to the Core*
          https://medium.com/@jennycohn1/americas-electronic-voting-system-is-corrupted-to-the-core-
          1f55f34f346e
          (Accessed: 2020-01-31)

[373]   Matthew Bernhard et al (2017) *Public Evidence from Secret Ballots*
          https://arxiv.org/pdf/1707.08619.pdf
          (Accessed: 2020-01-31)

[374]   Matthew Bernhard et al (2017) *Public Evidence from Secret Ballots*
          https://arxiv.org/pdf/1707.08619.pdf
          (Accessed: 2020-01-31)

[375]   Ask TOG (2001) *The Butterfly Ballot: Anatomy of a Disaster*
          `https://www.asktog.com/columns/042ButterflyBallot.html`
          (Accessed: 2020-01-31)

[376]   Nick Corasaniti, Sheera Frenkel, Nicole Perlroth (2020) *App Used to Tabulate Votes Is Said to Have Been Inadequately Tested*
          `https://www.nytimes.com/2020/02/03/us/politics/iowa-caucus-app.html`
          (Accessed: 2020-01-31)

[377]   Thomas Brewster (2015) *191 Million US Voter Registration Records Leaked In Mystery Database*
          `https://www.forbes.com/sites/thomasbrewster/2015/12/28/us-voter-database-leak/`
          (Accessed: 2020-01-31)

[378]   FoundTheStuff (2015) *Entire US voter registration record leaks (191 million)*
          `https://www.reddit.com/r/privacy/comments/3yinij/entire_us_voter_registration_record_leaks_191/`
          (Accessed: 2020-01-31)

[379]   Satoshi Nakamoto (2008) *Bitcoin: A Peer-to-Peer Electronic Cash System*
          `https://whycryptocurrencies.com/files/bitcoin.pdf`

[380]   bitcoin.com (no date) *Bitcoin Whitepaper: A Beginner's Guide*
          `https://www.bitcoin.com/get-started/bitcoin-white-paper-beginner-guide/`
          (Accessed: 2020-04-19)

[381]   BitcoinNews.com (2018) *BitcoinNews.com Daily Podcast 5th November 2018: The Bitcoin White Paper*
          `https://bitcoinnews.com/news/bitcoinnews-com-daily-podcast-5th-november-2018-the-bitcoin-white-paper/`
          (Accessed: 2020-04-19)

[382]   Cobra-Bitcoin (2016) *Amendments to the Bitcoin paper*
          `https://github.com/bitcoin-dot-org/bitcoin.org/issues/1325`
          (Accessed: 2020-04-19)

[383]   Blockchair (no date) *Bitcoin / Whitepaper*
          `https://blockchair.com/bitcoin/whitepaper/`
          (Accessed: 2020-04-19)

[384]   Stackexchange (no date) *How is the whitepaper decoded from the blockchain*
          `https://bitcoin.stackexchange.com/questions/35959/how-is-the-whitepaper-decoded-from-the-blockchain-tx-with-1000x-m-of-n-multisi/35970`
          (Accessed: 2020-04-08)

[385]   Wikipedia (no date) *Network effect*
          `https://en.wikipedia.org/wiki/Network_effect`
          (Accessed: 2020-03-17)

[386]   Zcash (no date) *How it works*
          `https://z.cash/technology/`
          (Accessed: 2020-03-17)

[387]   jeffq (2017) *On the linkability of Zcash transactions*
          `http://jeffq.com/blog/on-the-linkability-of-zcash-transactions/`
          (Accessed: 2020-03-17)

[388]   U.S. Department of the Treasury (2018) *Treasury Designates Iran-Based Financial Facilitators of Malicious Cyber Activity and for the First Time Identifies Associated Digital Currency Addresses*
          https://home.treasury.gov/news/press-releases/sm556
          (Accessed: 2020-03-17)

[389]   statista (no date) *PayPal's net number of payments from 1st quarter 2014 to 4th quarter 2019*
          https://www.statista.com/statistics/218495/paypals-net-number-of-payments-per-quarter/
          (Accessed: 2020-03-17)

[390]   Visa (no date) *Small Business Retail*
          https://usa.visa.com/run-your-business/small-business-tools/retail.html
          (Accessed: 2020-03-17)

[391]   Avalanche Labs (no date) *Scalable and Probabilistic Leaderless BFT Consensus through Metastability*
          https://avalanchelabs.org/QmT1ry38PAmnhparPUmsUNHDEGHQusBLD6T5XJh4mUUn3v.pdf
          (Accessed: 2020-03-17)

[392]   Blockchain Analytics (no date) *Bitcoin (BTC) network electricity consumption*
          https://www.blockchainanalytics.pro/btc/electricity-consumption/
          (Accessed: 2020-03-17)

[393]   WorldData (no date) *The world in numbers*
          https://www.worlddata.info/
          (Accessed: 2020-03-17)

[394]   CoinShares Research (2019) *Bitcoin Mining Network Report December 2019 | Research | CoinShares*
          https://coinsharesgroup.com/research/bitcoin-mining-network-december-2019
          (Accessed: 2020-03-17)

[395]   Blockchair (no date) *Bitcoin addresses*
          https://blockchair.com/bitcoin/addresses
          (Accessed: 2020-03-17)

[396]   Daniel Morgan (2017) *The Great Bitcoin Scaling Debate—A Timeline*
          https://hackernoon.com/the-great-bitcoin-scaling-debate-a-timeline-6108081dbada
          (Accessed: 2020-03-17)

[397]   Mike Hearn (2016) *The resolution of the Bitcoin experiment*
          https://blog.plan99.net/the-resolution-of-the-bitcoin-experiment-dabb30201f7?gi=c2a62f310034
          (Accessed: 2020-03-17)

[398]   Jamie Redman (2019) *Core Developer's 300kb Block Proposal Bolstered in Bid to Push Lightning Adoption*
          https://news.bitcoin.com/core-developers-300kb-block-proposal-bolstered-in-bid-to-push-lightning-adoption/
          (Accessed: 2020-03-17)

[399]   Blockchain.com (no date) *Size of the Bitcoin blockchain*
          https://www.blockchain.com/charts/blocks-size
          (Accessed: 2020-03-17)

[400]   BitInfoCharts (no date) *Bitcoin Hashrate historical chart*
          https://bitinfocharts.com/comparison/bitcoin-hashrate.html
          (Accessed: 2020-02-27)

[401]   bitcoin.it wiki (no date) *Wallet import format*
         https://en.bitcoin.it/wiki/Wallet_import_format
         (Accessed: 2020-02-27)

[402]   Bitcoin (no date) *BIP-39 wordlists*
         https://github.com/bitcoin/bips/blob/master/bip-0039/bip-0039-wordlists.md
         (Accessed: 2020-02-27)

[403]   Wikipedia (no date) *SHA-1*
         https://en.wikipedia.org/wiki/SHA-1
         (Accessed: 2020-02-27)

[404]   Eric Griffith & Kyle Kucharski (2019) *7 Huge Bug Bounty Payouts*
         https://www.pcmag.com/news/7-huge-bug-bounty-payouts
         (Accessed: 2020-11-13)

[405]   Monero Stack Exchange (2016) *Monero inception - how did bitmonero become monero?*
         https://monero.stackexchange.com/questions/1011/monero-inception-how-did-bitmonero-become-monero
         (Accessed: 2020-11-13)

[406]   Bitcoin ABC (2020) *New release: Bitcoin ABC 0.22.0 is available to download*
         https://blog.bitcoinabc.org/2020/08/18/new-release-bitcoin-abc-0-22-0-is-available-to-download/
         (Accessed: 2020-11-13

[407]   noise (2020) *If the IFP in Bitcoin Cash activates, it suggests that cryptocurrencies are doomed to centralization*
         https://read.cash/@noise/if-the-ifp-in-bitcoin-cash-activates-it-suggests-that-cryptocurrencies-
         are-doomed-to-centralization-86ff8006
         (Accessed: 2020-11-13)

[408]   GitHub (no date) *Farcaster RFCs*
         https://github.com/farcaster-project/rfcs
         (Accessed: 2020-11-23)

[409]   Seth Simmons (2020) *A Brief Breakdown of Monero's Ongoing Network Attacks*
         https://sethsimmons.me/posts/moneros-ongoing-network-attack/
         (Accessed: 2020-12-29)

[410]   siesta (2020) *workaround for nodes being killed*
         https://www.reddit.com/r/Monero/comments/kjrub1/in_honor_of_people_who_work_on_christmas_eve/
         ggyiids/
         (Accessed: 2020-12-29)

[411]   BitPal (no date) *A self-hosted payment processor*
         https://bitpal.dev/
         (Accessed: 2021-05-07)

Index

Plots have their page numbers in *italics*.

CPSIA information can be obtained
at www.ICGtesting.com
Printed in the USA
LVHW071505100621
689907LV00006B/223